Advance Praise for *Work in Progress*

"I love any book about a dog-fearing paperboy, wasp-stung lawn-mower, bumbling busboy, nearly-electrocuted caddy, popcorn-popping usher, bored assembly-line worker, sunburnt bank teller, pot-smoking undergrad, and ambitious 'corporate tool'... who ends up a priest! Funny, charming, inspiring, and wise—this is a memorable memoir."

—Stephen Colbert, comedian and writer

"To my shelf of well-worn books by Father James Martin, I add his moving, hilarious new memoir about summer jobs. With a keen eye for detail, he renders his quest as swashbuckling as any action tale—and as unlikely. The kid who busses tables at fifteen and puffs spliffs as an Ivy-Leaguer who'll land in the corporate world. But a chance encounter with the late Trappist monk Thomas Merton transforms this business dude into a novice in the Society of Jesus. There is no greater quest or romance than this. Martin's graceful storytelling voice and keen eye for detail makes this his most layered and lyrical effort. I hope he calls it *Portrait of the Artist as a Young Jesuit*. Like Joyce's book, I suspect Martin's will garner a cult readership."

—Mary Karr, author of *Lit* and *The Liars' Club*

"James Martin's tender memoir helps us to be in the world in the way that God is: compassionate, loving, and kind. With an utterly relatable trajectory of job experiences and graced, human encounters, we are witnesses to an eventual vocation, anchored in the God of love. This book will make you smile and compel you to remain in the present moment. It will also help you to recognize God, so quickly, in the here and now of your own life."

—Greg Boyle, SJ, author of *Tattoos on the Heart* and recipient of the Presidential Medal of Freedom

"*Work in Progress* is an evocation of a time and place that is both quintessentially American and quintessentially Catholic. Think *Leave It to Beaver* meets *The Seven Storey Mountain*. Richly descriptive, James Martin suggests that we can encounter the sacred everywhere, whether we are sitting on a stool in an ice cream parlor or kneeling before an altar. This is his best writing yet."

—Mary Gordon, author of *Payback* and *Reading Jesus*

"A fascinating account of a young man eager to work hard. All the way from mopping floors in an ice cream shop and caddying at a ritzy golf course straight to the Wharton Business School and right into a junior executive position at GE in New York City. 'Hungry like a wolf,' young Jim was, hungry to be somebody, hungry to use his mind, make good friends and a whole lot of money. Then comes the soul weariness, the stress, which tears up his stomach and paralyzes his brain with migraines. Suffering, the saying goes, either breaks us or breaks us open. This hungry wolf discovers his deepest hunger, and opens to God's invitation to personal friendship, and he learns how to pray. Life in the Jesuits thrusts him into Nairobi, Kenya, with Mother Teresa's Sisters to serve poor people and homeless people and the LGBTQ community and into his true gift—writing—which now gives us this fascinating, honest, vulnerable account. I love this book. Read it. Perhaps it will do for you what it has done for me: feed the hungry wolf of my very soul."

—Sister Helen Prejean, author of *Dead Man Walking*

"*Work in Progress* is a frank, charming, self-effacing, and very funny reminiscence of those hard summer jobs in our teens that, despite their miseries and mishaps, help us to find out who we really want to be. This is 'Jimmy' Martin at his finest."

—Ron Hansen, author of *Mariette in Ecstasy* and *Atticus*

"*Work in Progress* began when Father Martin's parents encouraged him to get out of the house and get a job. He did—and now we have the benefit of their wisdom. So sit back and enjoy. Laugh, be entertained, shed a tear, and be reminded of your own coming of age. See how ice cream cones, putting greens, and assembly lines helped to shape the life of a priest whose honesty and vision have much to say to all of us. What's in a summer job? Start reading and you'll discover more about yourself and about the God who loves us."

—Archbishop John C. Wester, Archbishop of Santa Fe

"Father Martin has written a wonderful, often hilarious memoir of his working life, from childhood jobs to priestly vocation, that captures the way in which our labor forms (and sometimes deforms) us, sapping us of a sense of meaning or offering us purpose. In Father Martin's hands, the various working cultures of his life show different views of how to approach human beings. He has a great eye for detail and for the telling anecdote, and we go from one delightfully sketched job to another before he finds his true work."

—Phil Klay, author of *Missionaries* and winner of the National Book Award

WORK IN PROGRESS

Also by James Martin, SJ

The Jesuit Guide to (Almost) Everything: A Spirituality for Real Life

Between Heaven and Mirth: Why Joy, Humor, and Laughter Are at the Heart of the Spiritual Life

Together on Retreat: Meeting Jesus in Prayer (e-book)

Jesus: A Pilgrimage

The Abbey: A Story of Discovery

Seven Last Words: An Invitation to a Deeper Friendship with Jesus

Building a Bridge: How the Catholic Church and the LGBT Community Can Enter into a Relationship of Respect, Compassion, and Sensitivity

Learning to Pray: A Guide for Everyone

Come Forth: The Promise of Jesus's Greatest Miracle

WORK IN PROGRESS

Confessions of a busboy,
dishwasher, caddy,
usher, factory worker,
bank teller, corporate
tool, and priest

JAMES MARTIN, SJ

HarperOne
An Imprint of HarperCollinsPublishers

Without limiting the exclusive rights of any author, contributor or the publisher of this publication, any unauthorized use of this publication to train generative artificial intelligence (AI) technologies is expressly prohibited. HarperCollins also exercise their rights under Article 4(3) of the Digital Single Market Directive 2019/790 and expressly reserve this publication from the text and data mining exception.

Unless otherwise noted, photographs courtesy of James Martin, SJ.
Photograph on page xii by Bill Cannon. Used by permission.
Photographs on page 292 by Howard Sherman. Used by permission.

Imprimi Potest: Very Rev. Joseph O'Keefe, SJ, Provincial Superior, USA East Province of the Society of Jesus.

WORK IN PROGRESS. Copyright © 2026 by James Martin, SJ. All rights reserved. No part of this book may be used or reproduced in any manner whatsoever without written permission except in the case of brief quotations embodied in critical articles and reviews. For information, address HarperCollins Publishers, 195 Broadway, New York, NY 10007. In Europe, HarperCollins Publishers, Macken House, 39/40 Mayor Street Upper, Dublin 1, D01 C9W8, Ireland.

HarperCollins books may be purchased for educational, business, or sales promotional use. For information, please email the Special Markets Department at SPsales@harpercollins.com.

harpercollins.com

FIRST EDITION

Designed by Jason Kayser

Library of Congress Cataloging-in-Publication Data has been applied for.

ISBN 978-0-06-269448-5

PRINTED IN THE UNITED STATES OF AMERICA

25 26 27 28 29   LBC   5 4 3 2 1

For my sister, who put up with me.

Well, you're not going to sit inside all summer.

—My mom

Of course it's not fun. Why do you think they call it work? If it were fun, they'd call it play.

—My dad

CONTENTS

CHAPTER 1

How the Bicentennial Wagon Train Almost Got Me Fired

1

CHAPTER 2

How Not to Be a Shiftless Troublemaker

41

CHAPTER 3

How Poltergeists, Aliens, and Bigfoot Prevented Me from Getting Rich

71

CHAPTER 4

How to Avoid Getting Struck by Lightning When Standing Next to a Bag of Metal Poles

93

Contents

CHAPTER 5

How to Pop Corn for Ten Hours and Not Lose Your Mind

145

CHAPTER 6

How to Be a Man and Not a Mouse

183

CHAPTER 7

How Not to Sacrifice Your Life for a Summer Job

215

CHAPTER 8

How I Became a (Sort of) Stockbroker and, Then, an Adult

245

CHAPTER 9

How I Graduated from College and Almost Met Grace Kelly

273

Contents

CHAPTER 10

How My Last Summer Job Turned Out
293

CHAPTER 11

How the Ice Cream Inn Prepared Me for Life
315

Acknowledgments
347

Credits and Permissions
351

Friends Meetinghouse, Plymouth Meeting, Pennsylvania. George Washington's horse is said to have stayed here during the Revolutionary War. Where Washington stayed was left unsaid. Perhaps at the nearby George Washington Motor Lodge. *(Photo by Bill Cannon.)*

CHAPTER 1

How the Bicentennial Wagon Train Almost Got Me Fired

IN THE SUMMER OF 1976, THE BICENTENNIAL WAS OMNI-present, especially if you lived in or near Philadelphia. And if you were in high school in or near Philadelphia, it was inescapable.

To mark the two hundredth anniversary of our nation's founding, the administration of Plymouth–Whitemarsh High School, whose mascot was the Colonial (a Revolutionary War soldier wearing a tricorn hat), renamed the driveway leading from the town's main drag into the school "Bicentennial Lane." That year, Bicentennial-themed posters were hung in the hallways, students attended Bicentennial-themed assemblies, and teachers assigned essays on Bicentennial-related topics in all our classes—including biology, in which we wrote papers on colonial-era scientists.

Along with another eager student, I was selected to declaim over the school's loudspeaker, once a week, a sixty-second snippet of American history called "Looking Back," usually centered on some famous personage of eighteenth-century Philadelphia, to the annoyance of every kid and probably most teachers. The last thing that a half-asleep high school student wants to hear about at 7 a.m. is the story of Benjamin Rush, father of American psychiatry.

One morning, our class was dragooned into attending a Bicentennial Assembly during which a local acting troupe offered up supposedly hilarious skits on American history and, at one point, selected unwilling students to participate onstage. Normally we'd be grateful for even the flimsiest excuse to miss a class, but after months of force-fed Bicentennial hoopla, we had had our fill. At one point during the skits, which were eliciting little enthusiasm, a frustrated actor called out to the crowd of bored students, "Hey! Would you rather be here or in class?"

"In CLASS!" yelled one brave kid. Thunderous applause rewarded his honesty.

Bicentennial specials on TV. Bicentennial sales at the grocery store. Bicentennial pull-out sections in the Philadelphia newspapers. When my younger sister, Carolyn, played her flute in a school concert that year, the music had, of course, a Bicentennial theme.

That summer, almost every kid in our neighborhood proudly wore the Stars and Stripes on practically every item of clothing. My sister and I sported red-white-and-blue Speedo swimsuits, though this may have had less to do with the Bicentennial and more with enthusiasm over the Summer Olympics. On Monday mornings after reciting the Pledge of Allegiance, and on Friday afternoons after the final class, we stood to listen to a scratchy recording of "The Star-Spangled Banner" broadcast over the school's ancient public-address system. A photo in my yearbook shows a cluster of students looking not patriotic but sullen as they face the flag.

How the Bicentennial Wagon Train Almost Got Me Fired

Overall, it was hard not to get tired of, blasé about, or even annoyed by the Bicentennial. It so thoroughly wormed its way into my consciousness that the covers of my notebooks that year are covered with doodles of the official Bicentennial logo: a five-pointed star surrounded by a curvy red-white-and-blue ribbon.

But even the most jaded observers took notice when our local newspaper, *Today's Post*, announced that the Bicentennial Wagon Train would be passing through my hometown, Plymouth Meeting, a Philadelphia suburb settled by the Religious Society of Friends, more commonly called Quakers, during the seventeenth century.

The "Meeting" in our town's name referred to a handsome Friends Meetinghouse constructed in 1708. The Meetinghouse, with the stone facade, red roof, and long porch common to Quaker meetinghouses in the area, is located in the town's center, about three miles from the high school. The town was settled by émigrés from Plymouth, England: thus, Plymouth Meeting.

It wasn't until decades later, in graduate theology studies, in a course called Christianity in America, that I came to understand not only the presence of Quakers in my hometown, but also the profusion of so many Christian sects in the area, including Anabaptists, Schwenkfelders, Moravians, Mennonites, and Amish. Their presence was the legacy of William Penn, who had been imprisoned in England for preaching and publishing "heretical" Quaker doctrines. In 1681, to pay off a financial debt, King Charles II granted Penn a charter for land in the colonies. ("Pennsylvania" means "Penn's woods.")

We learned the bare bones of that saga in the third grade, when our social studies classes focused exclusively on Pennsylvania history, outlined in three textbooks: *ABCs of Pennsylvania*, *It Happened in Pennsylvania*, and *Your State Pennsylvania*.

In graduate school, I learned that William Penn hoped that his new colony might be a "Holy Experiment" in religious tolerance and he actively sought out religious groups being persecuted in Europe. So it wasn't until many years after leaving Plymouth Meeting that I understood why our neighbors included not only Catholics, Presbyterians, and Jews, but also Quakers, Moravians, and members of the Church of the Brethren.

Several battles of the Revolutionary War were fought in the area—my sister and a friend once found a Revolutionary-era cannonball in some woods near our house—and the Meetinghouse was used as a hospital after the Battle of Germantown in 1777. A local legend has George Washington's horse spending a night in the Meetinghouse stables, where I played as a boy. Oddly, the story centered on his horse, not the rider. Where General Washington bunked was left unsaid. A few miles away, also memorializing his visit, was a somewhat less historic motel built in 1958: the George Washington Motor Lodge.

A large timber shed with dirt floors located behind the Meetinghouse could still stable a few horses, though I never saw a horse within miles of the place. Instead, an old tire swing hung from one of the rafters by a thick, dusty rope that chafed your hands. The stables could be accessed from my neighborhood by cutting through a colonial-era graveyard, filled with slim, tilting marble gravestones whose incised letters had long been worn away, visible signs of death that kids joked about during the daytime but were careful to avoid at night.

Across the street from the Meetinghouse is Abolition Hall,

which hosted antislavery speakers like Frederick Douglass, Harriet Beecher Stowe, William Lloyd Garrison, and Lucretia Mott. The hall was built above the eighteenth-century carriage shed of George and Mary Corson, which itself served as a stop on the Underground Railroad, the network of secret routes and hiding places for people who had escaped slavery and were making their dangerous way from south to north, from the late eighteenth century to the end of the Civil War. (When I heard about this as a boy, I imagined physical railroads in tunnels running underneath our town.) The location was no accident: The Quakers were among the first Christian groups to condemn slavery, and the Plymouth Meeting Anti-Slavery Society was founded in 1833. (Two of its founders were George Corson and his brother Joseph.)

Next to Abolition Hall is the home of Thomas Hovenden, an Irish-born artist (and son-in-law of George Corson) who often depicted African Americans in his work and whose massive painting *The Last Moments of John Brown* hangs in the Metropolitan Museum of Art in New York. He is buried in the Quaker graveyard.

But other than those few local sites, and a large mall, the small suburb of Plymouth Meeting wasn't well-known, certainly not outside the Philadelphia area. One of my Jesuit friends continually forgets the name of my hometown and often says, "How are things in Pilgrim's Hat?" Another friend used to misremember it as "Friendly Quaker."

So the Bicentennial Wagon Train was a big deal. It would be a cavalcade of horse-drawn covered wagons originating in California, Washington, Nevada, Montana, Colorado, and other states where the wagon trains of old had ended their pioneering journeys. In the summer of '76 the Conestoga wagons would make a reverse trip to Pennsylvania, in a Bicentennial Pilgrimage. Its destination was nearby Valley Forge, and they would arrive on July 4.

I couldn't believe my luck. They would drive (or whatever you call it when something is pulled by a team of horses) right up Ridge Pike, one of the main thoroughfares in town. It was like a celebrity coming to town, something that didn't happen for real until a few months later when President Gerald Ford, campaigning for election, stopped by the Plymouth Meeting Mall. I was only a few feet away from him in a crowded atrium, just missing the chance to shake the Presidential Hand. But a friend reported that President Ford's hand all but engulfed his own when he shook it. "That's why he was such a good football player," observed my dad, ever the sports fan.

I was also excited to see a real covered wagon: The only ones I had seen outside the movies were in Conestoga, a nearby suburb where the eponymous vehicles were built. A weathered replica was parked in front of the Conestoga Mill Restaurant & Bar, a favorite watering hole for some of my older cousins.

A celebratory brochure pasted in my scrapbook reads, "As an appropriate tribute to the Nation's 200th anniversary, we will roll the wagons once more. Once more we'll take to the wagon trails. But this time we'll head *Eastward*. Back to the Cradle of Liberty. A pilgrimage to the birthplace of the nation." (Note the italics, as if this were difficult to comprehend.)

More important for me, the wagon train would pass in front of the Ice Cream Inn, where I was working in the summer of '76 as a fifteen-year-old busboy and dishwasher.

How the Bicentennial Wagon Train Almost Got Me Fired

• • • •

Standing alone in a parking lot next to a shopping center, the Ice Cream Inn featured roughly twenty-five tables in a dark, wood-paneled dining room decorated with vaguely Early American décor. The popular family-owned restaurant offered simple fare—burgers, hot dogs, club sandwiches, fries, and the like, as well as its famous ice cream, made fresh every day and stored in an immense walk-in freezer.

The owner, a kind, middle-aged man named Mr. Clare, was justly proud of his restaurant's elaborate ice cream concoctions, like crushed-cherry sundaes, difficult to find elsewhere. The Ice Cream Inn also had unconventional ways of creating their own flavors. For their chocolate-mint ice cream, for example, rather than using green mint ice cream and adding chocolate chips, they added mint flavoring to chocolate ice cream.

Rum raisin was a favorite among patrons. With me too. That summer my official job title was "busboy/dishwasher," but it could have been more accurately described as "busboy/dishwasher/ice cream eater." Gradually, though, after consuming endless quantities of rum raisin, and also washing the huge plastic storage tubs and rinsing out half-eaten bowls of the sticky-sweet concoction, I'd had my fill. By August it turned my stomach. Today I can't stand either the taste or the smell of rum raisin ice cream.

Inside, to the right of the entrance, was a take-out section, wildly busy in the summer. Outside was a take-out window around which congregated swarms of high school kids, idling away the summer nights with ice cream cones and milkshakes, as they flicked away even larger swarms of mosquitoes and gnats. In the main dining room was a counter, upon which waitresses slapped down orders and which opened into a small kitchen area. In the kitchen, high school and college-age boys a few years older than me scooped out homemade ice cream, slung burgers, and set it all on the counter for the waitresses to collect after a bell was dinged.

This was the first job that gave me a paycheck. At fifteen, and a high school sophomore, I had to apply for state working papers, since I was still underage in the Commonwealth of Pennsylvania. This meant filling out an application through our school's guidance office and also undergoing a physical exam from our family doctor, which I considered excessive. While I was no star athlete, I was certainly capable of scooping ice cream, even though, as I would discover, it was often frozen solid.

The thrill of getting working papers that summer was outstripped by the thrill of my first paycheck. The Ice Cream Inn paid us in a curious way—maybe legal, maybe not—with dollars and coins stuffed in pocket-size beige envelopes. On the outside, Mr. Clare listed my hours and wages, with deductions, which my dad patiently explained after I asked, "Where did all my money go?" I kept the envelopes for years in a dresser drawer as a sign of juvenile accomplishment. The salary was minimum wage: $2.30 an hour.

It was not my first job. My parents were adamant about my working from as early as age thirteen. Before the Ice Cream Inn, I had already worked as a paperboy and a lawn mower. We were not wealthy, probably solidly middle class, and my earnings were going to a college fund, and to pay for the essentials of a teenager's social life in the 1970s: clothes, movies, bowling, skating, tennis, street hockey equipment, pizza, ice cream, and record albums.

But the Ice Cream Inn was my first official job, as my parents said, one that required a nerve-racking, sweaty-palmed interview while seated at one of the Early American tables.

I kept a journal from that year, which I was amazed to find when my mother moved out of our house in Plymouth Meeting ten years after my father's death. To record what I expected to be the monumentally historic events of the Bicentennial celebrations, I faithfully kept a daily diary for one year, filling up two cardboard-bound, wide-ruled composition books, but stopped when the year had ended. It was surprisingly moving to read the entries in preparation for this book, akin to meeting my fifteen-year-old self again, who was given to expressing strong opinions about almost everything, RECORDING IMPORTANT EVENTS IN ALL CAPS and using lots of exclamation points!!!

Most entries focus on school: funny things that happened in class, amusing comments said over the lunchroom table, onerous homework assignments, teachers I liked and disliked ("What a jackass!"), social events with my classmates (visits to the mall, lists of what movies we saw, and recaps of bowling and tennis matches predominate), and now-historical incidents noted in passing. (I didn't like Richard Nixon but liked Gerald Ford.) Family events (my father's long business trips, my sister's cross-country meets, and my mom's cooking) fill the gaps when there wasn't much going on at school.

According to my journal, I started the job search in March, filling out applications at Burger King, McDonald's, Thrift Drug Store, Strawbridge & Clothier (a local department store), Baskin-Robbins, Dairy Queen, the Ice Cream Inn, and, since someone told me that they were hiring high school kids, the post office.

"The lady told me that she was lucky to have her job!" I wrote in my journal. "So obviously I wasn't going to get one."

On April 14, I heard from the Ice Cream Inn: "YAY! I GOT A JOB!!" I was happy I landed a job and relieved that I wouldn't have to visit any more fast-food chains, ice cream joints, or department stores to fill out applications.

Recently, visiting my mom's retirement community, I saw a high school–age kid sitting in the lobby, interviewing for a job with the kitchen staff. Instantly that adolescent experience returned: nervously filling out forms while sitting across the table from an adult who didn't know you. How rare that was for kids then: All the adults we knew were either relatives, neighbors, or teachers.

After my interview with Mr. Clare, I was worried I wouldn't get the job and just as worried that I would get it and then somehow screw it up. So after my elation came anxiety.

On my first day, Mr. Clare gave me the official busboy's uniform: a white short-sleeved polyester smock with round metal buttons, which I wore over my faded, flared blue jeans and Adidas sneakers. That simple uniform filled me with immense pride because it said, "I have a real job!" It was my responsibility (read: my mom's) to wash the smock after every shift, since it was stained daily with chocolate, vanilla, butter pecan, rum raisin, and the other flavors of the day, along with a healthy dose of Coke, burger grease, cherry syrup, and whipped cream. The shifts were either daytime from 10 a.m. to 6 p.m. or nighttime from 6 p.m. to midnight.

For the daytime shifts I pedaled my Schwinn bike the fifteen-minute ride from our home; at night my father shuttled me back and forth. Our town was safe, but my parents were terrified of my getting struck by a car in the dark, probably not an unwarranted fear.

My father and I didn't talk much on our short drives, for two reasons. First, my dad was taciturn, at least with me. He had a great sense of humor that came to the fore mainly when he was telling jokes in a crowd, which could reduce him (the joke teller) to tears of laughter, but otherwise he was reserved, like many of the fathers on our street.

The second reason we didn't talk much is that I was overly focused on the social aspects of the job: how I fit in with the older kids, what other people thought about me, and whether I was cool. And those were the last things I wanted to talk about with my dad, my mom, or anyone for that matter. One of my chief concerns was getting people to like me.

My position at the Ice Cream Inn lay at the nadir of the organizational hierarchy. At the top of the ladder was Mr. Clare, the owner, who was used to having high school and college kids in his employ; he was patient, gracious, and encouraging. Then came the no-nonsense but very patient manager, George, who worked as a bricklayer on the side, and Gladys, the middle-aged hostess who greeted, seated, and cracked wise with customers. Then came a few adult cooks, perhaps in their twenties and thirties, who mainly kept to themselves. Not Gladys, who was always a lark. "There are two things you can do inside," she would say, to scandalize the high school kids. "One is playing cards. And I don't like playing cards!"

At the top of our social hierarchy were the ice cream servers, older high school and college-age boys brimming with testosterone-fueled confidence who dazzled patrons with the speed and dexterity with which they scooped ice cream; placed it into glass containers—petite metal cups for single scoops; clear fluted glasses for sundaes; goblets for bigger sundaes; tall glasses for floats; and curvy, banana-shaped glasses for banana splits—ladled on toppings such as coconut flakes, chocolate chips, or walnuts; and then tossed them onto the counter and loudly dinged the bell. Despite the predominance of customers ordering ice cream concoctions, the kitchen and dining room always smelled of burgers on the grill.

The boys shouted out the names of the flavors and the toppings as they filled their orders, taking special pleasure in the name of the gooey mixture of walnuts and heavy syrup kept in a square plastic tub next to the pistachios: "Wet nuts! Hahaha! Who wants more of my wet nuts?"

A few of the older boys grilled hamburgers and made sandwiches alongside the adult cooks. From the counter, waitresses (usually high school or college-age girls) retrieved the burgers and ice cream and carried them to the customers.

At the bottom of both the organizational and social hierarchies were the busboys, consigned to the hectic dining room and the enormously hot back room, where we washed the dishes. We busboys were forever miffed that the waitresses never shared their tips with us, even though we set and bussed the tables. This seemed unjust, almost criminal, and so was not only a reliable cause for endless complaints, but also an effective social glue among the summertime busboys.

Time behind the counter was a privilege for the busboys. I always felt like I was auditioning when I was there, trying to be funny or cool, and never sure if I succeeded. My journal for my first day, June 5, gives a good (if excited!!!) summary of the job:

> I'm a busboy/dishwasher/cleaner/everything!! It's so hectic. I clean dishes in the kitchen & then start out to bus tables. It's really hard & I wear a uniform that's white and gets real dirty. Then I bus tables and clear them off & then take them back to be washed. Then I bring everything out again & stack it & put it away. There's not a lot of people around at 6 but at about 9:00 it's <u>soooo</u> busy!!! I work from 6–12 at night. I hope I work more than that during the weekends. Then I cleaned up the store & mopped, took out the garbage. It's so hectic. Whew!!!

The counter that opened onto the dining room made for some perilous moments. A boy once placed a chocolate sundae on the countertop and prepared to polish it off with the required whipped-cream topping. Distracted, he mis-angled the canister nozzle and sent a powerful jet of whipped cream past the sundae, arcing over the counter, and into the dining room, where it landed on a customer, as I wrote in my journal, "all in her hair and on her dress," prompting her to leap from the table with a yelp.

Horrified, the boy ducked behind the counter. Still horrified but wanting to be helpful, he grabbed a rag from a ledge under the counter and, still crouching on the floor, deftly flung it over the counter. It landed with a splat on the table, knocking over a glass of water, flooding the table, and dousing the customer and her family. More yelps.

"Sorry!" he yelled out from his hiding place.

A middle-aged man, apparently her father, jumped from the table and approached the counter. The ice cream scooper cowered even farther underneath it.

The man peered over the counter as we recoiled. "Where is he?"

Like a timid animal emerging from its burrow, the boy crawled from under the counter and sputtered out an explanation. The father threw the offending rag into the boy's chest. My journal registered surprise that the manager didn't find out. "He doesn't even know now!"

It was the most exciting thing that happened that week. That night we celebrated in the parking lots with whippets, the bullet-shaped nitrous-oxygen canisters that powered the whipped-cream dispensers. Inhaling the fumes was supposed to give you a mild high, but it just made me dizzy.

As often happened, something mortifying was turned into a triumph for the boy, as he repeated the story over and over, each time increasing the amount of whipped cream and changing where it went, from splattering her shirt to spraying her entire face. "Ha! You should have seen her! She was *covered* in whipped cream!" he said as he took a hit on a whippet. Another guy smoked a cigarette as he listened to the story. I listened too and tried to look coolly nonchalant.

I wondered: *If I had made a mistake like that, would I be able to laugh about it?*

Probably not. I was too intent on not messing up, not so much to impress my bosses or do a good job, but so the other employees wouldn't deem me unworthy of respect. I wanted to be as cool as they were. So I tried hard to do everything the right way: mop the floors, rinse the dishes, load the dishwasher, bus the tables,

How the Bicentennial Wagon Train Almost Got Me Fired

carry out tubs of ice cream from the freezer. Above all, not say or do anything that would mark me as uncool. Nonetheless, I had my own share of foul-ups. The Bicentennial Wagon Train would figure into the worst of them.

The lion's share of my energy was expended on bussing tables and washing dishes. The back room was hot, crowded, and exceedingly noisy, as the busboys lugged in heavy metal trays, about three feet long, two feet wide, and eight inches deep, filled with forks, knives, and spoons; half-emptied coffee cups; red plastic glasses still filled with ice water; dinner plates with half-eaten cheeseburgers mashed on top of stale fries; cigarette stubs emptied from the ashtrays (from a time when you could still smoke inside a restaurant)—all overlaid by a stratum of emptied cups and glasses of melted ice cream and warm milkshakes, as well as the various nuts (dry and wet) and toppings and sprinkles, called "jimmies" in Philadelphia, which meant that people constantly shouted, "Jimmy, we need more jimmies!"

A busboy's job was to clear the tables, empty the ashtrays, load everything into the metal tray, and then wipe down the tables. Then we carried the load into the back room, rinsed the dishes out in the sink, and loaded the industrial dishwasher, which sanitized everything in a minute or two. The dishes and glasses were scalding when they emerged from the dishwasher, the cutlery almost glowing, and early on I burned my fingers repeatedly. And if the overheated glasses were filled with ice cream too soon after coming out of the dishwasher, they would shatter instantly.

Afterward I'd return the cleaned plates to the dining room, stack the ice cream glasses behind the counter (warning the scoopers which glasses were too hot), and set the tables. I didn't do that last task often at home, so I was forever forgetting the correct placement of the silverware.

Once done, I would bus more tables, while another busboy was washing his tray in the back room. It was a kind of ballet: in and out of the dining room and the back room, one busboy washing dishes, the other bussing tables, each of us avoiding one another as we came in and out of the two swinging doors, one next to the other, always using the right-hand one. At the end of the day, I mopped the restaurant floor, bagged the garbage, and tossed it into the dumpster, around which the guys were already gathering for cigarettes, beer, marijuana, or whippets. Whipped cream fights were common after work as well, sometimes in the kitchen, sometimes outdoors.

It was hard work that required both strength and dexterity, but once you got the hang of it, it was easy. Busy and boring at once, two regular traits of most of my summer jobs.

At least they let us have the radio on in the back room, and that summer it seemed that only two songs were being played. The first was "Let 'Em In," by Wings, Paul McCartney's band, which I considered a weak substitute for the Beatles, who had broken up a few years before. One of the employees at the Ice Cream Inn on whom I had a crush liked the song, and therefore so did I.

But the song that aired even more frequently was "Afternoon Delight," by the marvelously named Starland Vocal Band, which peaked at #12 on *Billboard* magazine's list of hits that year. (Like many of my friends, I assiduously tracked the progress of pop songs and visited a nearby record store to pick up a weekly flyer listing the Top 50 hits.) Nothing conjures up memories of that summer faster than the opening bars of this bouncy song, which was popular among my friends mainly for its risqué lyrics. Knowing the meaning of an "afternoon delight" was considered a mark of coolness.

> Gonna find my baby, gonna hold her tight
> Gonna grab some afternoon delight
> My motto's always been "When it's right, it's right"
> Why wait until the middle of a cold, dark night?

The only consistent highlight of the job, besides being able to listen to the radio, was taking the full "creamers"—the small, plastic, single-serving cream containers for coffee—that lay unopened on the bottom of your bussing tray; squeezing them between your thumb and forefinger; and popping them, sending a mini-geyser of cream into the sink and sometimes onto the ceiling. "Don't pop the creamers!" said Mr. Clare to the dishwashers. We ignored him. How could you not pop the creamers?

In a few days, I felt at home over the sink. The restaurant floor was more of a social challenge, since almost everyone was older, so I took solace in mastering the dishwasher without burning my hands and having fun with the creamers.

"I worked a lot for four days," I wrote on June 27. "It's OK. The people in there are moody. They're nice to you sometimes & sometimes they're not."

I wasn't old enough to make the ice cream, but that didn't mean I didn't cadge some. And though I worked hard, and grew more confident in the job, I never shook the feeling that I was the kid, an occasional target for the older boys, from my high school and others nearby, who at best tolerated my presence, the three years' difference in age delineating a teenage social chasm. Most of the older boys were taller, bigger, and more confident than I was. I tried my best not to do anything to invite opprobrium, and mainly succeeded, but failed once, spectacularly.

One day in July was especially busy. I had worked every night that week and the weekend before. Late in the afternoon, I raced back and forth between the back room and the dining room. I couldn't figure out why it was so crowded: Lunch was over, there were no high school sporting events since school was out for the summer, and there didn't seem to be any groups celebrating some kid's birthday, the most common reason for a large party.

Around 4 p.m., I emerged from the back room to discover a dining room utterly emptied of customers. Where did they go?

It seemed impossible for everyone to leave together, because they weren't all in one party but several smaller ones that arrived at different times. But what did I know?

I laboriously cleared the six or seven tables. Oddly, the meals were half eaten, some not even touched. At the time my summer reading ran to stories of mysterious creatures like Bigfoot and aliens, so I briefly wondered whether all the customers had been sucked up into a spacecraft that had landed atop the Ice Cream Inn, piloted by aliens who were perhaps initially interested in sampling some rum raisin ice cream.

If I left dishes on the empty tables, George would notice, so rather than ask questions about the sudden disappearance of all our patrons, I hurried up and bussed. Gladys was absent from her post too, which seemed strange. Maybe she was on her break.

I filled a bussing tray with plates, glasses, and ice cream containers from three tables and was barely able to lug it to the back room. I placed it into the sink and started rinsing, shoved all the dishes into the dishwasher, and closed the door with a satisfying *thunk*. I returned to the still-empty dining room and bussed another few tables and took that second tray into the back room.

I was proud of bussing all those tables so quickly. Surely I would win plaudits from the management and, more important, the older kids.

Over the rushing noise of the dishwasher, I heard a commotion in the dining room.

"HEY!" said several voices at once. "Heyyyyy!"

Then, "Where's our food?!"

I knew instantly that I had made a mistake. But what?

Before that day, whenever I read a novel that described a character "bursting" into a room, I found it faintly ridiculous. But George *burst* into the back room, throwing open the swinging wooden doors so hard that they slammed against the wall. I turned around so quickly that I nearly sprayed him with the big hose and nozzle we used to rinse off the dishes, which was still tightly gripped in my wet hand.

"Jimmy, what did you *do*?" he said.

"Nothing!" I said, my voice rising an octave, which mortified me. "I bussed the tables!"

This was the first of many times when I thought I had done a good deed, only to find I had screwed up. It's always a shock to go from thinking, *Didn't I do a great job?* to *What did I do wrong?* in a few seconds.

An elderly man barreled his way into the room, shouting, "Where's my FOOD?"

"Uh," I said, eloquently, as I stared into the sink, contemplating the half-eaten hamburgers and melting ice cream sundaes still in my bussing tray. I still didn't know what I had done wrong, but it seemed to have something to do with taking his food, and everyone else's, prematurely. But no one had been in the restaurant. Where had they gone? And why had they returned?

Speechless, I tried to puzzle out what I had done wrong after trying so hard to do right.

"They were watching the Wagon Train!" said the assistant manager.

Despite the endless coverage in the local papers, I had forgotten that today was Bicentennial Wagon Train Day! Upon seeing the long-awaited caravan through the half-curtained windows, every one of the customers had leapt from their tables, mid-meal, and bolted outside to stand under the eaves of the Ice Cream Inn and watch the Conestoga wagons and people in faux-Western garb making their stately way down Ridge Pike.

"Wow!" I said, momentarily forgetting the trouble I was in. "The Bicentennial Wagon Train is here?"

"Where's my goddamned FOOD?" shouted the customer.

At a loss, I reached into the tray in the sink and pulled out what I imagined was his sundae. Out it came. And I remember this as clearly as anything from that summer: sticking out of a modest scoop of our famous homemade vanilla ice cream, still in its frosty little silver cup, where a cherry might be, was a wet cigarette butt.

"Is this it?" I said as I held it up. I knew it seemed ridiculous, and borderline offensive, but I didn't know what else to say or do. Heat raced to my cheeks as I flushed in shame.

"That's not *funny*!" said the customer. "You idiot!"

"I was just bussing the tables! Everyone was gone! How was I supposed to know?"

This would be a pattern for many years. Rather than admitting a mistake, my first instinct was to defend myself. Of course, no one told me where everyone had gone. (It was early in the day so not many other employees were around, save the cooks, who probably didn't notice what was going on at the tables.) Still, the more mature route simply would have been to say, "I'm sorry."

But at age fifteen, I was unable to do that. It took a few years to realize that when you make a mistake (even one that you don't think warrants the treatment you're getting), you should probably just apologize. "I'm sorry" goes a long way.

By the same token, the customer was being a jerk.

"We'll refund it of course," said George. "And make you a new meal right away."

The customer approached me, red-faced, as I stood over the sink.

"It better come outta *his* paycheck," said the customer, jamming his meaty finger into my stained smock.

George nodded noncommittally. The customer smiled what I can only call an evil grin. He seemed to enjoy my being humiliated. I thought, *Why is he being so mean?*

"Idiot!" he shouted, as he banged open the swinging doors and left the room.

I thought: *When I grow up, I will never treat anyone like this.* Today I couldn't imagine berating a fifteen-year-old dishwasher, or frankly a fifteen-year-old anyone or any sort of laborer. In an instant, I learned not to mistreat someone who has less power than me. My busboy humiliation was as effective a lesson against being mean or cruel or insensitive as a year's worth of homilies.

On the verge of tears, I felt that this was undue punishment for doing my job. But I was too upset to say anything articulate. I wanted to explain but was deathly afraid I'd cry, about the worst fate for a boy in those days. "Baby!" was the epithet used for boys who cried, or, even worse, "sissy" or "fag," or worst of all, "fairy."

It was the first time I felt the sting of anger over being mistreated at work. It wouldn't be the last. What I remember most was a feeling of powerlessness. At that age, it was impossible for me to respond. First, the two men scolding me were older, and I had been brought up to respect adults. I also understood that I had no real power. Working papers alone do not make a confident adult. Second, I was mortified that I had made a mistake and that others would hear about it.

After the customer left the back room, George, sympathetic, reassured me that I would not have to pay for it. (That would have taken a few weeks.) Fortunately, the Bicentennial Wagon Train was sufficiently long (there were a lot of wagons) that after my humiliation, I was still able to watch the Conestoga wagons roll by, with the rest of the staff. Men wearing cowboy hats and jeans and women in sunbonnets and gingham dresses waved cheerfully at us as the horses pulled their wagons down Ridge Pike.

As I stood there, one busboy nudged me and said, good-naturedly, "Man, did you really just f—k up like I heard you did?"

At midnight, after mopping the restaurant, I told my dad in the car what had happened. He sympathized and said something that he repeated often: "Work isn't supposed to be fun. Why do you think they call it work? If it were fun, they'd call it play." Decades later, a whiskey manufacturer sponsored a nationwide contest inviting readers to send in life lessons from their fathers. My sister submitted that quote and it made it into the full-page ad, which ran in *The New York Times* and *The Wall Street Journal*. She framed the ad and gave it to him for his birthday. It hung in our recreation room until he died twenty-five years later.

The Bicentennial Wagon Train doesn't come to town every day. Neither does an entire restaurant bolt from their tables, leaving behind half-eaten plates of food. So I wasn't overly worried about screwing up like that again. For the next few days, whenever I bussed an empty table, the other busboys would joke, "Are you sure they're gone?" The waitresses ribbed me too. They'd peer past the Early American curtains and say, "Hey, Jimmy, the Wagon Train is back!" Usually I laughed about it. Other times, depending on my mood, it embarrassed me.

My bussing snafu did not dim my Bicentennial enthusiasm. The entry for my journal on July 4 is written in red ink and blue ink and covers four pages, describing the day's events: President Ford's visits to Independence Hall and Valley Forge (where he addressed the modern-day pioneers who had journeyed on the Wagon Train); "Operation Sail," a tall ships gathering, and fireworks, both in New York City; bells rung across the country; and events in Williamsburg, St. Louis, San Francisco, and Washington, DC, all of which we watched on TV. Closer to home was a picnic in our backyard with my grandmother and great-aunt, both immigrants from Sicily, which concluded with our singing "Happy Birthday, USA" over a red-white-and-blue birthday cake lit up by sparklers. My journal reads, sincerely but grandiloquently, "This is undoubtedly the greatest country in the world & I'll fight for it and its principles against everyone."

Despite any Bicentennial-related mishaps at work, by August I felt like a pro: faster at cleaning the tables and more adept at washing dishes. I felt proud to walk into work every day, knowing that I had acquired some new skills: how to use the industrial dishwasher, how to bus tables quickly, and even how to make a few ice cream concoctions. Plus, I became a whiz at using our big industrial mop, with its thick wooden handle and long, white, cotton loops at the end. To use it, you had to dunk it in soapy water and wring it out with the "side press wringer" that was attached to a big, square, yellow bucket on four wheels.

I'm not sure why I ended up enjoying mopping—maybe because it was an "industrial mop," not like the smaller ones we used at home on our linoleum kitchen floors, and so it made me feel like an adult. And I enjoyed making something dirty into something clean. Years later, when I entered the Jesuit novitiate, we used the same kind of mop to clean our kitchen floor, so at least there was one thing I knew how to do as a novice.

As the summer wore on, I was even allowed to scoop ice cream when things got busy. "Not too much!" was Mr. Clare's refrain. Once I made a "Telstar ICI," our pièce de résistance, a monster sundae made of several scoops of ice cream, chocolate sauce, various toppings (including wet nuts), and whipped cream. We always watched to see whether the customer could finish it. I never figured out why it was called the Telstar unless its round shape resembled the communications satellite launched in 1962. Maybe Mr. Clare was an aficionado of satellites. I had no idea what he did outside the restaurant: I still felt odd speaking to adults who weren't either my mom and dad, my neighbors, or my teachers. Mr. Clare could have been an astronaut, for all I knew.

Even by the end of the summer my job performance was not

flawless: The long banana-split glasses were especially slippery when wet, and I dropped (and broke) more than a few in the sink that summer. Worse, one day I accidentally knocked a gray-haired woman in the right temple with the corner of my tray as I bussed the table next to hers. As I angled the heavy tray above her head while she was seated (a big no-no), she suddenly stood up.

Bang! The accidental collision drew blood—hers, though from the look on her face she probably would have gladly spilled a little of mine.

She said, "You moron! What's *wrong* with you?" George came over to apologize.

Melted ice cream from a gap in the corner of the metal tray trickled onto her shirt, mixing with blood. "Sorry, sorry, sorry," I said as I watched her bleed onto her tie-dyed T-shirt. George refunded her meal and apologized again.

"Haha," said one of the busboys, who had enjoyed the show. "Nice job almost killing that old lady."

Besides the occasional injuring of customers, the monotony of the bussing/washing/bussing cycle was broken by unusual visitors. One day I overheard a family seated at a table by the window speaking a foreign language, something one never heard in our white-bread town. I edged in closer. They were speaking *French*!

Like other kids in my junior high school, I had started language classes in seventh grade, at age twelve, so I had been studying French for three years.

I made sure to bus the table next to theirs, casually sidling up to them and saying "Bonjour," hoping desperately that the other employees would overhear and be dazzled by my command of the French language. (They didn't, so they weren't.)

Initially I had some success. "I saw two little kids come in with two adults," I wrote in my journal. "When I was bussing a table I heard the little kids speaking French & the adults weren't. They were so happy when they heard I spoke French. What I did was to describe a chocolate sundae. I did pretty well! Except I didn't know how to say whipped cream."

They were from Montreal. Why the kids spoke French but the adults didn't I couldn't tell. The kids peppered me with rapid-fire questions in French. First they asked what to see in Philadelphia for the *Bicentenaire*. That was one word we all knew from French class, where our Bicentennial-themed lessons centered around the Marquis de Lafayette, who had fought in a famous battle with the Continental Army a few miles from our high school, in the town where many of my classmates lived: Lafayette Hill.

After laboring to direct the kids to the Liberty Bell, I switched to English, realizing that when confronted with native French speakers, even children, I was too nervous and could barely string together a few sentences. Talking with my French teacher and my classmates was a lot easier. The adults, who spoke English, intervened. So I said *au revoir* and retreated to the Anglophone safety of the kitchen. Years later I read Fran Lebowitz's aperçu that when one visits France (or Quebec for that matter), one realizes that residents there took their French classes more seriously than you ever did.

My failure to communicate with our Quebecois customers was a disappointment, and not only because of my three years of French. My mom majored in French in college, taught French for a time, and worked as a French-language translator for an international business in downtown Philadelphia before marrying my father in 1959.

Growing up, my sister and I would often be serenaded by French songs and regaled with stories about my mom's halcyon summers at Middlebury College's intensive summer-language program in Vermont and the summer she visited Europe with her girlfriends after college. Rarely did we see her happier than when showing us her color slides of the trip, which came out on special occasions and were projected onto a grainy white movie screen set up in our living room, and narrating her youthful adventures by reading from her travel journal, which had a fraying green leather cover and thin robin's-egg-blue pages, all held together by a thick rubber band. Her European diary was one of the few possessions she kept all the way until her stay in a nursing home.

When my sister and I were older, my mom worked as a substitute (pronounced *sub-zee-toot* in Philadelphia) teacher in junior high schools and high school. I was so proud when she went to work in her camel-colored twin set, with a thin, gold 1970s chain necklace, looking smart, capable, and professional. I was proud of my mom in general: She was a bright woman with a great sense of humor. Clever, well-read, and confident.

However, my friends ragged on me whenever they had her in class. "Jimmy, I had your *mommmmmmy* today." On the rare occasions when she was *my* teacher too, despite my pride in her accomplishments, I slunk down in my chair, mortified that my mom might call on me in class. She would not have been *heureuse* about my performance at the Ice Cream Inn.

Worse was an encounter at our local swim club, called Ply-Mar (after "Plymouth Meeting" and "Whitemarsh," the neighboring town), which I blame on a film.

During freshman year of junior high, in Mr. Sherman's French class, we watched an endless series of black-and-white films of early 1960s provenance, with young men wearing fedoras and young women in big skirts, all speaking stilted and rather silly dialogue that focused on saying hello, asking how every single person in the scene was, replying that you were very well, and painstakingly introducing all your friends to one another one by one. When that was over, they would talk about items of clothing, what they liked to eat, and where they would be traveling. Apparently, everyone in France was exceedingly polite, always greeting one another with the same precise formality: "I am happy to make your acquaintance." The films, produced by Encyclopedia Britannica, repeated the banal conversations featured in our textbook *Je Parle Français*, which would again be repeated by us in live playlets performed in class.

By the end of the school year, we knew all the characters, especially the star, Margot, her friend Anne, and Margot's uncle. Strangely, he was called not by his first name, like Uncle Pierre, but always *Mon Oncle*. After reading their conversations, watching them in the films, and acting out their scenes in class, we knew all these interchanges by heart. (Amazingly, I recently discovered these films online and was happy to discover that I had accurately remembered the snippets I had carried around in the French section of my brain.)

In the very first film, Mon Oncle and his friend Monsieur Price are chatting with Margot outside a classroom building. After a round of formal greetings, asking after one another and being assured that everyone is *très bien*, Margot exclaims that she is late for class. After excusing herself and saying *au revoir*, she turns and walks up a staircase. As the two men stare at her backside, Mr. Price says, "*Elle est charmante.*" She is charming. "*Oui, char-

mante!" says her uncle with emphasis, as they continue to leer. Naturally, as teenagers in the 1970s, we found this more than a little *louche* and therefore hysterical.

One film saw Margot introducing her friend Josette to one of her professors. Margot was constantly meeting new people and introducing them to everyone else:

Professor: Good day, Margot.
Margot: Good day, sir. How are you?
Professor: Very well. Thank you, Margot. And you?
Margot: Very well, thank you. Sir, do you know Miss Bilodeau?
Professor: No, Margot.
Margot: Permit me to present to you Josette Bilodeau.
Professor: Good day, miss.
Josette: Good day, sir. I am happy to make your acquaintance.
Margot: Josette is Canadian. She is from Quebec.

At that point the professor said, "*Ohhhhh, VRAIMENT?*"—"Oh, really?"—with an exaggerated emphasis that we found hilarious. Why was it so weird that someone was from Quebec?

For the rest of the year, whenever I shared a boring piece of news with my friend Barb, we would deploy that phrase to mock its banality. "I have an algebra test tomorrow," I would say.

"*Ohhhhh, VRAIMENT?*" Barb would say. As befits twelve-year-old seventh-graders, we found this the height of hilarity and worth repeating several times a day.

One day at Ply-Mar, as I was eating some Freeze Pops with friends, my mother waved me over to where she was sitting, in the shade of a maple tree, in her green mesh lawn chair. She had struck up a conversation with a woman visiting from Canada who spoke French. My mom told her *en français* that her son was studying her native language.

I stood there in my stars-and-stripes Speedo, a flower-power towel around my sunburnt shoulders, holding a grape Freeze Pop, trying to remember how to start a conversation.

I began with the formal greeting that Margot always used: *Je suis heureux de faire vôtre connaissance*. I am happy to make your acquaintance. My mom's friend smiled. Then I asked where she was from.

"*Je suis du Québec*," she said.

Unable to stop myself, I blurted out, "*Ohhhhh, VRAIMENT?*"

My mom was aghast. Frowning, the woman said in English, "Yes, I'm from Quebec. Is that so hard to believe?" I stood speechless, grape Freeze Pop juice dripping onto *la terre*.

Our foreign-language teachers in both junior high school and high school were superb. I would end up taking six years of French and two of Spanish. Amazingly, our energetic tenth-grade French teacher, Mrs. Paulos, assigned us to read not bland textbooks, but something else entirely: the classics of twentieth-century existentialism.

"You're reading *what*?" my mother said, after we were assigned Jean-Paul Sartre's *Huis Clos* (*No Exit*), set in hell, with its stupefyingly depressing insight, *L'enfer c'est les autres*. "Hell is other people." Now there's something inspiring for a skittish high school student looking for life lessons! I still have my copy from junior high and was amazed by some of the notes and translations written in the margins: "There is no need for a devil. We torture each other." Also the English translations for words such as "sadist," "infanticide," and "leather whips."

I wonder if these books would pass muster in today's more cautious environment. After all, it was in *Huis Clos* that I first ran across the term *lesbianisme*, which Mrs. Paulos had to explain to our class. Also on our list of high school texts was *L'Étranger* (*The Stranger*) by Albert Camus, with its famously nihilistic introduction: *Aujourd'hui, maman est morte. Ou peut-être hier, je ne sais pas.* "Today, Mom died. Or maybe yesterday, I don't know."

In later years, we would read Jean Anouilh's play *Antigone*, which took as its inspiration Sophocles's drama and emphasized the need for resistance under totalitarianism (*Antigone* premiered in 1944 during the Nazi occupation of France), and André Gide's *La Symphonie Pastorale*, a dark tale about religion, morality, and sexuality. At the time, I had no idea how fortunate I was to be introduced to this kind of intellectual fare at a young age. Our English classes were equally rigorous: Any skills I have as a writer I learned first in junior high.

Madame Paulos and Monsieur Sherman were two of several dedicated but probably underpaid teachers who helped me fall in love with foreign languages, even if I can no longer remember the *subjonctif plus-que-parfait* tense. But I remember those teachers, and many others in those years, opening up new worlds for me. It didn't hurt Mrs. Paulos's *enfant terrible* image when a few girls from our class were invited to dinner at her home and reported that in her kitchen was a large sign that read "F—k housework!"

By the time I left the Ice Cream Inn in August, I still may have been a middling French student, but I was a whiz at bussing tables and washing dishes. Years later in a Jesuit community, someone complimented me on my dishwashing after dinner and I joked, "I'm a professional!"

Working in a restaurant was a tough job, physically demanding, but it had three perks. A steady paycheck was one, occasional whippets were another, and free ice cream a third. But I rarely felt like I fit in with the older crowd; being on the low end of the work totem pole was an emotional struggle. As an adolescent, I had always been chatty, sometimes to a fault. My three consistent U's (Unsatisfactory) on my elementary-school report cards were "Uses Free Time Wisely," "Keeps Desk Area Neat," and "Refrains from Excessive Talking." And I was blessed with many friends, so I was forever talking excessively in school. In algebra class that year, our teacher moved me to the far end of the classroom to prevent me from speaking to my friends. But at the Ice Cream Inn I found myself red-faced and tongue-tied among the older kids.

On June 12, I wrote in my journal: "The kids at the place are okay. I guess they're not super-nice but they're not super-mean and everyone cuts up everyone else. It's sort of stupid."

"Sort of stupid," but, on the other hand, by the end of August I had more money than ever. Even though I had been worried that I wouldn't see my friends, they all stopped by for ice cream. I made sure to visit them at their jobs too. My journal includes detailed accounts of all the friends from junior high who dropped by that summer to say hi (and ask for free ice cream). I wanted people, everyone really, to like me, so I took careful note of which friends visited.

That was an easy way to see friends during the summer. All my classmates except the rich ones had jobs. These ranged from staffing the counters at McDonald's or the local burger chain called Gino's; to working as movie theater ushers, lifeguards, or caddies; to working at their parents' businesses. Visiting friends at their summer jobs was a lark, often designed to get them in trouble:

stealing candy from a movie theater display case, reaching over the McDonald's counter to steal fries, or getting a free round of miniature golf. You didn't just visit your friends; you had to embarrass them into illicitly giving you something for free and then talk endlessly about it later.

Summer jobs were hardly a rarity in the US in the 1960s and 1970s. In the two decades before I was born (the 1940s and 1950s), the number of kids working when school wasn't in session was even higher. In 1978, the summer I graduated from high school, according to a study by the Pew Research Center, more than half (58 percent) of all teens were working in summer jobs. The percentage went up and down over the next few decades until it began to drop in the 2000s, reaching a low of 28 percent in 2008.

Lately, that figure has edged back up to about 36 percent. But while most summer jobs for teens are still in the old standby areas of food (e.g., the Ice Cream Inn and McDonald's) and retail, among wealthier families these traditional low-paying teenage jobs are being replaced with unpaid internships in offices, to burnish future college applications. One could argue that white-collar internships help students get into better colleges and therefore represent a better long-term investment. But young people working in office internships are often insulated from the kinds of challenges faced by low-wage workers. As ever, for poorer kids and poorer families, there is less choice involved; many young people have to work in whatever jobs they can get, during both the summers and the school year, to help put food on the table.

Overall, though, in the middle classes in the US, the almost universal expectation that a teenager would work in the summer has declined. When I look back on my own experiences, then, I see something of a vanished age. Because it seemed that not half of my friends, but *all* my friends, were working. And I was expected to do so until I graduated from college.

This book is mainly a snapshot of a few years of being thrown into a series of jobs for which I had zero training when I was a boy, then a teenager, and finally a young adult. I had never set foot in a restaurant kitchen before working as a busboy; I had never stepped onto a golf course before working as a caddy; and I had never seen a factory floor before working as an assembly-line worker. And few of the skills you learned in one job prepared you for the next: Knowing how to mow lawns does not help you bus tables; knowing how to bus tables does not help you caddy; knowing how to caddy does not help you on an assembly line. So I nearly always felt unsure of myself. Uncomfortable. Unsettled. Uneasy. All feelings I disliked.

I did it because I needed the money. My parents were not poor but not rich. And if I wanted to make money to enjoy life as a teenager and, later, support myself as a college student, like most of my peers I had to work a series of summer jobs (and fall and winter ones). Fifty years later, I look back on my adolescent willingness to jump into these situations with something resembling wonder.

I tell these tales chronologically, summer by summer, except for this first chapter, since the Ice Cream Inn was my first paying job (and the Bicentennial Wagon Train was too much fun not to tell first). And if you're a fan of snafus, you won't be disappointed: I'm not the hero of these stories—more a hapless teenager who learns in each job, even the ones I loathed, something about work, about what it means to be an adult, about people, and about life overall. The story closes with college graduation and my time in corporate America before entering the Jesuits, a job that technically started in the summer, so it counts.

One area I'm not going to focus on is my experience dating and falling in love, mainly because I doubt many readers want to hear about the romantic life, even the early one, of a priest. In short, I dated during high school and college, had frequent crushes, went to a seemingly endless series of dates, parties, dances, and proms, had a few kisses and hugs and the rest, and tried to act cool about it all, as most kids in that era did. There's not a whole lot to tell, and besides, since most of my dates are still alive, I doubt they'd want me to tell any tales, tall or otherwise. The summer job stories are funnier than the dating stories anyway.

To that end, this is mainly a lighthearted tale. But a darker time comes in the summer between my junior and senior years of college, since no one's life is free from suffering. Even a teenager's life. That almost unbearably sad time marks a shift in tone in the book, because it marked a shift in my life. Things changed. So did I.

Since it's hard for me *not* to see things through this lens, this is also a spiritual memoir, though maybe not the kind you're used to reading, if you read those sorts of things. There is not one single dramatic conversion moment, where I shamefacedly rue the past, weep remorsefully, and transform into a pious soul who rejects the things of the world. It's more of a gradual transformation. Besides, the world's not such a bad place. Peach ice cream, for example, is pretty great.

But everyone's life is a spiritual journey, whether they know it or not. So while some of these stories may not seem explicitly religious, grace was there, mainly in what I was being taught about life. When I was young, I wasn't aware of that. Now I am.

At the end of the book I recount what led me to become a Jesuit priest, but, as I said, that doesn't mean that I regret everything that came before, mainly because I think that what came before, even the embarrassing parts, led me to where I am. As an aside, I hereby apologize for any behavior or language that offends. I've cleaned things up but also want to accurately recount, as nearly as I can, what happened. As I often remind people, I wasn't always a Jesuit priest. My high school and college friends will remind you of that too.

This is a spiritual memoir from a different angle, then, told "slant," as Emily Dickinson might say. I'm writing not only to share what I learned from these jobs, but also to remind readers of the ways that grace works through all our lives, no matter who we are or how ordinary our daily activities may seem.

The lessons learned were also not accompanied by a blinding light, like Saul's experience on the road to Damascus. Often enough, they were smaller ones: Work hard, be on time, apologize when you need to, forgive frequently, ask if you don't know something, don't misuse power, pay attention to those who are struggling. Don't be mean. Be kind. Listen.

Speaking of listening, I am blessed with a good memory for conversations, people, events, and especially places: I'm usually able to remember what a room, house, building, or even a natural setting like a meadow or backyard looked like years after I saw it. Often all I have to do is close my eyes and I can more or less re-create the scene.

You may, however, wonder how I remember conversations from decades ago. Not long ago I read a review of a memoir that excoriated the author for putting conversations in quotation marks, as if the author had perfect recall. My answer is that I can fairly easily remember an important interchange, a clever turn of phrase, a helpful insight, or sometimes an insult. Some things burn themselves into one's memory. Obviously, though, I didn't have a tape recorder with me during my summer jobs, so I've tried to re-create the conversations as best I can remember.

Names, however, are more difficult for me to remember. So you won't see a lot of names in this book, other than those of family members and close friends, which is for the best anyway. One of my rules for writing a memoir is that in any story where someone behaves badly, I will change the name and sometimes even the sex of that person, so as not to embarrass the person if he or she is alive and reading this.

Sequences, I'm sometimes fuzzy on too: what happened first, second, third. As for recounting the stories overall, you'll have to trust me, though there will probably be some places where my memory has embellished things. I'm sure I got a few things wrong, despite my speaking with old friends, reading through my journals, poring through scrapbooks, and doing as much fact-checking as I could, even visiting all the places that are still standing.

So if one of the busboys from the Ice Cream Inn is reading this and I mistold the story of your misfired whipped cream that landed in that girl's face, I apologize. In fact, I apologize for any faulty memories in this book.

For example, I had long remembered a prank against me as malicious, when a glance at my journal showed that it wasn't at all.

On my last night at the Ice Cream Inn, at the end of August, I was given the standard farewell for all summer employees. My journal describes it in some detail. It was a surprise to read it almost half a century later: "My last night of work was Friday the 27th and on everyone's last night they get it and I got it too: 21 buckets of water on me and I was thrown into the dumpster. I knew it all night and at the end we all just laughed about it. I'm glad I worked this summer and I made over $300. I guess that's pretty good, I think. I'll probably return next year if I can't find a better job."

I can vividly recall the experience of being doused with water on a humid summer night; picked up bodily by two older boys; swung back and forth as the busboys, servers, and waitresses all called out, "One, two, *three*"; and then sailing over the edge of the great green monster and landing, not uncomfortably, in a heap of trash-filled bags, empty ice cream tubs, and used whipped cream canisters. I felt like an Olympic high jumper clearing the bar. The surrounding detritus smelled of spoiled ice cream and French fries. They fished me out and gave me a swig of warm beer to celebrate.

And even with the Bicentennial Wagon Train debacle, knocking that lady on the head with my tray, and breaking a few glasses, I was proud of holding down my first real summer job. Putting on that smock every night filled me with a pride I hadn't known before.

Years later, I would read St. John Paul II's encyclical on labor, which begins with this ringing declaration: "Through work man must earn his daily bread and contribute to the continual advance of science and technology and, above all, to elevating unceasingly the cultural and moral level of the society within which he lives in community with those who belong to the same family." I'm not sure I felt all that, but at age fifteen, still somewhat unsure of myself, I was proud to have a job and earn, if not my daily bread, then my daily rum raisin.

Despite my predictions, I wouldn't return to the Ice Cream Inn. By the spring of the next year, I concluded that I didn't like being cooped up during the summer. So I'd look for a job that was outdoors.

But, as I said earlier, being a smock-wearing, mop-wielding, whippet-sniffing, creamer-popping, rum-raising-eating, banana-split-boat-breaking, dumpster-thrown busboy wasn't my first real summer job. That had come two years earlier.

Feel free to stub out your cigarettes on my nine-year-old face. Ashtray courtesy of the Cub Scouts.

When being chased by dogs, or critiqued for his poor aim, this eighth-grade paperboy was not smiling.

CHAPTER 2

How Not to Be a Shiftless Troublemaker

I'M NOT SURE WHY I AGREED TO TAKE A JOB WITHOUT the promise of being paid. But when you're thirteen, you don't have much bargaining power.

A modest income was promised to young boys (occasionally girls) by the publishers of *The Conshohocken Recorder* and *The Weekly Advertiser,* two minuscule newspapers published in the Philadelphia suburbs, probably not that different from many other local papers at the time. The way the income was earned by those who delivered it, however, was unusual.

It's hard to imagine a time when anyone would want to read these weekly ten-page tabloids. As its name suggests, *The Advertiser* was crammed with ads for local businesses, next to brief articles about local doings. *The Recorder*, I guess, recorded local news, but like its competitor, supported itself by advertising the same pizzerias, barbershops, and insurance agencies that placed identical ads in our local church bulletin.

Decades before the internet, there were far fewer places to get news, and decades before cable and streaming, there was far less to watch on TV. In the Philadelphia area we had the Holy Trinity of Channels 3, 6, and 10 (NBC, ABC, and CBS) plus whatever you could find on UHF: Channels 17, 29, and 48, whose fare ran heavily to *Gilligan's Island* and *The Flying Nun* reruns, 1960s Japanese anime cartoons like *Astro Boy* and *Marine Boy*, and black-and-white movies from the 1950s and earlier. In that entertainment wasteland, why not peruse the papers to see what *The Advertiser* was advertising and *The Recorder* was recording?

The two papers published enough local tidbits to pique anyone's interest. Often enough you'd spy a photo of a classmate or neighbor, spotlighted for bringing in the most cans to a food drive sponsored by a school or church. Some sort of canned food drive always seemed to be going on. You'd turn a page and see your next-door neighbor posed next to a precariously tall tower of cans of peas, peaches, and stewed tomatoes, the last of which I was forever urging our family to donate, so miserable was I when my mother served it. I had a hard time imagining anyone eating the slimy red mess, no matter how poor, hungry, or desperate.

Our neighbor across the street recommended to my parents the paperboy job for me. Delivering papers at a young age would be good for me, said my dad. When you were a kid, things that sounded frankly awful were always good for you. Like stewed tomatoes.

My dad meant "good for me" in terms of "building character." I, however, was interested not in building character, or learning any moral lessons, but in building my bank account.

My parents gave me a weekly allowance of five dollars to compensate me for my house chores: taking out the trash on Wednesdays, drying dishes every night, mowing the lawn during the spring and summer, raking leaves in the fall, shoveling the walk in the winter, and vacuuming our rugs every weekend. In the 1970s, that last task was harder than one would suppose: Our orange-yellow-and-red wall-to-wall shag carpet in our faux-wood-paneled recreation room came with a plastic yellow rake so you could make sure the high shag pile was "standing up" so the vacuum could suck up cookie crumbs from late-night snacks and pine needles from when we were dumb enough to set up a Christmas tree on a shag carpet. "Did you rake the rug?" was a common question from my mom.

Delivering *The Recorder* was the first time I would get paid for a job outside the house.

Every week a green pickup truck pulled into our driveway and dumped onto the blacktop a stack of flattened newspapers, which landed with a loud *thwack*, along with a box of about a million powdery, dry, green rubber bands.

Then, in our garage, often with my dad and sometimes my sister, I would roll several hundred papers, encircle them with the rubber bands (which often snapped and, wasplike, stung your fingers), jam them into a green cloth sack emblazoned with the words "The Recorder," and stuff the bag into the wire basket perched on the handlebars of my blue Schwinn Speedster bike. There was no question of carrying the bag through the neighborhood on foot because, filled with papers, it weighed fifty pounds, probably half as much as I did at the time.

The sack, crammed into my bike basket and straining at its

canvas seams, was absurdly heavy, which made steering nearly impossible, especially at the beginning of the route when the bag was full. The slightest turn of the handlebars meant the bike lurched violently to the side as the weight of the papers took control of the steering. I cycled through the neighborhood and flung papers on the lawns (or porches and steps, if my aim was good) of every house, since everyone got a paper, whether they wanted one or not.

You didn't subscribe to *The Recorder*. It just appeared on your doorstep every week, unbidden, to be read, tossed away, used to line a birdcage, or left on the lawn to disintegrate in the rain or snow or slush. I delivered it to everyone. That meant a two-hour bike ride through our neighborhood, rain or shine.

That bizarre business model made the weekly collections an exercise in frustration, since no one was obliged to pay. Every month, I would dutifully clip my metal money changer on my belt and soldier out to accost every householder in our neighborhood, a task that took several hours. My income was whatever I could collect, less the cost of the papers and rubber bands, which I paid the publisher. Sometimes my neighbors gave me nothing except a cold stare.

Usually I did collections after dinner, which made it not only frustrating, but frightening. I was worried not so much about the dark or being mugged (if that happened I could scream and someone would come to my aid, I figured optimistically) or being kidnapped (a common fear among my friends despite our knowing a total of zero kids who had been kidnapped) or seeing a "flasher" (which I didn't understand, though I knew it had to do with a naked man opening his raincoat, which I could never see the point of), but about something more ordinary: dogs.

• • • •

An unaccountably high number of large, menacing dogs prowled around unleashed in our neighborhood, which I found incredible. German shepherds seemed to patrol every yard, as if guarding some suburban stalag.

One cool fall afternoon I was coasting down Kings Road, under the red and orange leaves of the maple trees that lined the sidewalks, my bike basket jammed with newspapers. Suddenly from someone's backyard an enormous German shepherd, tan with a black snout, spied me and began barking furiously. He gave chase for four or five houses, trying to bite my legs with his surprisingly white teeth, and I can still remember my heart racing as I sped downhill, worried that I would flip over my handlebars. Everyone knew that flipping over your handlebars was the worst thing that could happen on your bike because, as our mothers told us over and over, "You'll break your neck!" I had never pedaled so hard going downhill and was going faster than I thought possible.

Even in my fearful exertion I thought angrily: *Who would let their stupid dog off the leash? What if I were walking? I'd probably be dead!*

As I pedaled, the dog snapped at my heels while I remonstrated interiorly with the offending family, fury fueling my adrenaline. Fortunately, I escaped, though I was too frightened for an hour to return to that street. It took almost that long for my heart to stop pounding. When I finally did return, it was so dark that I could barely see, and so each house was a potential trap, as I imagined the same dog lying in wait for me, along with his mean dog friends.

This was one of many times when I imagined what would happen if a dog attacked me. *What was the best way to confront a dog?* I wondered as I walked up to each house. The only solution, I thought, was a gun, though a thirteen-year-old paperboy with a loaded weapon was not something people would want to see when opening their front doors. Maybe I should buy mace, which I had heard about but wasn't sure what it was: a spray? Early on I brought a big stick, which I found in the woods across the street from our house, but pedaling a bike, balancing the handlebars, throwing papers, and carrying a stick proved impossible.

"They only attack you if they smell fear," said one of my friends, but that made no sense at all. Since dogs could attack you, I was frightened. I was doomed.

The other time I was "attacked" on my paper route, a dog raced up to me, probably out of curiosity. I was so startled that I turned immediately, and my basket was so filled with papers that the bike swerved and I lost my balance and landed on the street. The dog sniffed at me contentedly until the owner came out and said what all dog owners say: "Don't worry! He doesn't bite!" Once, my friend Joyce's German shepherd leaped out of the front door when I was dropping off some homework and took a bite out of my yellow windbreaker, leaving behind its dog saliva. The hole was there for as long as I had the jacket.

After I completed the paper route, whether delivering or collecting, I was grateful to return to our house, often in the dark, where my mom, without fail, would have dinner on the table precisely at 6 p.m. My family was a loving one, not perfect of course, but breakfast, lunch, and dinner were unfailingly on time, with near military precision. My favorite dinner at the time was canned crab, with cream of celery soup and peas, all served over rice, with toast, which we ate a lot on Fridays, being Catholic. Another Friday standby was Mrs. Paul's Fish Sticks (or, if we were splurging, crab cakes) and Kraft's macaroni and cheese. And Saturdays were for cheesesteaks.

As the daughter of Sicilian immigrants, my mom was justly proud of her spaghetti and meatballs and her peerless chicken soup, served with a Sicilian egg-and-chicken frittata we called *froscia* (pronounced *FRAW-sha*), which we ate with Heinz's sweet relish. My sister and I would sometimes take to school leftover *froscia* sandwiched between two slices of Wonder Bread, to the horror of our classmates in the cafeteria: "What's *that*?" Her Sicilian meat stuffing for Thanksgiving turkeys (ground beef, raisins, chopped boiled egg whites, along with celery and onions and plenty of sage and poultry seasoning: Try it!) was also tops. On the other hand, my mom's experimental meals were not always successful: Meatloaf stuffed with melted mozzarella cheese was a memorably bad, gooey mess.

My mom was also assiduous about what we would today call food safety, avoiding anything that could possibly cause illness, especially raw meat: "Well done" was the norm for everything, and anything that could possibly go bad was kept in the fridge. The only exception was Nature Valley Granola, a breakfast cereal that debuted the year before, in 1973, and famously contained no preservatives. I begged my mom to buy it after I saw so many TV commercials. It seemed so healthy! So moral! So *noble*! Like I was helping the environment by eating cereal with no added chemicals.

Unfortunately, one morning in our kitchen, while listening to "Kodachrome," Paul Simon's song that was in heavy rotation on the radio, I ate a bowl of old granola. A few hours later, in Mrs. Donnelly's eighth-grade English class, when we were reading Jack London's short story "To Build a Fire," I was spectacularly sick, vomiting all over my book. "Oh no, Jimmy threw up!" said one girl, somewhat superfluously. Mrs. Donnelly gamely put her hand on my shoulder and tried to lead me to the boys' room, but I ralphed on her too. My friends returned the book to my house the next day, and I had to open it up to "To Build a Fire" and hose it off in our backyard. For our English class, it was the undisputed highlight of the week. A few years later, in our junior high school yearbook, the theme of most of my friends' farewell messages ran heavily toward, "Remember when you threw up in Mrs. Donnelly's class?"

Apart from not tossing away that one spoiled box of granola, a clean, healthy, and well-ordered household was one way that my mom showed her love. Not simply verbally (she often said "I love you") and physically (she often hugged and kissed my sister and me) but by making sure the household was well run. That meant cleaning the house, washing our clothes, driving us to doctors' appointments (and to school when it rained), and, above all, making sure meals were precisely on time. So when I returned from my paper route in the dark, dinner was always, unfailingly, *there*.

Darkness was a common theme in 1974, when the energy crisis, caused by the oil embargo from OPEC (Organization of the Petroleum Exporting Countries) in the Middle East, prompted the US government to make daylight saving time permanent. Fuel consumption, it was explained, would decrease as Americans used the extra evening sunshine for heat and light. That meant that for several months, clocks would "spring forward" but not "fall back." Thus, on the East Coast the sun didn't rise until 8:30 a.m.

On school days, that meant waking up in pitch-dark and walking to the bus stop with a flashlight. There we'd stand in the dark and talk and try to act cool and complain about school and spit on the sidewalk every few minutes. (Spitting, a regular pastime of many boys in our neighborhood, showed how cool and/or tough you were.) Between going to school in the dark and doing my collections after school in the dark, I started to feel like a bat.

Despite my parents commending my industriousness, I also felt like an idiot collecting money for *The Recorder*, a paper no one subscribed to. I wanted the money, but this was an odd way of earning it. Or not earning it.

At every door I thought: *Why am I delivering papers that no one wants? I should be delivering a real paper, one that I'd get paid for. And was that barking I just heard?*

Someone would come to the door, occasionally holding a dog back, which started barking as soon as I rang the doorbell. I could hear the owner shouting, "SHUT UP!" I wondered why dogs barked at the doorbell. *They've heard it before*, I thought, silently reproaching the dog. *It's a person at the door, where they always are. How dumb can you be?*

I always took a step back, remembering Joyce's German shepherd and absentmindedly touching the bite hole in my jacket.

The rest of the conversation always fell into the same pattern, with as much numbing regularity as the old films we watched in French class:

Me: Hi. I'm collecting for *The Recorder*.
Homeowner (*holding back a snarling dog*): The what?
Me: *The Recorder*. The newspaper?
Homeowner: Don't worry. He doesn't bite.
Me (*looking at the dog's remarkably white teeth*): Uh . . .
Homeowner: We don't get it.
Me: Uh, yeah, you do. I deliver it here every week.

Homeowner (*pointing to rolled-up paper on the lawn*): Oh, that rag? We throw those out.

Me: Oh. Well, you only have to pay if you want to.

Homeowner: How much?

Me: A dollar fifteen.

Homeowner: A dollar fifteen for a paper that I don't read and didn't ask for?

Me: Yes. I guess. Sorry.

Homeowner: Hold on. (*Disappears while the dog eyes me, then reappears with coins.*) Here.

Me: Thanks. (*Joyfully places four quarters, one dime, and one nickel into my money changer.*)

Homeowner: By the way, your aim stinks. If I'm going to pay for it, throw it on my steps, not on the lawn, which is where I usually see it.

Me: Okay.

Homeowner: Do you play baseball?

Me: I'm in Little League in the summer.

Homeowner: Well, you should practice your throwing. I hope you're not a pitcher. Hahaha.

Me: I'm not. I play right field. (*Dog barks, door closes, dog continues barking.*)

Repeat about two hundred times. The job was door-to-door begging. I hated it.

When I told my father that I would say "sorry" to the homeowners, he said, "What are you apologizing for? You haven't done anything wrong." I was forever apologizing for things I hadn't done, just to avoid conflict. I didn't want to offend anyone or cause conflict. Even then, at thirteen, I wanted everyone to like me.

"Keep at it," said my dad. "It's good for you. It builds character."

I had other reasons for sticking with it. Chief among them was a powerful desire to buy a pup tent that I had seen in the Sears catalog. Even now, I'm mystified by the appeal of a pup tent: I hated camping.

A few years before starting my paper route, I had finished my stint with the Webelos, the next step up from Cub Scouts but preceding Boy Scouts, and that meant at least one camping trip.

Webelos stood for "We'll Be Loyal Scouts," but the pronunciation of the singular form of the word was an absurdly easy source of mockery at school. If you had to pick a worse name for an organization of adolescent boys, you could do no better than what the Boy Scouts had chosen. "Hahaha. We blow? Who do you blow?" We Webelos heard that every time we wore our bright blue uniforms to school.

I was in Webelos for only a year or so, since I didn't have the enthusiasm to be a Boy Scout, much less an Eagle Scout, the final stage of scouting, which, from what I heard, required an almost fanatical devotion. As a younger boy, however, I enjoyed being a Cub Scout, making it to Bobcat, Wolf, and Bear Scout status, which sounds impressive, betokening battles with each of those forest creatures that left you bloody but triumphant—but in fact they were classifications given to any Cub Scout in the first, second, third, and fourth grades.

Cub Scout meetings were only a few blocks away, so I could walk even at a young age to see Mrs. Nelson, our friendly den mother and mother of a friend from my school. The Nelsons were also one of the few families who gave me money for *The Recorder*. At her house we made papier-mâché pumpkins constructed around balloons for Halloween, decorations for Christmas (even though Mrs. Nelson was Jewish, we made Christmas-tree chains from loops of multicolored construction paper), and learned about what was then called "Indian lore," centering on the people who had once lived in the area, the Lenni-Lenape.

I loved being a Cub Scout, especially the arts-and-crafts part and the Hawaiian Punch and Chips Ahoy! cookies served at all the meetings in our den mother's recreation room, which was, as in my own house, covered in thick shag carpeting, all the better to hide the crumbs from all those cookies.

My career as a Cub Scout was memorialized with a photo of me in my uniform, which our den mother that year, Mrs. Greenfield, snapped in her backyard. The next week, after our photos were developed, we all gathered in her den. There, we carefully cut the photos out in the shape of a circle and affixed them to the bottom of a heavy glass ashtray so you could see the photo through the glass. It was a testimony to the mores of the era that everyone's parents were assumed to smoke, or at least to need an ashtray for guests. That night I proudly took it home as a gift to my parents. For the next few decades, they would stub out their cigarettes on my smiling Cub Scout face, sans irony or regret. After my mom moved out of our home, I received it as a gift.

I was also enamored of the uniform. I wasn't overly concerned with clothes—which at the time ran heavily to Keds sneakers, multicolored striped or plaid bell-bottom pants, short-sleeved shirts with half-zip necks, long-sleeved shirts with wide collars, and colorful polyester "Apache scarves" worn around our necks. Everything came from the local mall or the Sears catalog.

But how could you not like the Webelos blue cap, blue shirt, blue-and-yellow scarf (and brass scarf clip with official insignia), and tiny pins that trumpeted your accomplishments? We Webelos pinned red-yellow-and-green ribbons on our shoulders, to which little medals were attached for every accomplishment: a tiny scroll for "scholar," a tiny palette for "artist," and a tiny running guy for "athlete." Even my school safety uniform, a white strap and belt with a gleaming silver metal emblem from the American Automobile Association, surmounted by an eagle, which you wore over your heart, couldn't hold a candle to the Cub Scout or Webelos getups.

The camping trip was billed as the year's high point. Plus, I would be able to go with my dad, which I thought would be fun. But what I envisioned as an exciting night in the woods, roasting marshmallows, eating s'mores, telling ghost stories, and being surrounded by wide-eyed Disney creatures before bedding down in a comfy sleeping bag, ended up being a sleepless night spent in an ice-cold wooden cabin next to snoring fathers and farting sons, followed by a miserable breakfast the next morning of stale Sugar Pops. At least the milk was cold. I couldn't wait to get home and sleep in my own bed. On the other hand, I got another cool Webelos badge for being an "outdoorsman": a tiny metal flying goose.

In any event, I wanted to buy a pup tent not so that I could do anything resembling camping, but so that I could have some privacy in our backyard. Our three-bedroom, one-and-a-half-bathroom, split-level house started to seem cramped as I grew older, and the balsa-wood doors to our bedrooms were hardly soundproof. I liked my bedroom, with one window that looked out onto our backyard, where I could watch the birds come and go, and another looking onto the side of our neighbor's house, where huge lilac bushes burst into lavender bloom in the spring. I liked the round braided rug that covered the simple wooden floor and made ridges on the soles of my feet, and I liked the patterned wallpaper with blue ships, globes, and treasure chests arrayed on a sand-colored background, which my parents and I selected from the boys section of a wallpaper sampler book. But I wanted a place where my parents wouldn't forever be saying, "What are you *doing* in there?"

I took a brief hiatus from delivering newspapers for our traditional two-week vacation in a rented apartment in Ocean City, a family-oriented (read: alcohol-free) resort on New Jersey's Southern Shore, where many families from Philadelphia cooled off in the summer. That August, my family would watch, on a portable black-and-white TV in another family's house, Richard Nixon announce his resignation from the presidency. "Well, that's that," said my dad, and we kids went back to watching a horror movie called *Fiend Without a Face*.

That summer I also volunteered, along with a few other friends, at our town's summer recreation program as a Junior Leader. The Plymouth Township Recreation Department sponsored a program for younger kids, which I had participated in as a boy, consisting of activities held at Ridge Park Elementary School.

Our elementary school was a textbook example of what is now called mid-century modern design but was then called just modern: a one-story, tan-brick building with a flat roof and tall windows that let sunlight stream into the classrooms. On Halloween, Thanksgiving, and Christmas the windows were nearly covered with cardboard witches and pumpkins, pilgrims and turkeys, Santas and wreaths. Built in 1962, a few years before I started first grade, Ridge Park was on a hill and sprawled over acres of land that overlooked our neighborhood. In the front, under a wide porch supported by slim metal poles, school buses exhaled kids in the morning and inhaled them in the afternoon. These were the "bussers." My sister and I were "walkers," because the school was only a mile or so from our house.

My participation as a Junior Leader that summer was memorialized in *The Recorder*, along with all the other kids in the program, in a clipping I carefully taped into my scrapbook. The article, "Plymouth Youngsters Don't Waste Summer," began on a surprisingly dark note: "Not all adolescents are shiftless troublemakers."

The summer program featured sporting activities that even the most uncoordinated kids could play: dodgeball (easy but lethal when the ball was aimed at your face), softball (easier than baseball since the ball was bigger), kickball (which anyone who could kick could play), volleyball (also lethal when facing a kid a foot taller than you across the net), box hockey (which I loved because it involved furiously whacking a small ball in a box toward a goal while the other person just as furiously whacked back), and all manner of races on foot. For the less actively inclined, there were board games: Monopoly, Risk, Stratego, The Game of Life, Chutes & Ladders, Game of the States, and, for the girls (yes, sexist, I know), Mystery Date, which was then heavily promoted on TV with an earworm tune.

"Mystery Daaaaate, are you ready for your mystery daaaate?" sang the man in the commercial. "Open the door for *your* mystery date!" The aim of the game was to land a promising young man. "When you open the door," asked the announcer, "will your mystery date be a dream?" There followed a guy wearing a suit jacket, and the girl swooned. "Or a *dud*?" There followed a guy dressed like a hippie. "Oh," said the crestfallen girl. No guy wanted to be a dud.

When it rained, we stayed indoors and used the school gym, playing endless rounds of dodgeball, volleyball, and "crab ball," which consisted of doing backward-bending crab walks and kicking an immense cloth-and-wire ball around the gym floor, only occasionally getting it anywhere near the goal.

Most days the kids also did arts and crafts, which meant making small boxes from popsicle sticks, potholders from colored cotton loops, and lanyards from "gimp," long, thin, brightly colored strips of plastic. I've never spent so much time around gimp, before or since. Also, we chaperoned the young kids on field trips to local places ranging from the fun (the Philadelphia Zoo) and the somewhat less fun but educational (Independence Hall and the US Mint in Philadelphia, where we all received a newly minted penny) to the truly fun-less (the 7-Up bottling plant and Stroehmann Bakeries in nearby Conshohocken).

The summer before, I had been to an actual day camp, called Sesame Day Camp, a few miles from our home, run by a Jewish couple and catering mainly to the many Jewish families in the area.

Many of my friends were Jewish, and by my count I attended twelve bar and bat mitzvahs, compared with zero First Communion or Confirmation parties. In fact, I knew no children who went to Catholic schools, which made for some strange moments after I entered the Jesuits: I knew the first few words of the Hebrew *berakah* (blessing) but didn't know how to say the Rosary properly. One day a few years ago, on a pilgrimage in Israel with about a hundred other Catholics, outside the walls of the Old City in Jerusalem, we ran into a procession for a young man's bar mitzvah, complete with a DJ singing "Hava Nagila." He playfully handed me the microphone and I started singing. Then, egged on by people throwing their hands over my shoulders, I danced a hora. "Did you learn that in an interfaith program?" one rather surprised Catholic pilgrim asked. "No," I said, "I learned it in junior high."

At the time, Catholicism was simply part of my life, like being Italian or Irish. Or having brown eyes and red hair. I gave as much thought to it as I did to my last name. It was important but simply there. I went to Mass and attended Sunday School classes for a few years when preparing for First Communion and Confirmation, and I prayed to God to ask for things, but I never saw religion as more than a "should." You should go to Mass; you should pray; you should be a good boy because that's what Jesus would want. But surprisingly few of my friends were Catholic; more were Protestant, or like my friends at Sesame Day Camp, Jewish.

I enjoyed Sesame immensely. A school bus picked us up every morning, and after a morning assembly we kayaked and swam and shot BB rifles, rode go-karts, sang songs, shot bows and arrows, and did endless hours of arts and crafts. Gimp predominated there as well. Why counselors and parents thought that we needed so many gimp lanyards and key holders is still difficult to understand. When my mom moved out of her house, I threw out about a dozen of them.

Sesame had a creek running through its wooded grounds, which meant lots of time spent hunting for crawfish and making half-hearted attempts at fishing but succeeding only in getting muddy. I loved camp, and they served the best hamburgers I ever had, before or since.

Decades later, I realized that Sesame Day Camp was only a few miles from where my mom lived in her new retirement community. One morning, after Mass, we drove to see it.

"Does this look familiar?" I said, remembering the pool, the burgers, and the gimp. My mom looked around, quizzically, from the front seat of the car.

"Not really," she said. "I don't think I've been here before."

"What do you mean?" I said. "You drove me here, right?"

"No, you took the bus, remember?"

"Well, you and Dad came to see the place before I came here, right?"

"Mmm, I don't think so," she said. "We knew the other families in the neighborhood had checked it out, so we figured that was good enough."

When I told a friend, she laughed and said that today a parent would probably examine the camp's website, perform a detailed investigation of its safety record, interview the owners and the counselors, inspect the site before they let their kids attend, and then text their kids throughout the day once they were there.

But in the 1960s and 1970s things were more relaxed, especially regarding kids and especially regarding safety for kids. And, most especially, regarding safety for kids in the summers. Kids were expected to be home for lunch and dinner, but otherwise we were expected, encouraged, almost forced, to be outside.

"What are you doing *inside*?" said my mother if she saw me paging through a book on a sunny day. Then followed several hours of what is now called "unsupervised time."

My parents were not careless; in fact they were more careful than most other parents in the neighborhood. My mother was often censorious of the way that some of our neighbors supervised, or rather didn't supervise, their kids.

"Look at *that*," she'd say as she saw a neighbor's child frolicking in the snow wearing a lightweight jacket, with no hat and no gloves. "They're going to catch pneumonia."

By contrast, my sister and I were bundled up even in mild

weather. Years later, Mrs. Ash, who lived across the street, told my mother that, to decide how to dress her kids, she would look at my sister and me, and then at our neighbors, who were somewhat less worried about the weather, and dress her children in between.

But common practices that even my cautious parents didn't mind but that would probably be frowned on today include:

- Not wearing a bike helmet (which would have made you a laughingstock and didn't exist anyway). Also, while not wearing your nonexistent bike helmet, playing "Chicken" with moving cars and trucks as you rode beside them on the street, with extra points for grabbing onto bumpers.
- Speaking of cars, never using seat belts. Especially when worn in the back seat of our 1964 Falcon, seat belts made it harder to dodge the cigarette ashes that my parents constantly flicked out the open windows of the moving car, which would, still burning, land on my sister and me in the back seat.
- Shooting BB guns and rifles at birds, cats, dogs, cars, houses, and other kids or, if you were lucky enough to have one, firing massive "Air Blasters," large plastic air guns usually filled with packed dirt, at other kids, often in their faces.
- Going to a highway overpass to drop dirt bombs, snowballs, rocks, or water balloons on passing cars.
- Setting afire the wispy white tent-caterpillar nests, lodged in the branches of trees, using gasoline and a match thrown in the general direction of the tree. Also, burning ants, beetles, and caterpillars with magnifying glasses under the hot sun. Finally, at night making a necklace of lightning bugs by stringing them together on thread, using a needle through their bioluminescent bodies. Sorry PETA.

- Hanging out in a friend's house for hours without telling your parents where you were. And, while there, throwing the neighbor's cat out the second-floor window with a homemade trash-bag parachute. (The cat was fine.)
- Eating paste (delicious!) and dried glue (not as tasty) in school and drinking water from a backyard hose.
- Putting over your head the clear, plastic wrap that covered your father's suits after they came back from the dry cleaner and pretending you were an Apollo 11 astronaut or a deep-sea diver. Extra credit for sucking the plastic wrap into your mouth, running to your mother, and saying, "I'm choking!"
- Sticking your bare legs over the curb and letting other kids drive over them with their bikes to cause purple bruises. My mother told me that I would have those bruises for my entire life. Fortunately, it was only for a few months.
- Playing with dangerous toys: Jarts were heavy metal lawn darts that you would throw like horseshoes, but they were also lethal metal projectiles that could easily take down an unwary kid. Creepy Crawlers were stretchy plastic insects made from plastic goop poured into metal molds; however, the goop needed to be baked in a superheated metal "Thingmaker" plate that burned many kids' fingers. Clackers involved two plastic balls on strings that were knocked together at a furious pace to make a deafening noise. Unfortunately, the clackers often shattered, sending plastic shards into kids' faces, and so were eventually banned. If none of these dangerous toys appealed, boys could always turn to their wood-burning kits, with red-hot metal pointers that were essentially juvenile branding irons; and girls could enjoy their Easy-Bake Ovens with temperatures up to 350 de-

grees. Many toys in the 1960s and 1970s seemed intent on burning children's fingers.
- Hitchhiking to school, hitchhiking to the mall, hitchhiking to nowhere just for fun.
- Exploring the woods at night, wandering aimlessly around the neighborhood after dinner in the dark, or going to strange houses in the dark and asking for money for a paper that no one had subscribed to.
- Perhaps most notable of all, walking to kindergarten at age four.

I asked my mom whether my memory about that last one was correct. "Sure," she said. She took four-year-old me the first few times to kindergarten, about a mile away, but then, she said, "I figured you knew the way so you could walk back and forth on your own."

I remember thinking, at four, *If anything happens, I can knock on someone's door.* Back then, someone's mother was bound to be home. We knew that because if you happened to trespass on someone's lawn or look like you weren't doing what you were supposed to be doing (i.e., walking to school) or even dawdling, someone's mom would stick her head out the window or open the door and say, "HEY! Would you do that on *your* property? What's your name?"

My mom's escorting me to school for the first few days continued through the first and second grades, but after that I was clearly old enough to fend for myself. I asked my sister, who has children of her own, what would happen now if a parent sent their four-year-old to kindergarten by themselves. "You'd probably get arrested for child endangerment," she said with a laugh.

Between working as a Junior Leader and delivering papers, I was busy. Some days I would also bag groceries at the local A&P grocery store, a job that took almost no brain power, save for figuring out how to protect an egg carton from getting crushed in someone's bag.

Supplementing my paperboy money, my grocery bag tips, and my allowance was a side job as a babysitter. The income was more reliable: You didn't have to beg for money.

I had several clients in the neighborhood, since in the wake of the Baby Boom every family on every block, except for the occasional elderly couple, had kids. On our way to elementary school in the morning when the weather was warm, the neighborhood kids would line a dozen bikes in front of the house across the street and bike to school together, making our stately procession through the neighborhood. On the way, our "bike line" ran into other kids on their bikes going to school, who joined our group, until it could be as long as twenty kids.

Kids were everywhere: nice ones, mean ones, ones you knew from school, older scary ones you stayed away from even though you knew their younger siblings, ones who wanted to be your friend but you didn't want to be theirs, and ones who you wanted to be friends with but they didn't want to be yours. You were always passing some informal game in the neighborhood featuring kids: street hockey, baseball, softball, kickball, football, hopscotch, tag, It, four square, Duck-Duck-Goose, Freeze Tag, Flashlight Tag, Red Light–Green Light, Mother-May-I, and, our favorite, which I'm sure would be called by another name today: Free All Slaves.

We always chose sides or who would be "It" with a series of

rhymes. Every kid stuck out a clenched fist, and one person would choose by pounding the top of each fist and chanting:

> One potato, two potatoes, three potatoes, FOUR.
> Five potatoes, six potatoes, seven potatoes, MORE.

The "more" person was "out." This lasted until one kid was left holding out a fist, making that kid "It."

Others had a call-and-response pattern, where the chooser posed a rhyming question and the last person whose fist was tapped would answer:

> Engine, engine Number NINE,
> Going down the Chicago LINE
> If the train goes off the TRACK,
> Do you want your money BACK?

Someone would answer yes or no, and the chooser would spell out, by banging on outstretched fists: "Y, E, S, and you are not going to be It, for this game of Red Light–Green Light." The last kid with a fist in the circle would be "It."

And my favorite, weirdly violent, choosing rhyme:

> My mother and your mother were hanging out CLOTHES.
> My mother punched your mother right in the NOSE!
> What color blood came OUT?

Purple was always the favorite answer: "P, U, R, P, L, E, and you are not going to be It for this game of . . ."

As far as we knew, no one's mother in our neighborhood had

ever once punched another mother in the nose while hanging out clothes or at any other time. But it was fun to imagine purple blood shooting out of someone's mother's nose and getting all over the white sheets hanging on the clotheslines that everyone had in their yard.

Kids were everywhere: choosing sides for games; walking dogs; climbing trees; mowing lawns; playing with dolls; getting scolded by neighbors for breaking a window or stepping in a flowerbed; getting yelled at by parents for walking in the street, racing, or popping wheelies on their Sting-Ray bikes; starting fires with dried leaves and magnifying glasses; playing games in the street; or just causing mischief. And in case one didn't cause enough informal mischief, the night before Halloween, when we strung toilet paper on the branches of trees in our neighbors' lawns ("TP-ing" a house) and threw eggs on their cars and at their houses, was called Mischief Night.

Kids, kids, kids. It was a seller's market for babysitters.

My best babysitting clients were our next-door neighbors, who had two younger boys, one my sister's age and one even younger, both relatively well-behaved.

"Next door" was a noun in our family. It was not "the next-door neighbors"; rather, "Did you see what next door did?" My mother used some Sicilian dialect with my father, and he said he learned it for self-defense. *I pressa porta*, she would say, dialect for "next door" or, more broadly, anyone in the neighborhood, and she would comment on behavior that she did not approve of with a roll of her eyes. Special opprobrium was reserved for people who were *cafona* and displayed boorish behavior.

My mom's mother, Rose, had emigrated from a small town

in Sicily called Nicosia, arriving in the United States in 1911 at the age of sixteen. She cried so hard on the voyage that upon arrival at Ellis Island, she was almost turned away by medical examiners who thought her eyes were red because of disease. (The ship that carried her from Italy to the US was the RMS *Carpathia*, which, the following year, would rescue survivors from the *Titanic* disaster.)

While in the US, she met her husband, Thomas, who had immigrated while still an infant to this country and whose family was from a small town near Nicosia. They met through an aunt, who was related to both by marriage. When my grandfather was about to be shipped overseas during World War I (he later was unable to go because he contracted the flu), he asked my grandmother, "Will you remember me when I'm gone?"

"How could I forget a face like that?" she joked.

I remember them as affectionate with each other, and a black-and-white photo I have shows them sitting on two wooden chairs at a party, both laughing, with my grandmother's left hand in her husband's right hand, on his lap; and her right hand on his left hand, which is thrown around her shoulder. I have no idea what their marriage was like, but the photo is a picture of joy.

My grandmother worked as a seamstress (later on, she would make some Halloween costumes for my sister and me) and my grandfather as a barber, for a time co-owning a shop in Philadelphia with a cousin and then working for the US Army in Aberdeen, Maryland, which necessitated time away from the family. My first memory (of anything) is of my grandfather cutting my hair while I sat on a metal highchair in the basement of my grandparents' home. I was three.

My mom was the youngest of three children. The eldest boy

was Lawrence (Uncle Larry to us), a veteran of World War II, and his younger brother, Louis, was a lively man who nonetheless struggled with depression. For my mother, family was paramount, and her Sicilian ancestry was an important part of her life. We're still in touch with our cousins in Nicosia.

We used a fair amount of Sicilian dialect growing up for words in two main areas: first, for things to be kept secret (like what was going on next door), and second, for topics not to be spoken about in polite company. So my parents often spoke in Sicilian dialect to hide things from my sister and me. Like news about *i pressa porta*.

When my parents were talking about my sister and me, we were *i carosse* ("the dear ones," pronounced, more or less, as *ee ca-daw-zha*), a phrase usually coupled with *N'di' niente*. "Don't say anything in front of the children." Eventually, after learning French and Spanish in high school, I could puzzle out what they were saying. One day I translated what I heard and my mom's face dropped. "Well," said my dad, "I guess we'll have to learn a new language."

Many bodily functions were camouflaged by Sicilian dialect, since they'd presumably be too embarrassing to say in English. (A few curse words were part of the lexicon too, like *fungu*, which I'm sure you can translate.) So the words for farting (and different kinds of farts), burping (and different kinds of burping), and shit and diarrhea were expressed in Italian. One day in first grade when I had a bout of diarrhea, I told my teacher in dialect, "I have *cagaredda*!" Mrs. Foster had no idea what I was talking about. When I went to Sicily decades later and my mother's relatives asked me what dialect I knew, I repeated all the words for farting and belching and diarrhea I could remember. When they stopped laughing, they told me some of the words were antique, from the time of my grandmother's arrival in the US in 1911.

The mother and father living next door (*i pressa porta*) were a favorite of my family, a groovy young couple about twenty years younger than my parents, with two kids, one my sister's age (who was three years younger than me) and the other a few years younger than that. They also had a dog named Chester, the source of both joy and sadness for me.

Chester was the best dog I could imagine, a breed that my mom referred to as a "doggy dog." I'm not sure what he was: a mixture of a lab, a golden retriever, and a beagle, maybe. Cream-colored and floppy-eared, he never got bigger than a puppy and had a marvelous, friendly, joyful disposition. As much as I was afraid of the German shepherds who chased me on my paper route, I adored Chester.

Chester came from a litter of puppies in the neighborhood, and our family had selected one from that same group: a black-and-white dog that I had already named Sneakers. Unfortunately, it turned out my sister was suffering from allergies, and so Sneakers went to another family. After I was told the bad news, I raced up to my bedroom, closed the door, threw myself on the bed, and wept into the blue chenille bedspread, crying over and over "Sneakers! Sneakers! Sneakers!" somewhat dramatically, as the ships and treasure chests on the wallpaper looked on impassively.

Babysitting was the easiest job around, especially with "next door." After making sure the kids ate dinner, finished their homework, and went to bed, you could watch TV, pet the dog, and chat on the phone with your friends, under the pretext of talking about homework. Usually, whatever parents retained your services also set out food for you: simple 1970s fare like Tang, a tart, powdered orange drink (used by the astronauts!); Snack Pack chocolate pudding cups; or Ding Dongs and Oreos.

It was certainly easier than delivering newspapers. Our neighbors were good tippers too.

Thanks to babysitting and my paperboy begging route, I opened a bank account at the Conshohocken Savings & Loan in a shopping center an easy bike ride from home. They gave me a buff-colored passbook so that I could see my balance grow. I checked the numbers often.

I loved the idea of being rich. My family was not well-off, so as a boy I thought that being rich was about the best thing that could possibly happen to someone. You could buy anything you wanted! Around this time, I started a coin collection, which I kept in blue cardboard Whitman coin albums under my bed. My father, who would often travel on far-flung business trips to India, Pakistan, and the Far East, would always bring back some foreign coins.

But my focus was American coins. My friend Marc, who lived down the street, had a collection bigger than mine that stirred up no little envy. From time to time, I would clip out order forms and send them, along with dollars and cents in an envelope, to the Littleton Coin Company, which would send me other, presumably more valuable, coins; occasionally, I would hang out at a coin shop at the mall, calculating what new pieces I could afford. I wasn't overly interested in the history of the coins, though I ended up subscribing to *COINage* magazine and enjoyed learning about the artists and the designs and the different grades of coins: G (good), VG (very good), F (fine), U (uncirculated), P (proof), and my favorite, BU (brilliant uncirculated). Mainly I hoped I would stumble on some rare coin that I would sell for a million dollars.

Then I wouldn't have to work and could stop collecting money for *The Recorder*.

I never bought a pup tent, since by the end of that school year I wanted to spend money on more important items: clothes and record albums. I also started to think about another job for the summer. I didn't want to deliver papers, which was difficult physically, scary dog-wise, and humiliating: I hated begging. This was no career.

In time, I graduated from *The Recorder* to a larger paper that charged its subscribers: *Today's Post*, which I delivered throughout the school year. I was happy not to have to beg any longer. When I said, "I'm collecting for *Today's Post*," the response was "Let me get my money," not a protracted debate with a neighbor while their German shepherd eyed me for dinner.

Still, collecting required riding my bike or walking all over the neighborhood for a few dollars in collections and maybe a few tips. For a summer job, I decided that I wanted something else.

Some of the older boys in the neighborhood mowed lawns, and since I was now doing that every week at home, why not do it for other people and get paid? Maybe I could invite other kids to join me and start a kind of lawn-mowing business!

My parents agreed to let me use our lawn mower. I thought about a name and logo for my lawn-mowing business, which I would start next summer and which, I was already predicting, would earn me hundreds, if not thousands, of dollars.

After all, how hard could it be?

This was several years before my lawn-mowing business failed, but I wanted to share a photo of my family, this one taken in my grandmother's row home in Philadelphia. I only wish I had kept those groovy gold-and-blue striped pants.

CHAPTER 3

How Poltergeists, Aliens, and Bigfoot Prevented Me from Getting Rich

HOW HARD COULD IT BE? WAS A QUESTION FOR ALL MY summer jobs, almost always answered with something along the lines of "pretty hard." Most of these jobs turned out to be physically, mentally, or emotionally hard. Sometimes all three. Except babysitting, which consisted of watching TV, talking on the phone, and drinking Tang.

But lawn mowing? How hard could it be? By age fourteen, I was mowing our lawn every week during the spring, summer, and fall. Fortunately, we had a new power lawn mower, a big red Toro that I loved starting.

Filling the tank with gasoline and pulling on the cord and hearing the enormous rumble as the engine revved to life made me feel like an adult. *Look at me!* I thought. *I'm mowing the lawn!* It was almost like driving a car—after all, our mower's noisy engine was powered by gasoline—which I couldn't wait to do in another two years. In fact, I liked starting the lawn mower too much. "*Jimmy! Don't pull so hard*," said my dad. "You're going to *break* it!"

Then he'd come out and show me how to do it. "Like this," he'd say, and pull harder than I did.

Every time I filled the tank or started the engine, I wondered whether it would explode. When I poured the pungent gasoline from the red metal gas can into the Toro's tank, it smelled like danger. Would a stone shoot up through the whirring metal blades and lodge itself in the engine and cause an explosion? Did the fact that my parents smoked when they came outside to check on my mowing progress mean that a cigarette ember would land on the motor, find its way into the tank, and set off a gas-fueled conflagration? Would yanking the cord too fast create a spark that would ignite the gas and destroy our backyard in a catastrophic fireball? I saw the disaster movie *The Hindenburg* that year, and from then on, I thought about the big blimp exploding every time I yanked on the cord. "Oh, the humanity!" I would say, as our neighborhood was flattened by my carelessness.

Explosions were, to my mind, just an accident away. I got this attitude from my mom: You could never be too careful. I felt that I was pushing a lethal device over the grass, though I had never known anyone in our neighborhood whose lawn mower had blown up.

Despite my fears, I was happy not to rely on a hand-push lawn mower, like my grandmother had at her row home in Philadelphia, and which I occasionally used to cut her lawn, to ill effect. It was like pushing through molasses, for all the good the dull, rusted blades did, which were probably last sharpened during World War II. On the bright side, I didn't have to worry about it exploding.

As may be evident by now, I spent a good portion of my adolescence in fear: of exploding lawn mowers, biting dogs, stinging bees, not to mention poison ivy (and oak and sumac), dentists, bullies, being called names, failing at sports, and so on. The list grew longer each year.

I also worried that I would suffer the fate of one boy in our neighborhood: While mowing his family's lawn, he accidentally ran over a nest of baby rabbits hidden in the grass, turning them into a bloody pulp. One of the toughest boys around, a few years older than me, he burst into tears and had to be consoled by his mom.

Every time I mowed, then, I was alert to possible rabbits' nests and burrows, which meant that every hole needed to be inspected. Any perfectly formed holes were sure to house a massive snake, probably poisonous, though I lived in the Philadelphia suburbs, not the Florida Everglades.

Then again, you could never be too careful. One day a large snapping turtle walked right out of the woods, across Kings Road and up our driveway. It lived for a few weeks on rations of lettuce in a cardboard box in our garage until it tipped over its temporary home and walked away, no doubt looking for higher-quality lettuce. We didn't even have time to name it.

Our lawn, a quarter of an acre, took me almost two hours to mow. This presumed that my mom or dad weren't monitoring me from the window, or even coming out to inspect my work, which meant more time, because it meant many do-overs.

I thought of my parents as the lawn police. They could get annoyed when I hadn't cut close enough to the trees or bushes or lamppost or fence, didn't make straight lines, or did a substandard job on the edging around the driveway and sidewalk. I had a low tolerance for criticism, a trait that unfortunately dogged me into young adulthood. Rather than simply accepting that I wasn't a good edger, or ask for help, or apologize, I took it as a personal attack.

"If you don't like it, do it yourself!" I once said to my mom, whose face clouded as she stood in the doorway.

"HEY!" shouted my father from a bedroom window. My parents would have made great spies, since they were always silently monitoring my and my sister's activities. "Don't talk to your mother like that!"

I sullenly started edging again.

Occasionally daydreaming, I would stop the lawn mower, still running, to look at anything that was more interesting than the grass, which was everything: an ant mound that I had avoided, a cardinal or blue jay in the trees, a flock of geese (now a nuisance, back then a rarity), or even a strange insect, even though most bugs grossed me out. Once, my mom caught me staring at something for a few minutes.

"What are you doing?" she shouted out the kitchen window.

"*Whaaaaat?*" I said. "I'm looking at a rock, okay?"

"You're wasting gas!" she said, taking a puff on her Kent and closing the window. "That costs money!"

You might think that, since I'm now a Jesuit priest, I was contemplating nature with a sense of religious awe. But that's not how I saw it then. If you had asked me whether I was admiring God's creation, I would have said, "No, I'm looking under a rock." Perhaps some true contemplation was going on, but I wasn't aware of it.

But there was one event in childhood, a few years before, that I now see as an early awareness of God. When it happened, I chalked it up as a strange experience and set it aside.

How Poltergeists, Aliens, and Bigfoot Prevented Me from Getting Rich

On most school days I pedaled my bike to Ridge Park Elementary School with the rest of our bike gang. But sometimes I rode alone. I loved sailing downhill to school, past the late-1950s split-levels, all constructed from the same architectural blueprints with enough variance in design to satisfy a town planner's heart: some with square windows, others with long windows paned in diamond shapes; some with doors that led to a living room on the first floor, others that opened onto a landing with a living room a few steps above the entrance.

Most of the homes in our neighborhood, including our own, were filled with Danish-modern furniture, then labeled "contemporary." In every house were low-slung chairs; maple coffee tables and end tables with spindly legs (with heavy crystal ashtrays on top); tall wooden lamps with oversize shades and tiles embedded into chunky ceramic bases; and giant metallic, moon-shaped chandeliers that hung from the dining room ceiling. By the 1970s, this décor was supplemented by thick shag carpeting and patterned wallpaper or vinyl faux-wood paneling. Nearly all the kitchens were decorated in either Harvest Gold or Avocado Green, including the blenders, crockpots, ovens, and refrigerators. And nearly all the houses were filled with kids.

I passed the house of older kids I was afraid of; houses of friends from school; the house of my Cub Scout den mother; houses with dogs (fast); the house of our school principal's secretary, Mrs. Voros, whose name made my parents laugh because in the first grade I told them that she was my "close, personal friend"; and the house of my friend Allison, whose backyard I would cut through to get to school more quickly, if I were walking. But mostly I biked.

At the bottom of a hill at the end of our street, you dismounted your bike to walk a few feet on pavement between two houses, at the end of which was a concrete staircase. At the top of those steps was a meadow, my memory of which remains intact, now fifty years later.

The meadow was nothing more than a small undeveloped plot of land bordered on the left by a sidewalk and a stand of oak trees, and on the right by the wide green baseball fields of our elementary school. In the fall and winter, you walked over the brown, frost-covered, desiccated oak leaves that crunched underfoot and sometimes traipsed through the shin-high snow.

But in the spring and summer, the meadow was a riot of life, filled with weeds, wild grasses, and all manner of wildflowers. It was a beautiful place, especially in the morning.

One spring morning, I hoisted my blue Schwinn bike to the top of the concrete steps, pedaled a few feet over the rutted dirt path that cut diagonally across the meadow, and stopped in the middle. Maybe my schoolbooks were falling out of my bike's metal basket; maybe I stopped to check that the Wacky Packages decals or Day-Glo Flower Power stickers on my bike weren't peeling off; maybe I had run over a stone and wanted to make sure that my tires weren't punctured. Whatever the reason, I stopped and set my feet down.

On this unseasonably warm morning, a sweet grassy smell came from the meadow. All around me was so much *life*: grasshoppers jumping from one blade of grass to another; Queen Anne's lace waving slowly in the sun; and wild yellow snapdragons, black-eyed Susans, white daisies, and wild strawberry plants in profusion. Even the flowering weeds looked beautiful: yellow dandelions, white clover, and purple thistles. Bees buzzed but they seemed friendly, uninterested in me, for the time being. A chorus of crickets chirred softly.

In the distance was my elementary school, which, though I complained about it, I loved. It was an inviting place, a space for learning and exploration. It felt, above all, safe and orderly—you knew you would be welcomed every day, you knew that the teachers would have carefully planned lessons, and you knew what was expected of you. Its quasi-monastic regularity appealed to me.

I loved almost everything about it, except the homework. I loved the First Day of School (always capitalized in my mind), when, wearing my new back-to-school clothes that my mom and I had picked out at the mall, I would walk or bike in the summery weather through our neighborhood into a new year. I loved looking at the minuscule insects that swam in brackish water drawn from a nearby stream, subjects we examined between two glass slides with our classroom microscopes; I loved finger painting (and the splattered smocks we wore to protect our clothes); I loved the fragrance of glue and paste (I also liked the taste of the latter); I loved celebrating almost every holiday, both secular and religious, by taping up cardboard decorations on the windows of our classrooms; I loved dressing up for Halloween and marching around the school parking lot with the rest of the kids in an ersatz parade; I loved the elaborate posters we drew for our social studies classes; I loved inhaling the sweet fragrance of the purple ink on the wet mimeograph pages (almost every kid pressed the newly printed sheets to their noses immediately after receiving them from the teacher); I loved covering my textbooks (which were used by dozens of kids before me, who signed their names in the back) with paper from shopping bags to keep them clean; I loved almost anything about the library—new books filled me with joy; and I loved nearly all my teachers. I loved school. It was one of the earliest sources of what I experienced as real joy.

On this sunny day, unlike other mornings, when you would pass (or be passed) by other kids on their bikes, no one else was in the meadow. So I stopped to take it all in, still astride my bike, my feet on the bumpy dirt path.

Suddenly I felt a strange sensation: a profound happiness coupled with a desire to stay in that meadow forever, to understand the source of this beauty, to know what was happening—to *possess* it all somehow. It was an odd experience that I didn't understand. But it seemed to point me to something else, something more, something beautiful, though at the time I had little understanding of what that meant. I just knew that I wanted to stay where I was.

At the time, I didn't see this experience as especially important, just a weird moment of daydreaming. Like looking under the rocks in our backyard. I got back on the bike seat and pedaled the rest of the way to school. Later I'd come to see this moment as one of the first times that I felt a longing for God.

On a recent fall day, I visited that spot, no longer a meadow but just a grassy area behind some houses that have been built during the past few decades.

The stairs I dragged my bike up back then are still there. So are the sidewalk and oak trees that border the field on the left, but the trees are enormous now, perhaps forty feet high.

I parked my car and walked toward the field from the direction of the elementary school, which looks as it did in the 1960s: an exemplar of mid-century-modern school architecture. The broad baseball fields are still there too, and as far as I know, the wire baseball backstops are the same ones used when I was a boy during Little League tryouts.

I approached the plot of land cautiously because I didn't know if any homeowners would feel that I was trespassing. Someone else was on the sidewalk ahead of me, so it seemed that this was public property. Soon the person left the area, and I was alone in the crisp air.

As I walked closer, I felt a sense of consolation, an almost physical pang of recognition: how well I knew this place. Each of us knows places that are part of our core memories and can move us deeply when we encounter them again—especially if we've not seen them for a long time.

Then I saw something that amazed me: The diagonal, rutted path we took as children across the meadow was still there, fifty years later, now a deep indentation in the ground, carved out by thousands of bike wheels and children's sneakers. The rut was filled with brown fall leaves, which had blown in and settled there, revealing the path I had taken as a boy as clearly as if someone were pointing it out to me—and perhaps someone was. In a flash, the memory of that morning came back to me, and on that chilly day it was suddenly spring again.

Other spots evoked similar feelings: Near the playground of our school was a field in which I would sometimes sit, surrounded by tall grasses and weeds, and just be quiet. Even in the fall, I would find a clearing, not far from the playground, and just sit, looking at the grasses waving in the breeze. Watching the grasshoppers and crickets. Studying the flowers. Listening.

Across the street from our house were "the woods," undeveloped acres of land with tall trees and rocks and cliffs where one could happily get lost. My friends and I constructed forts and dwellings from rocks and sticks, climbed up and down cliffs, and generally explored, trying not to get too dirty; trying not to get poison ivy, oak, or sumac; and trying not to get eaten by bears, which we were sure were nearby. There weren't any grizzly bears in the area, but you would see the occasional deer. Unlike today in the suburbs, where deer proliferate, destroy flower beds, and are seen as pests, seeing a deer back then gently poke its nose from behind a tree was a rare treat, like seeing a unicorn.

Deeper in the woods we played on undulating hills, perhaps ten feet high, made of a mysterious white substance, which I thought was discarded material from a nearby steel factory. My friend Carol insisted that it was simply lime. Plymouth Meeting sat over immense deposits of limestone, which formed the basis of an industry that began in the town in the late 1600s. On a corner near the Friends Meetinghouse were well-preserved outdoor stone limekilns that processed lime for fertilizer for farms and whitewash for painting houses.

After a few hours in the woods, we would come home covered with the stuff, making our jeans look as if we had bathed in talcum powder. Years later, it dawned on me that this might have been asbestos, perhaps dangerous refuse from a nearby factory.

One day at a fundraising event a few years ago, I was seated next to an investigator from the Environmental Protection Agency whose area of responsibility was suburban Philadelphia. "I've always wondered about something," I said, and gave her the general location of the suspected asbestos.

She emailed back a few days later: "Your friend Carol was right. It was lime deposits. You'll be fine!"

Overall, I found the natural world captivating, except when it was stinging or biting me. Or making me itch. Poison ivy and poison oak and, worst of all, poison sumac were also to be feared. One summer I managed to get poison sumac on my hands, which not only swelled up but exploded in dozens of small white bubbles that required liberal dosings of calamine lotion and wearing thin white gloves, both a misery in the hot weather. I was on the lookout for poison-anything when I was mowing the lawn, and since you could never be too careful, I assumed any plant with leaves, save the trees, was poison-something.

Still, I loved the outdoors, was enchanted by birds, poring over Roger Tory Peterson's *Field Guide to Birds* and trying my hand at sketching local birds, and so I didn't mind mowing our lawn. Plus, I figured if I got paid for mowing lawns for other people, it would make being outside even more enjoyable. And again: How hard could it be?

That question was answered on the first day of my new job. My first customers were the Burkes, a lively Irish American family a few doors down from us whose garrulous father told great jokes. Their eldest son had moved from home and their youngest son was too young to mow, and back then most daughters didn't mow lawns. So Mrs. Burke asked my mom if I would mow her lawn for a princely sum. I couldn't wait to get my ten bucks.

At this point I had moved on from saving for a pup tent to spending my money on clothes and records: I was amassing a collection of 45s, my first purchases being "Delta Dawn" by Helen Reddy and "The Morning After" by Maureen McGovern, the theme from *The Poseidon Adventure*, the disaster movie I had seen three times a few years before. "A gigantic wall of water—heading directly for the ship!" says one of the crew members of the doomed ship. I found the story of a rogue wave overturning an ocean liner terrifying, which was of course the point. The scene of a man hanging from an upside-down Christmas tree, bolted to the floor, which had become a ceiling, gave me (literal) nightmares. That summer at our local pool, we would all sweep our hands across the top of the water to create a mini-tsunami and shout, "It's a gigantic wall of water!"

The first morning of my lawn-mowing business—a humid morning a few days after the end of school—started with my pushing a lawn mower from my family's shed through our neighborhood to Mrs. Burke's house. The cicadas were singing their metallic song from the maple trees, but they were drowned out by the Toro's plastic wheels, which, rolling across the sidewalk, made more noise than I had expected.

I thought merrily, *This is such a great job! What a beautiful morning! I'm going to make so much money—and get a great tan!* I already thought of mowing lawns as a business and planned to buy a pickup truck (even though I still couldn't drive) and bring together all my friends in my lawn-mowing business (even though I don't think my friends were interested in mowing any more than they had to), with me as president. And I already had designed a logo. I was interested in heraldry and coats of arms and enjoyed painting with watercolors, so I sketched out a crest with a lawn mower in the middle and two crossed rakes (even though I didn't do much raking) with the legend: Martin Lawnmowing.

One neighbor stuck his head out the window as the lawn mower rolled noisily down the sidewalk around 8 a.m. "Hey, Jimmy," said *I pressa porta*, "can you not make so much noise?" Mrs. Burke's house was only a few houses away, so in minutes I was knocking on her door and getting detailed instructions on how she liked her lawn cut. I nodded thoughtfully as she told me, paying little attention to what she was saying, thinking instead of how I'd spend the ten dollars plus the inevitable tip for my superior work.

After a half hour of what I thought was top-notch mowing, I drew close to the bushes on the side of the Burkes's house, and then saw something strange: It looked like someone had stuck a white papier-mâché pumpkin, like the ones we made in Cub Scouts, into one of her bushes. *How odd*, I thought, as I slowly inched closer. *What were the Burkes sticking into their bushes?*

When something buzzed angrily past my ear, I realized what it was: a nest of paper wasps the size of a basketball. Suddenly I noticed many more wasps flying in and out and around the huge, now seemingly malevolent, nest. In response, I did something I often did. I froze with panic: frightened, confused, and embarrassed.

I was (1) frightened for obvious reasons. As wasps flew in and out of the nest, their skinny legs dangling from their evil black-and-yellow striped bodies, I was terrified of getting stung. Now they were flying all about me, and who knows whether they could smell fear, like a dog could. Did wasps have noses? I was (2) confused, because I didn't know what to do. Bravely continue mowing? Ask Mrs. Burke if she would mind if I didn't mow near the nest? Call off my first day of work? Maybe give up on lawn mowing altogether? That was often my default: If the smallest thing went wrong, I'd be tempted to give up on the entire project.

Most of all, I was (3) embarrassed because I was afraid. Feeling fear humiliated me. I felt that, *as a boy*, I should be less afraid, I should know what to do, or I should at least be brave. (Sexist yes, but that is how boys thought in the 1970s, or at least how this one did.) Boys should be brave. Boys should be tough. Boys shouldn't be afraid of wasps. Later in life, a Jesuit called this "shoulding all over yourself." Still, it was probably not unwise to be leery of a basketball-size nest of wasps a few feet from my face.

Of course, I could have just done the adult thing: ask Mrs.

Burke for advice. She was a nice lady and surely would have just counseled mowing around it.

In the end, too embarrassed to ask and too afraid of getting stung, I carefully maneuvered the Toro around the bush, ducking and holding my breath as wasps dive-bombed me. I was happy when the morning was over and felt that I had more than earned my ten dollars. I wheeled our lawn mower back home and told my mom, who was never one to brush off a fear. "Be careful!" she said. "If you get stung too many times, you could go into shock!"

While lawn mowing was an improvement over begging for newspaper payments, it swiftly lost its appeal. I was happy to be outside and work on my tan, but it was sweaty, dirty, buggy, sometimes waspy, work. Many of my customers wanted me not only to mow the lawn, but to edge around the sidewalks and driveways, rake leaves and debris, clean out a gutter, or paint something: a curb, a shed, a doorway. Sometimes I was more handyman than lawn mower. "Can you put the trash cans on the curb?" "Can you rearrange my shed?" "Can you clear out that poison ivy?" And my favorite, "Can you clean the dog poop off the sidewalk, please?"

Plus, I saw for the first time one of the biggest roadblocks in my quest to earn money and/or start a lawn-mowing business: I didn't like working in the summer. I much preferred not working. I was starting to play tennis with friends more often. That summer, I even enjoyed band camp, having joined our junior high school's marching band (the Marching Patriots) as a not-especially-talented trumpet player. But what I liked to do most of all was read.

Our backyard porch was nothing fancy, just a concrete slab covered by a simple roof supported by a few wooden posts. But it had my favorite place to sit: a green plastic chaise lounge next to a low brick wall. I could sit there for hours in the summer, trying to identify all the birds that flitted around, with Roger Tory Peterson's guidebook beside me: sparrows, blue jays, cardinals, robins, juncos, grackles, and starlings. Mainly I just read.

My selection of books at the time ran largely to what I considered adult fare, and the mountain I had set myself to climb that summer was William Manchester's *The Glory and the Dream*, a two-volume, fourteen-hundred-page history of the United States from 1932 to 1972. I wanted to read something long, important, *impressive*.

My commitment to self-improvement often flagged, and I would go back to reading Hardy Boys knockoff adventure books, Agatha Christie mysteries, and, when I was younger, the books I purchased from the year's Scholastic Book Fair at school, which was one of the highlights of my young life.

Once or twice a year, the Scholastic company, which decades later made billions of dollars from the Harry Potter series, would visit our elementary school for the Scholastic Book Fair. The company would set up mouthwatering displays of new books in our auditorium, with titles like *The Arrow Book of States*, *Encyclopedia Brown Finds the Clues*, and my all-time favorite, *Danny Dunn and the Homework Machine*, in which our hero builds a machine that, not surprisingly, does homework. As I recall, Danny, the hero of a series of books that focused on science (like *Danny Dunn and the Smallifying Machine*, whose plot should be obvious), also made money from his homework machine, which appealed greatly. I read *The Homework Machine*, first published in 1958, three times and didn't think it was possible for any book to ever be as good.

Students would either buy the books at the book fair or, if the selections were sold out, order them by ticking them off on a paper form and bringing in a check from their parents. A few weeks later, a big box would arrive in your homeroom filled with new books, which your teacher would distribute. It was almost as good as Christmas—and maybe better because it didn't require a visit to church. At other times during the year, teachers would hand out order forms, and again, a few weeks later, the books would arrive. Seeing the box appear in class filled me with an almost intoxicating joy. I know that sounds over the top, but that's how I felt about reading, about books, and about reading Scholastic books in particular. Occasionally a "bookmobile" would pull up in the driveway outside our school and we students could indulge our appetites for even more reading. If I thank my parents for encouraging me in school and my teachers for helping me learn to read, I have to thank Scholastic for making reading so exciting.

Supplementing our elementary-school reading diet was a marvelous little flyer called *Weekly Reader*, which in a few pages told you wholesome stories about animals, political leaders, kids who had done some amazing feat, and especially men and women who had made notable scientific achievements, most especially astronauts. Neil Armstrong and Buzz Aldrin walked on the moon when I was in third grade. Like every other family in our neighborhood, we watched the moon landing on television and took photos of the broadcast: meaning we pointed our Kodak camera at the TV screen. Astronauts were a big deal in the 1960s: For a few years I proudly carried an Apollo 11 lunch box.

Between homework, Scholastic Book Fairs, *Weekly Reader*, the bookmobile, and the books lining the many bookshelves in our house, I read a lot. Often I read the same things over and over, immersing myself in lighthearted series like *Encyclopedia Brown*, about the clever and somewhat smug boy detective who solved ridiculously easy mysteries; *The Happy Hollisters* (an entire family of mystery solvers); and young-adult novels like *Island of the Blue Dolphins*, the engrossing tale of a girl stranded on a remote island off the coast of California; *The Old Man and the Boy*, the tale of a young boy's relationship with his wise, kind, and patient grandfather, who teaches the boy life lessons between bouts of fishing and hunting in the North Carolina woods and shorelines (and which I read a few years ago and found to be borderline racist, something that escaped me as an adolescent); *From the Mixed-Up Files of Mrs. Basil E. Frankweiler*, in which two resourceful runaway kids hide out in the Metropolitan Museum of Art in New York and in the process identify a lost statue by Michelangelo; and a Scholastic book about a group of kids who find a bag of a hundred pounds of popcorn called, not surprisingly, *100 Pounds of Popcorn*, which would presage a future summer job. In between all of these was a steady diet of Peanuts comics collections: *Here Comes Charlie Brown!*, *Very Funny, Charlie Brown*, *Good Ol' Snoopy*, and my only reading foray into religion at the time, *The Gospel According to Peanuts*.

Sometimes I would sit on our living room floor and leaf through the art books my parents kept in the house. They had a series from the great museums of the world: the Prado, the Hermitage, the National Gallery. "What are you reading?" said my mom one day when I was very young.

"A book on the . . . Loo-*voor*."

"Oh, the Louvre," said my mom in perfect French. And then, "Go outside and play. It's such a nice day!"

But around the time of my lawn-mowing business, that is, around age fourteen, my favorite genre was books on the supernatural by the prolific author Brad Steiger, whose series of inexpensive paperbacks covered ghosts (including a taxonomy of different types), as well as Bigfoot and UFOs, with titles like *Strangers from the Skies* (about alien visitors) and *Strange Guests* with the fantastic claim on the cover, "True, scientifically authenticated stories of the unseen, uninvited, unexplainable forces that take possession of places, things, and people."

I must have read one of Steiger's books on ghosts ten times. At dinner, I would offer detailed explanations of how poltergeists operated, scaring my little sister, and dilate on all the nuances of the supernatural world: "Did you know that a *vardogr* is a ghost that sounds like you and enters the room before you do, like it's your spirit coming in *early*?" When mowing lawns, I couldn't wait to get back to the porch and read about how certain ghosts walked a few inches above the floor in the houses they were haunting because *that's where the floors were when they lived there a hundred years ago!*

One of my nephews recently asked me what the appeal of these rather strange books was, and to be honest, I'm not sure, other than it seemed endlessly fascinating that this other world could somehow exist within the realm of our own. Perhaps this foreshadowed my interest in religion and spirituality, but at the time it was less a vocation than an avocation. I just couldn't get enough of ghosts and poltergeists, not to mention aliens and Bigfoot.

"Jimmy!" my mom would say. "Can't you talk about something else? How did the Phillies do today?"

Tied with Brad Steiger's oeuvre were books by Jean Shepherd, the estimable American humorist. My father owned a beat-up copy of Shepherd's collection of picaresque short stories about growing up in the Midwest during the Depression, *Wanda*

Hickey's Night of Golden Memories, which includes Shepherd's memorable account of being unexpectedly drunk and spectacularly sick during his senior prom. (When I went to my own prom, I made sure not to drink, remembering his ornate description of vomiting up his meal.)

None of my friends shared my enthusiasm for Jean Shepherd or even knew who he was, despite my importuning them to read him and even loaning them copies of his books. About a decade later, in 1983, when the film *A Christmas Story*, based on Shepherd's story "Duel in the Snow, or Red Ryder Nails the Cleveland Street Kid," premiered around Thanksgiving, I made sure to be the first in line. But I was one of only a handful of people at the cinema at our local mall. It wouldn't be until the film was shown on television, and rerun frequently, that it would become a holiday classic.

I would have been happy that summer with a steady diet of Brad Steiger and Jean Shepherd. Rather than mowing lawns, and making money, I preferred to read about poltergeists and *vardogrs* and growing up in 1930s Indiana as I sat on the porch and tried to figure out whether that was a junco or a sparrow that landed on the clothesline. But just when I got comfortable, my mom or dad would poke their nose outside the back door and say, "Did you mow any lawns today?"

By the end of the summer, several customers had hired me to mow their lawns weekly. But I started to dread the work: the heat, the bees, the poison ivy, and the grass clippings that never seemed to leave my clothes or shoes, much to my mother's chagrin. "Wipe your feet!"

When pedaling my bike past the houses of my clients, I would wax wroth to see the grass growing back, as if it were a personal affront. The grass was growing to *annoy me*. So I stuck to mowing just a few yards in our neighborhood, despite my parents entreating me to solicit more clients. "Don't you want that pup tent?" my dad would ask. "I don't want it anymore," I would say, to excuse my growing indolence.

The low point in my fading lawn-mowing business happened at a house where an elderly woman lived who was exceedingly kind and often invited all the neighborhood kids over for vanilla ice cream and Oreos. But she had a giant black dog that ran around off the leash, a strike against her. I was happy to mow her lawn since her yard was flat and presented few struggles. Plus, ice cream and Oreos.

One day, I was trying to mow close to her shed. Thanks to my parents, I knew I needed to get closer to everything when I was mowing lawns. Get closer to the sidewalk, get closer to the tree trunks, get closer to the side of the house, and so on. Angling the lawn mower's wheels so that I could reach those last few blades of grass was my constant concern. My other concerns were how I would best spend the money I earned, whether there were any dogs or bees around, whether I was getting tan, and when I could get home and read more about ghosts.

In the process of getting close to the shed, the lawn mower inadvertently banged against an outer wall. The dog barked at me from inside the house and I turned to look.

Suddenly I felt a searing, shocking, blistering pain above my right eye. Wasps! I had accidentally dislodged a wasps' nest (in Philadelphia, a *wahss-ness*) hidden under the eaves of the shed. Out they poured: an angry, living, evil cloud. Stung on my hand! On my back! On my *face*! As I flailed about, the lawn mower still

How Poltergeists, Aliens, and Bigfoot Prevented Me from Getting Rich

rumbling, I said what every American teenager would say at that moment: "F—K!" Apologies, but I said it over and over and over and threw my hand over my already swollen eye. I had never felt such intense pain.

I raced home, where my mom applied ice wrapped in a paper towel to my rapidly swelling eye.

When I calmed down, she said, "Where's the lawn mower?"

"Back in Mrs. Dobrynin's yard."

I couldn't believe how much a wasp's sting stung. It felt unfair: I hadn't done anything to them! *Stupid wasps!* My response to animals or insects biting, stinging, menacing, or in any way inconveniencing me was usually out of proportion to what had happened: I wanted to kill them. Not the most generous of impulses, but there it is. I took great pleasure in the widely held belief that a bee immediately dies after it stings you. Wasps, I wasn't so sure about.

For the rest of the summer of junior counseling, tennis playing, band camping, and reading about aliens and poltergeists, I continued mowing lawns in a desultory way, eventually setting aside my ideas for a multimillion-dollar business, storing my clever logo in a desk drawer in my bedroom, and getting excited about going back to school. Also, I noticed I was more grateful for rain, when my lawn mower could stay in the shed, where it belonged.

The next summer, I vowed, I would not work outside. Something indoors would be much more civilized. At least fewer bees. Which is how I ended up at the Ice Cream Inn.

At age sixteen, I felt too old to go trick-or-treating with my neighbor Carol on Halloween, but we decided we couldn't pass up the candy. Thanks to a beard from a burned cork, I'm a "hobo" (a costume that would probably be frowned on today), and Carol is a "graduate." (Not her real hair, she would want me to tell you.)

CHAPTER 4

How to Avoid Getting Struck by Lightning When Standing Next to a Bag of Metal Poles

"MAYBE TOMMY CAN GET YOU A JOB AT THE CRICKET Club," said my mom cheerfully.

In the winter of 1976, I told my parents how much I had disliked working as a busboy at the Ice Cream Inn the summer before. This was not the first time they'd heard my complaints, which started almost as soon as I put on my busboy smock. I didn't want to be stuck inside washing dishes in that hot back room. I didn't want to get yelled at for clearing the tables if another wagon train came by, which was unlikely since the Bicentennial was over. I also wondered whether I had done too many whippets, though I didn't tell my mom that. One busboy told me that they'd make you go blind (after he gave me one to sniff). My eyesight seemed okay, and I had done only a few over the summer, but you could never be too careful.

Mainly I thought it would be pleasanter to work outside, though I certainly didn't want to mow lawns. This would be a continuing pattern during the summers: I don't like working inside, so I'll work outside next year. I don't like working outside, so I'll work inside next year. Eventually, I realized that I didn't like working *at all* in the summer. I'd rather sit on the porch and read about *vardogrs*.

My mom and dad, however, were resolute about my working. This came not only from their own strong work ethic, perhaps stemming from their Depression-era upbringing (both were born in the early 1930s), but because we weren't well-off. If I wanted to attend college, I needed to supplement whatever they could afford to pay. Also, as I got older and my life became more social, I needed more than the five dollars weekly allowance for the endless movies my friends and I saw. I bristled at my parents' constant encouragement to work summer jobs, but today I appreciate the work ethic they instilled. "What are you going to do this summer?" didn't mean "How would you like to relax?" and certainly not "Where do you want to go on vacation?" but "Where will you work?"

The year before, I had tried to get a job at a golf club a short drive from our house. "I hope to be a caddy at Green Valley," I wrote in my journal from that year. "I'd be outside, walk wherever I want and get a pretty good salary." Admirable goals, but I'm not sure what I meant by walking wherever I wanted, as if caddying meant strolling around a golf course, admiring the flowers and identifying birds.

My plans to "walk wherever I want," that is, caddy, would be foiled that year.

One Saturday in February, I gave it my all. My journal recounts the story, including, for some reason, what I ate that morning: pancakes, bacon, orange juice, and a grapefruit. Like many teenage boys with a zooming metabolism, my appetite was boundless, but unlike many of my peers, my journal (you could stop right there; I don't imagine many of my male classmates were keeping diaries) often pauses to praise my mom's spaghetti sauce, critique the price of a hamburger at Ponderosa Steakhouse after bowling with friends, communicate my awe over the varied toppings at a free salad bar (listed one by one), or share my rapture over Welsh rarebit at a restaurant in Philadelphia, a dish I considered the *ne plus ultra* of fine dining. After school, I would usually down half a cheesecake, at night a ham sandwich, and on summer nights an ice cream float, which made my dad say, "Do you have a hollow leg?"

After that heart-stopping breakfast it was time to find a summer job, stopping at nothing, not even using a clever tactic from my mom—employing a little sartorial subterfuge. In my journal I wrote: "One of the first things I did was call Green Valley Country Club to see if I could be a caddy there. They said to come over. I got all dressed (put on my Villanova shirt cause my mom said the guy was Catholic and Vill. is a Catholic college). I drove over (w/ Carolyn) and I went back to talk to Mr. Butera. He said there weren't any openings. They only need 30 kids and they have 65 now!! Then I went to the Ice Cream Inn but they were closed."

This was one of several jobs I applied for, as I traipsed from one sticky counter to the next: McDonald's, Burger King, Dairy Queen, and Karmelkorn, where owners and college-age assistant managers told me either I was too young or they were booked up. Eventually the Ice Cream Inn called me back and offered me a summer of rum raisin and whippets.

But this summer, at sixteen years old, I wanted to be outside.

No more stuffy dining rooms and hot dishwashing machines for me. That's when my mom encouraged me to call my cousin Tommy, an assistant golf pro at the Philadelphia Cricket Club, a place I had heard of during family gatherings but had no clue about. What was cricket anyway?

The more I thought about being a caddy and suggesting to golfers which club to use, the more ridiculous it seemed. Didn't you have to know something about golf? I had never golfed before. On Sunday afternoons, however, my dad would often watch golf on TV, and I found the announcer's bland voices comforting but ultimately boring.

My dad was an avid sports fan, fond of watching almost any sporting event on TV or listening to it on the radio. A few years prior, in 1974, during a rare family outing to the Academy of Music in Philadelphia, when the Flyers were in the middle of the Stanley Cup playoffs, my father surreptitiously brought a tiny transistor radio with him, its slim cord snaking sneakily from his suit jacket pocket to his ear. During one soft movement of some forgotten symphony, he leaped from his seat, clapped his hands together silently, and whispered, "Score!"

An athlete when he was younger, my father's baseball and football days ended after he injured his knee in the Army Reserves when a Doberman pinscher chased him on a training maneuver and he slipped in a hole and twisted his medial meniscus, which I didn't understand but it sounded painful. Hearing about my dad being attacked by dogs didn't help me in the fear department, especially on my paper route. "Dobermans are *dangerous!*" my mom said often.

Neither of my parents golfed, though my mom and dad kept a set of dust-covered clubs in the crawl space, the half-basement of our split-level house. Golfing was mainly for rich people, not us. Nor did I know any schoolmates who golfed. I'm sure I could have found a few if I'd asked, but it seemed bizarre and dull: hitting a ball down a field and chasing it. Tennis was more my sport.

My lukewarm interest in most sports was probably a disappointment to my dad. His command of the most arcane sports knowledge astonished me. A safe Christmas gift for him was the latest edition of *The Baseball Encyclopedia*, something that bored me to tears but over which he could pore for hours, even though he already seemed to have memorized its contents, especially anything having to do with the Phillies. I'd rather read *The Arrow Book of Dirt*.

I grew up hearing about Shibe Park, later renamed Connie Mack Stadium, where the Phillies played until it was torn down and replaced by Veterans Stadium. In fact, my dad took me to the final Phillies game at Connie Mack in 1970, and we (with permission) tore off and took home one of the wooden seatbacks, with a seat number in fading white paint, a treasure I stored under my bed until my mom sold our house after my father's death, decades later.

On the one hand, I was proud that my dad could hold his own on any sports topic with any father in the neighborhood; on the other, I was embarrassed that no matter how hard I tried, I could never evince much interest in watching sports or do as well as I would have liked playing them. I enjoyed collecting Topps baseball cards and "flipping" them to win new ones from friends, but other than knowing the megastar Phillies players who were household names in those days (Jim Bunning, Larry Bowa, Mike Schmidt), I wasn't all that interested. (One benefit of buying all those baseball cards was a constant supply of the dry, hard, rectangular squares of bubble gum in each pack, which at the very least built up my jaw muscles.) For several years I kept a scrapbook dedicated to the Mets pitcher Tom Seaver, mainly because I had written a letter to him for a class project and he kindly answered. Some of my friends, however, could talk to my dad in detail about sports while I was tongue-tied. Once when my dad drove me and a friend home from school, the two of them had an in-depth conversation about Bobby Clarke, the Flyers star, while I sat mute, ashamed of my lack of knowledge and interest.

The best I could manage was watching *ABC's Wide World of Sports* on Saturday afternoons, though mainly to see the introduction where every week the same unfortunate skier sailed off a ski jump and wiped out spectacularly as the announcer, Jim McKay, intoned about the "agony of defeat." "You would think he'd learn from last week," my dad would joke.

My parents had tried to fuel my interest in sports. I dutifully signed up for Little League as soon as I was old enough, as well as what we used to call Bitty Basketball, which for years I thought was Biddy Basketball, as if we were on a team of elderly women.

The most humiliating moments were tryouts, when I stood in front of dozens of kids (most unknown to me, but some classmates and friends) on a baseball diamond or basketball court to try out for a team, and then be chosen (or not chosen) depending on my skills or lack of them. Everyone ended up on a team, but there was some arcane process of selection among the teams' coaches, pitting hapless twelve-year-old batters, catchers, and pitchers against one another. This meant that for Bitty Basketball tryouts I donned an ill-fitting polyester tank top and shorts and was told to dribble, shoot a foul throw, and do a layup, none of which I did well—and all this in front of my peers.

If you wanted to design an event to cause maximum adolescent embarrassment, you could do no better than basketball tryouts in ill-fitting polyester clothes in front of one's peers.

Nor was I an ace at baseball, and tryouts on my school's baseball diamond were equally nerve-jangling, though during the seasons I often connected with the ball, once hitting a triple and once making an unassisted double play. I could bat well, but my throwing arm, as *The Recorder* subscriber (or nonsubscriber) pointed out, needed work. As did my fielding.

My first year in Little League I was chosen for the Rams and immediately relegated to right field. That seemed a pleasant enough place to stand, and the field at my elementary school had a beautiful view of our neighborhood. Only a few years ago did I learn that this position was where managers often put the weaker players, because most batters are right-handed and hit the ball to left field. At least my ignorance at the time spared me that mortification.

But I was mortified enough. My dad tried hard to pique my interest and was grimly patient at helping me practice. One year, he was the assistant coach for the Rams, happily coaching me and the other boys on the team. I enjoyed playing catch with him after dinner to hone my skills. But when I got on the field, if I struck out or missed a ball, I felt that I was letting him down. Some of the saddest words he ever uttered were "That's okay, Jimmy!"

I realize now that this was one way my father showed me love: through sports. His own father had died at age forty-nine, when my dad was only eleven. (While my mom's parents emigrated from Sicily, my father's grandparents were of Irish descent.) After my grandfather's death, my dad's older sister, Marguerite, and her husband, Andy, along with their two children, moved back into the family home in the Philadelphia suburb of Upper Darby to help my grandmother care for her two younger children. One of my cousins recently described my grandmother, who died at age sixty, when my father was twenty-three, as "tough." My dad often said that he was in effect raised by his older sister and her husband, both kind and generous people. I knew neither of my grandparents on my father's side, both of whom were long gone by the time I was born in 1960.

In recent years, I've wondered if my dad's losing his father at a young age and living with his "tough" mother made it harder for him to express affection. He tried his best to be loving and often, like my mom, told me he loved me. And he was proud of my success in school. "Great job, pal!" he would say, clapping me on the shoulder after I brought home a good report card.

But another way to show that love was through sports: playing catch in our backyard, driving me to tryouts and practices, and volunteering as a coach. My father loved sports and so naturally wanted me to love sports too. In this desire he was expressing love. I imagine other boys (and girls) my age had the same experience. There's a reason that so many men cry at the scene in the 1989 film *Field of Dreams* when the main character, played by Kevin Costner, miraculously meets his (dead) father as a young man and says, "Wanna have a catch?"

The next year, on the Hawks, I played second base (an upgrade from right field) and got a few hits (plus that triple and unassisted double play) but never shook the feeling that I was not made for Little League, much less Bitty Basketball. I couldn't wait for the seasons to end, though oddly, I enjoyed playing baseball and softball with friends, when there wasn't any pressure. Baseball, softball, and kickball were much more fun without crowds of parents and friends looking on and clapping when you struck out. I was never any good at basketball and hated playing it. Also, with basketball there was no chance the game would be rained out.

My mom would say, "Even if you don't like sports, why not read the sports pages so you can talk about them with your friends?" Years later, she would tell a newly married friend of mine: "You want a happy marriage, Peggy? Read the sports pages!"

Gamely, I tried but found it a chore to keep track of the box scores and players and teams and leagues. I enjoyed going with my family to Phillies and Eagles games at Veterans Stadium and Flyers games at the Spectrum, and I'd later love high school and college football games, but reading the *Evening Bulletin*, a Philly paper, to examine box scores seemed like another assignment from school: Memorize the names of the presidents and then memorize the starting lineup for the Phillies. I'd much rather read about some unsuspecting couple being abducted by aliens or the best way to test your house for ghosts.

Tennis was another story. I'm not sure why I was able to play that game better (at least not as bad, and I always had a lousy serve), but I played constantly in the summers as a teenager. Perhaps because there wasn't a team depending on me, or because missing a ball wasn't racked up as a strike (with an umpire calling it out loudly in case anyone missed my mistake), or because getting hit by a tennis ball was less painful than getting hit by a baseball rocketing from someone's bat, or, most likely, because I wasn't on display in front of a crowd of parents and neighbors, it was fun. Racing to where the tennis ball was headed and returning the ball was also easier than dribbling a basketball, which I found nearly impossible. And perhaps because this was a sport my father was not much interested in, there was less pressure.

But I loved playing tennis with friends as often as we could snag a court at the local swim club or the nearby high school, right off Bicentennial Lane, sometimes twice a day. My journal is filled with lists of tennis games (and bowling, though I considered that less a sport and more a pastime), whom I played with, whom I beat, who beat me, and what the score was. My friend Gary was my most regular partner; we were evenly matched and were able to challenge each other to get better. And after band practice was over in the afternoon, I would hone my skills with an unusual contraption.

My parents bought me a heavy, round yellow piece of plastic, shaped like a half-dome, to which was attached a thick, yards-long rubber band, the end of which was stapled to a tennis ball. It worked under the same principle as paddle ball. (You can still find them online under "Tennis Ball Trainer.") I stood in the street in front of our house for hours, moving only when cars drove by, with the ball making a satisfying *thunk* when the racket hit it right, working myself into a tennis trance, into the waning hours of daylight. More than once I broke the rubber band, which sent the ball rocketing down our street into the dark. "Be careful! We're not buying you another one!" my mom would say. "And don't get hit by a car!"

I also loved street hockey, playing it often after school with Gary and other boys down the street, often in front of my friend Arthur's house a few blocks away. Essentially, the game consisted of whacking an orange plastic ball, or your friend's shins, until one was in the net or the other started bleeding. We played it in all kinds of weather, until it got dark. I loved it and was pretty good at it too.

One of the graces of age is not being afraid to say that you're decent at some things and stink at others. As a teenager, the thought of admitting my lack of aptitude in any sport was too much to bear.

I expended so much energy pretending that (1) I knew something about baseball, (2) I had watched last night's game, or (3) I was good at it myself.

Like everyone else in my neighborhood, I rooted for the Phillies, the Eagles, the Flyers, and the Sixers and so did my family—especially my cousins Marguerite and Mary Beth, who were *friends* with some of the Flyers, which I thought akin to knowing Jesus, since both Jesus and the Flyers seemed equally revered and equally distant. Our 1970 Ford LTD sported a bumper sticker that read "Only the Lord Saves More Than Bernie Parent," referring to the legendary Flyers goalie.

The Flyers' 1974 dramatic Stanley Cup victory was memorialized in a record album of the play-by-play commentary of the final game, which my dad played frequently on our Magnavox stereo console in the living room. Side Two ended with longtime Flyers announcer Gene Hart shouting, "The Flyers win the Stanley CUP! The Flyers win the Stanley CUP!" with as much fervor as someone announcing the Second Coming of Jesus. In keeping with the quasi-religious devotion of Philadelphians, the album was called *God Bless the Flyers*, a nod to the superstition that if the team played a recording of the 1940s singer Kate Smith singing "God Bless America" before a game, then they would win, but also a not entirely irreligious hope that God would indeed bless the Flyers. But while I celebrated the Flyers' victories and jumped up and down when they won the Stanley Cup, I didn't live or die for any of these teams.

More to the point, it's a relief to say, "I'm not that good at baseball and basketball but pretty good at tennis and street hockey." A relief because there is nothing to prove. And while a natural proficiency at a skill is a gift, not being proficient doesn't mean that you're any less valuable a person. As a teenager, I wish I had understood that each person has a unique set of talents. To quote the Apostle Paul on another matter, "There are a variety of gifts."

Interestingly, St. Paul occasionally used sports metaphors in his writing, as when he compared living the Christian life to running. "I have finished the race," he says in the Second Letter to Timothy. Still, I doubt that St. Paul would enjoy trying out for Bitty Basketball in a polyester tank top and shorts while the rest of the apostles critiqued his lousy dribbling skills.

But at sixteen that insight—it's okay to be good at some things and not so good at others—was beyond my emotional capabilities and probably beyond those of most kids at that age, then and now.

Nonetheless, my journal is crammed with references to tennis, bowling, skating, and street hockey, which follow a pattern of describing how the games were arranged, what happened and who said what, and what we ate afterward. (I was a big fan of the Ponderosa Steakhouse.) One day I fumed that I was beaten at tennis by my friend Joyce, *a girl*, and vowed never to let that happen again.

There is an exception to these lighthearted journal entries about sports—nearly unbelievable fifty years later, since I had buried the memory entirely: an entry reporting an eighteen-year-old boy with whom we played street hockey who was arrested for raping five women. "He forced some women to do things with him at gunpoint," I wrote. "I only played with him when he came out to be a goalie . . . It gives me the creeps." The next day at school, according to my journal, he was all we talked about, especially my friend Joyce, who lived on the same street he did.

Violence was rare for our neighborhood in the 1960s and 1970s—rape nearly unthinkable. Everyone I knew felt comfortable playing street hockey late into the night, biking home from the swim club in the dark, or knocking on the doors of houses owned by people you didn't know to trick-or-treat for UNICEF, to ask them to buy oversize chocolate bars to support the Cub Scouts, or to give money to a paper they didn't subscribe to.

One of our neighbors was once having an argument with a former boyfriend, and a police cruiser raced to the house. Later, police officers came to our house to question us, an event so unusual that it warranted five consecutive pages in my journal.

Crime was nearly unheard of, and into the night you could find kids biking, walking home from Little League in their uniforms, or playing street hockey. I remember hitting that tennis ball in the street until it was so dark that I couldn't see it at the end of its rubber band. "You'll strain your eyes!" my mom would say as the fireflies winked on and off. Overall, I felt safe.

Golf, the focus of my new summer job, fell in an undefined middle ground in my sports landscape: between basketball, which I was terrible at, and tennis, which I was good at. I had never golfed so I could not say whether I was good or bad.

A few of my older cousins, none of them wealthy, golfed. My cousin Tommy, on my mother's side, was the best of the lot. He began caddying at age fourteen at the Philadelphia Cricket Club, a tony country club a half-hour drive from our house. Founded in 1854, the Cricket Club bills itself as the nation's oldest country club. Tommy's younger brother, Ricky, three years older than me, also worked there as a caddy, from ages fourteen to twenty-one.

Six years older than me, Tommy was an impressive guy: tall, confident, and a terrific golfer who caddied at the Cricket Club through high school and later worked in the Golf Shop while studying at Temple University. Like the rest of my family, he came from working-class roots, growing up in the Wissahickon section of Philadelphia. After graduating from college, Tommy became an assistant golf pro. Even after his workday at the Cricket Club was over, he often played a round.

So he was naturally enthusiastic when I nervously called to ask if I could caddy. "Of course, Sport!" he said.

Tommy had a nickname for everyone. His brother Ricky was "Opie," after the character in *The Andy Griffith Show*, and my dad was "Joe Garagiola," for my father's oft-remarked-upon resemblance to the former baseball player and current smiling, bald television sportscaster. I was either "Ace" or "Sport" or Jimmy, the name my family and friends used until roughly high school.

Tommy promised to put in a good word for me with the caddy master, but my suspicion was that, given his position at the club, it wouldn't be much of a problem. Left unsaid was the fact that, unlike Tommy and Ricky, I had never set foot on a golf course.

One humid morning in June, after putting the final touches on eleventh grade, I donned what I judged to be a reasonable facsimile of golf clothes: a polo shirt, a pair of long pants, and Adidas sneakers. At the time, I wasn't sure why it was called the Cricket Club and never saw anyone playing anything other than golf. Even if they did play cricket, I wouldn't have recognized it: I had a vague sense that it was British but didn't know if it was played with mallets or rackets or paddles—and whether or not a horse was involved.

The Cricket Club was an imposing place, obviously the domain of wealthy people. And my job there marked the first time I was around rich people in any number. Our family sometimes drove through the Main Line, the Philadelphia suburbs in which "old money" resided. "This is where all the rich people live," said my parents as we drove through Devon or Paoli, straining to see the immense brick mansions that were hidden behind tall trees. Years later, I read Paul Fussell's book *Class*, which dissects the various classes in American society with as much precision as we dissected frogs that year in school. His taxonomy of classes includes the "top out-of-sight" class, who live in houses you can't even see. Reading that phrase, I remembered those family car rides when I was a boy.

My prom date in junior high lived in a big, two-story brick house with an attic, a few miles from our split-level homes, and so she was considered rich. But as far as I knew, most of my classmates and everyone in our neighborhood were solidly middle class. One exception was Joe Frazier, the heavyweight boxing champion, who lived a few miles away, in Whitemarsh, a wealthier suburb. Two of his children, both tremendous fun, were in high school with me, and once I ran into "Smokin' Joe" in the supermarket and told him what a fan I was. The man my dad called "Champ" when he met him playfully put out his huge fist for me to punch, which I did, and he pretended that it hurt.

At the Cricket Club everyone was rich, was trying to be, or was trying to appear to be.

The course was immaculately kept, with rolling hills and magnificent trees, and, well, you probably know what a golf course looks like. This would be one of the most enjoyable parts of the job: simply being there, walking on the soft green grass, admiring the majestic trees, and catching sight of an interesting bird. At night, I'd try to identify them in my Roger Tory Peterson guidebook. Maybe it wasn't "walking wherever I want," as I hoped in my journal, but it was a pleasure, even a joy, to be surrounded by a picture-postcard view every day and to breathe in the almost constant fragrance of freshly cut grass.

The clubhouse was a series of long white buildings with dark gray roofs, looking like a group of private homes jammed side by side. I don't think I set foot in the clubhouse proper very often, if at all, except to use the bathroom. Certainly not to eat. The caddies were assigned to the caddy shack, a shedlike garage with a few benches, mere yards from the first tee, where we waited for the caddy master to assign us to golfers. Often golfers requested the senior caddies, grizzled older men in their fifties and sixties whom we called the Super Loopers, a loop being the circuit a golfer makes on the eighteen holes.

On that humid morning, my dad drove me to the Cricket Club, located in a wealthy suburb about thirty minutes from our house, and dropped me off. I found my way to Tommy in the caddy shack. He was dressed in a white polo shirt and long, dark pants and a pair of immaculately white golfing shoes. With his long, dark hair and mustache, Tommy was something of a fashion plate. After briefly introducing me to the caddy master, Tommy said he was going to teach me all he knew about caddying.

As usual, when confronted with something I didn't know much about (in this case I knew nothing), I felt embarrassed, almost ashamed. But Tommy, patient and knowledgeable, said that all I had to do was listen and watch. Tommy's confident personality and obvious acumen with the game commanded respect; as a result, he got away with things that others would not have, such as giving everyone nicknames and, once, dumping a bucket of cold water on some caddies from a bathroom window that overlooked the caddy shack. I asked his brother Ricky recently what their reaction was. "Oh, they thought it was funny! Everyone loved Tommy!"

Under the broiling sun, Tommy shot a round of golf, as I caddied. The first lesson was the proper way to carry a bag: over your right shoulder and pushed behind you, so it didn't drag on the ground or trip you up and so you could keep your hand protectively over the clubs.

At first the bag was lighter than I expected. But it grew heavier throughout the morning, and by the eighteenth hole my shoulder ached. In time, I got used to carrying around the bags, even two bags at once, and I must have gotten stronger, even though I wore out the right shoulder of several T-shirts that summer.

As we loped down the fairway of the first hole, I realized that I didn't know Tommy well, having seen him only at family gatherings—Easter, Thanksgiving, Christmas, weddings, and funerals—and rarely having extended conversations with him. The six years between us in age was an oceanic difference: I felt like a kid next to him. I wasn't used to talking with him, or with anyone his age, and was a bit tongue-tied around him, even though he was kind and helpful.

Tommy patiently offered advice about which clubs to offer the golfer: Use the driver off the tee, irons for approach shots, wedges around the greens, and putters, of course, for the green. He also taught me the right way to pack a golf bag, clean the balls in the metal ball-washers (with the inevitable jokes about ball-washers appropriate for his teenage cousin), and retrieve balls from the water hazard with a long extending metal wand with a ball-size loop on the end. I would do this often that summer for chagrined golfers who wanted their balls back but were mortified that they had lost them. One golfer got angry after I said, "I think it went into the pond." "Water hazard!" he snapped. I learned to keep my mouth shut. And to bone up on my golf lingo.

Tommy was tremendously knowledgeable. I could tell he was holding back at first, but soon words and phrases poured forth from him like water—"fairway," "rough," "bunker," "aprons," "carpets," "front nine," "back nine"—as well as his advice on how to treat the golfers, how to react when they were not doing well, and, most of all, how, when the golfer was putting, a caddy should never stand in his line of sight or commit the cardinal sin of stepping on the green in between the golfer and his ball. "Never do that," he said, calmly but firmly.

Tommy also gave me an easy-to-remember tip for where to stand when your golfer was putting: "Look at either his belly button or his ass." Meaning, stand either directly in front of him or behind him. "No one wants to see their caddy standing to the side, distracting him." *Okay*, I thought, *I got all that.*

But when Tommy started describing which clubs to use for different shots ("a five iron goes farther than a nine iron"), I panicked. How could I remember all this? It was like trying to learn a semester of geometry in a few hours—and I was having a hard enough time in geometry class. I realized I should have brought a piece of paper to take notes.

"You got all that, Sport?" he said in his high-pitched, gravelly voice.

I nodded dumbly.

"Good job!" he said. "You'll do great!"

When we returned to the caddy shack, the caddy master, a gruff but friendly man nicknamed Muttsy, grilled me, in a brief interview: Had I ever played? (No, I admitted.) Was I strong enough to carry two bags? (Yes.) Was I willing to work hard? (I told him a few stories about the Ice Cream Inn, which seemed to convince him.) Chief among his concerns was my treating the guests courteously. That, I said, I could do well. At the very least, I treated the non-paying newspaper subscribers well and didn't yell at homeowners who failed to warn me about bee-infested sheds. I did refrain from telling him that I had drawn blood with my bussing tray.

After a cursory review of my newly minted Social Security card and a glance at my frame, he said, "Okay, show up tomorrow at eight and we'll see how you do." The other caddies eyed me suspiciously. I seemed to have a knack for choosing summer jobs with confident older boys ready to size me up.

In the afternoon, my dad picked me up and I repeated what Tommy had taught me. But I told him I didn't think that I'd be able to remember all the different clubs.

"That's okay," he said, "you'll get the hang of it."

My dad was probably hoping that I would be better at caddying than I was at basketball. "Tommy will take care of you. If you have any questions, just ask him. Maybe you'll even get to golf." Maybe golf would be more like tennis than basketball, I thought, as I imagined myself hitting perfect shots down the fairway, the other caddies looking on in awe. "You're a natural!"

The next day I leaped out of bed at 6 a.m. and dressed. I couldn't believe that I was doing this. *Which club do you use for a long shot? Which one for a short one? What do I know about golf anyway? Am I insane?*

But I piled into our car at 7 a.m. and took off for golfing glory.

At least I could drive. A few months before, I had turned sixteen and passed my driver's exam. Drivers' Ed was a popular course in high school, though it meant taking the course with a gruff gym instructor whom I'll call Mr. Smith.

Students were elated that they were taking Drivers' Ed and on their way to becoming legal drivers, but they were somewhat cowed by Mr. Smith. Like other gym teachers, he also taught health class, which in junior high and high school seemed to focus on three topics: sexual maturity (which included watching a deeply uncomfortable movie about puberty called *From Boy to Man*), drinking (my journal records that we saw an anti-alcohol movie called *Drink, Drank, Drunk*), and, even more, avoiding drugs (we read the popular book *Go Ask Alice*, a 1971 cautionary tale about a teenage girl with a drug addiction).

Health class was supposed to prevent us from using drugs, especially pot, but the endless lessons about the various drugs and their effects just made me more curious. The effects of LSD (which for the record I never used) were described in terms that were so florid, so outrageous, so, well, psychedelic that had they served LSD in the cafeteria the day our teacher talked about it in health class, every kid happily would have put a big fat serving on their tray.

Drivers' Ed consisted of not only an in-class portion, to prepare us for the written exam, but also nerve-racking sessions in a car with Mr. Smith, driving around town and onto major highways as he shouted, "NO!" and pumped the brakes, bringing the car to a screeching halt every few minutes. One of his standard lectures was how, if you crashed your car, your sun visor could "crack your skull open" if it was angled incorrectly. We pitied Mr. Smith for his unenviable job of teaching teenagers how to drive, but we feared him more.

The only other teachers I feared as much were the industrial arts teachers, whose classes included wood shop, where we sawed, drilled, hammered, screwed, and sanded and made a nice wooden toolbox; metal shop, where we poured molten steel into molds and I made an eagle, which, after being nailed to a wooden plaque I had made in wood shop, hung in my family's recreation room for the next thirty years; and mechanical drawing, the least interesting of the three shop electives, which consisted of drawing containers and boxes and buildings with rulers, compasses, and protractors on special crinkly paper. This being the 1970s, while we boys were sawing wood and melting steel, the girls were baking cakes and learning how to sew in home economics classes.

The shop teachers, like the gym and health teachers, seemed a different breed from the other teachers: tougher, terser, tenser. "Not like that," my wood shop teacher would say with admirable economy as he yanked a saw from my hands. "Like this."

Driving with Mr. Smith near our parish church one day, I spotted a suspicious obstruction on the road ahead: a perfectly shaped black metal cube the size of a Kleenex box, which looked exactly like the parts of UFOs that Brad Steiger was always writing about. That year I would also start watching the TV series *In Search Of*, hosted by Leonard Nimoy, who had played Mr. Spock on *Star Trek*. I wasn't a Trekkie, but *In Search Of* was just as engrossing as Brad Steiger's books, since it examined not only poltergeists and Bigfoot, but ESP, the Loch Ness Monster, ancient civilizations, and of course aliens, all with Leonard Nimoy's deep but creepy voice. And the sinister black metal cube on the road ahead of us now easily could have fallen off an alien spaceship.

But most likely it fell off a truck. An experienced driver could easily avoid it, but back then I wasn't sure whether I should drive around it and into the lane of oncoming traffic, or drive over it and let it pass underneath the car. In my confusion I ran directly *over* it with my left wheel, creating a horrible clattering noise, as if the car were coming apart, and sending Mr. Smith and me flying up toward the roof of the little green Pinto hatchback we were driving.

"What the hell are you DOING?" he shouted as he slammed on the brakes. We lurched to a stop and almost hit the dashboard. I was glad that the sun visor didn't crack my skull open.

Embarrassed, I sputtered that I was trying to avoid the cube by going over it since it looked like it would fit under the car, or the chassis, and I could just pass over it instead of hitting it and, uh, uh . . .

"Don't EVER do that AGAIN!" he yelled. "You could RUIN the CAR! This is the SCHOOL'S CAR!"

I thought I was going to cry, and Mr. Smith was the last person I wanted to cry in front of. Then I got angry: Mr. Smith probably hadn't even seen that metal box, or whatever it was. Aliens were always leaving strange things behind, so I briefly wondered if it could be something we should turn in to the FBI. Anyway, why did he have to be so grumpy about it? Here was another lesson learned: Don't scream at an already nervous teenager. To be fair, Mr. Smith probably had to live with the fear of constant car crashes while at the mercy of student drivers. Sullenly, we drove back to the high school. Well, I was sullen. He was steamed.

The school's tense driving lessons were supplemented by my patient though slow-burning father, who drove me to a local park after my December birthday, where we practiced parallel parking and making three-point turns in a snow-plowed parking lot, untroubled by other cars. Something about the sessions reminded me of our baseball practices because I would often mess up, and mess up in front of him, but I eventually learned how to drive, thanks to Mr. Smith and my dad. And began to enjoy it.

The driving test was another matter. One Saturday, I drove with my dad to the Pennsylvania Department of Motor Vehicles office in Norristown, a few towns over, and waited in the lobby on a green plastic chair. I was so nervous I thought I was going to vomit. Or faint, though I had never fainted. Or vomit and faint. I had purposely avoided Nature Valley Granola that morning.

Having already passed the written portion of the exam, all I had to do now was the driving part. Here's what you had to do: Start the car (easy!), drive around in the parking lot (also easy!), drive in highway traffic (not as easy but still easy), do a three-point turn (harder, but I had mastered it), and parallel park (hardest of all).

Driving between a series of orange traffic cones, in and out, was also part of the exam. My friend Ernie regaled us in class one day with his story of slowly and painstakingly snaking his way in and out of the orange cones, being extra careful not to bump one, to the dismay of the state trooper, who barked "Faster!" When Ernie floored the gas pedal, the car lurched back and forth through the cones, the man's head snapping back and forth in the car. "SLOWER!" he shouted. Ernie told that story again and again, his own head whipping back and forth to increasing laughter, until our homeroom teacher told us to shut up.

When the tall state policeman entered our powder-blue 1972 Gran Torino, I felt my heart in my throat. With his gray uniform, mirrored sunglasses, and broad-brimmed black hat, he looked not only menacing but annoyed, even though it was his first test of the day. (I made sure to arrive early: School rumor had it that troopers were more cheerful in the morning.) Who could blame him?

Being driven around by nervous teenage drivers was not a job to be envied. At least Mr. Smith taught gym and a few health classes and knew all the slang for marijuana. Then again, I bet the state trooper did too.

I was more nervous about this test than the SATs. More was at stake socially. While only a few people knew your SAT scores, *everyone* knew who could and couldn't drive, who had and hadn't passed the test, and how many times it had taken them. And unlike the SATs, the results were obvious to anyone: You either were or were not driving yet.

"Start the car," he said.

No problem! The Gran Torino rumbled to life.

Then he led me through some easy steps, until we reached the orange cones. Thinking of Ernie, I went slowly. But not too slowly. I started to worry that he could smell my fear, like the dogs in my neighborhood.

"Faster, please," he said. I sped up and accidentally hit one of the cones. *Damn it! How could I do that?* Heat rushed to my cheeks.

"Sorry," he said, scribbling on a piece of paper, which he tore off his pad and handed to me. "You failed." I felt like I had struck out in a Little League game. "Strike One!" was a terrible thing to hear. I almost cried but didn't think that the trooper would be sympathetic.

When I returned to school on Monday, I had to tell my friends—including Gary, who not only had passed his driver's test, but also got a cool two-toned, powder-and-dark-blue Camaro for his sixteenth birthday, which he drove to school—that I had failed. How it added coals to the fire of my jealousy—even though he wasn't trying to make me jealous—when Gary generously drove me home from school that week. There was no way my parents could afford to buy me a car. I was grateful for the rides Gary gave me: We had been friends since elementary school, and his parents were unfailingly kind to me. (His bar mitzvah was also one of the best parties I had ever been to.) Also, his car had a first-class stereo; and it seemed that every time I was in his Camaro, Queen's "Bohemian Rhapsody" was playing on the radio, so soon I knew all the lyrics. But at the time I was often incapable of being happy for someone else's good fortune, in this case Gary's Camaro. It wasn't until years later that I realized how entering into someone else's joy is itself a joyful thing.

In the Jesuits we have an expression: "Compare and despair." If you compare yourself to someone else, you usually focus on your own mixed bag of good and bad experiences. My life was a mixture of the good ("I'm doing well in school, have a lot of friends, and am healthy") and the bad ("I stink at baseball, am lousy at basketball, and just failed my driver's test"). But we tend to compare that with what we see as the other person's "perfect life" ("He has a Camaro!"), forgetting that everyone's life is a mixed bag. So when you compare your own mixed-bag life with what you falsely perceive as the other person's perfect life, yours always loses out. It's a rigged game, as an older Jesuit once said. The key is recognizing that everyone's life is a mix of good and bad. But it would take me years to realize that. For now, I was stuck comparing, and in this case I compared myself to everyone who could drive.

Thanks to Strike One, I remained in abject misery until the next weekend.

When I struck out for the second time! During this iteration, I saw a stop sign, which seemed to be on the right-hand side of a parallel lane next to mine, facing me. That is, the sign was in a lane going the opposite direction but was pointing toward me. That sounds odd, I know, but that's how it appeared. Or maybe my nervous brain didn't register it correctly. I didn't know whether the sign applied to me or not, since it was not where a stop sign usually is, so I drove past it.

"STOP!" yelled the new but just as menacing state trooper.

I stopped.

"You went through a STOP SIGN!" Which of course was a no-no. "You've failed. For the second time, I see," he said as he flipped through his clipboard disdainfully.

When I got to school the next day, I was mortified. Everyone knew that if you failed a third time, you had to wait for another six months—a year, said one kid. "Two years!" said another. Happily, the next round was more successful, no flattened cones and no run stop signs, and when the trooper said, "You passed," I felt like I had won the Nobel Prize in Driving.

I loved driving, and in the weeks after I passed my exam, I wanted to drive everywhere. After a few weeks my parents relaxed about letting me use the Gran Torino.

From then on, my dad also wouldn't have to drive my sister and me to church on Sundays, which he often did when my mother wasn't able to go. On the important feast days—Christmas, Easter, and so on—we would never miss Mass and went together as a family. But on ordinary Sundays, things were more relaxed. Sometimes my dad would stay in the car in the parking lot and read the sports pages of the Sunday edition of the *Evening Bulletin*. I once asked him why he didn't want to go into church. "I've been to church enough for one lifetime," he said. "Now it's your turn!"

One June morning, I got into the Gran Torino and took off for my first day at the Cricket Club, windows down, listening to, as I did that summer, Rita Coolidge's "We're All Alone" on the radio.

Something about Rita Coolidge's sultry voice and plaintive tones captivated me. I wasn't lovesick, though I had a few crushes that summer. We had played that song at our Student Council Disco Dance that year (since I was president of the Student Council, I had some pull in what songs were played). "Turn it off!" people shouted, begging for more Donna Summer.

I was so happy to be able to drive! Plus, I could sing along with Rita Coolidge without anyone complaining.

Close the window, calm the light.
And it will be *all riiiiight*!
No need to bother now.
Let it out, let it all begin.
Learn how to pretend.

Rita Coolidge understood me, although I had no idea what she was talking about.

Thank God I could drive. How embarrassing it would be to show up in front of the Super Loopers with your dad or, worse, your *mom* driving you to the Cricket Club. Even though I was nervous about caddying, I was excited: I had a new job that would let me work on my tan. No more washing dishes in a dark, hot room. Goodbye, Ice Cream Inn! No more begging people to pay me for newspapers they didn't want. Goodbye, paper route! No more having to maneuver a lawn mower around basketball-size wasp nests. Goodbye, mowing lawns!

When I got out of the car on that humid day, I pictured myself confidently strolling behind a golfer, casually pushing my Phillies cap above my brow and stroking my chin thoughtfully as I considered which club he should use, and then, after examining his bag, selecting the perfect club, which I gave to him so that he could drive the ball clear down the fairway into the hole, clap me on the back, and say, "You have an intuitive knowledge of golf, Jim," and hand me a twenty-dollar bill and then invite me to work at his law firm next summer.

I parked the car and walked down a sloping driveway and underneath a connecting bridge that linked the clubhouse to the caddy shack. The smell of the fresh-cut grass filled me with a sense of purpose. Also, I thought, *I'm glad I don't have to mow any more lawns.*

My elation evaporated when I entered the caddy shack. Twenty pairs of unwelcoming eyes stared at me. My presence (and most of the caddies knew that I was Tommy's cousin) meant that there was one less chance that they would get to go out. There were always plenty of golfers, but as an inexperienced caddy, I often felt I was taking a job away from a more experienced caddy, which was everyone else.

Nonetheless, I was chosen by Muttsy within a half hour and paired up with a caddy a few years older than me, who took a dim view of my lack of experience. "I hope you can keep up," said my fellow caddy as he walked ahead of me. I was determined to.

We were caddying for a pair of women golfers, and I was careful to give my golfer exactly the clubs she requested. On weekdays, the women golfers went out early; the men, later in the day, usually after lunch, though that schedule was more flexible on weekends. That morning, my golfer kept slicing the ball (shooting inadvertently to the right) and the other hooking it (to the left). A few weeks later I would "double bag" for two women who did the same thing, which meant that I was constantly crisscrossing the fairway, from roughs on the left to roughs on the right.

My fellow caddy was more intent (as he should have been) on catering to his golfer than on teaching me the ropes. At times, I felt overwhelmed, especially worried that the players would ask me for advice, though for the most part that summer the golfers, both men and women, didn't need anyone to tell them what club to use, only to carry their bag for a few hours in the sun. But on my first loop, I didn't commit any mortal golfing sins, didn't drop the bag or any clubs, and seemed to pull it off. At the end I got the standard fifteen dollars, with a few dollars tip. The cash felt good in my pocket. Unlike my paper-route begging, I was guaranteed to get paid, and unlike the Ice Cream Inn, there were no deductions.

Most golfers kept in their bags their clubs, balls, tees, and maybe a towel. But from time to time, a golfer used their bag like a locker, which added to the weight. One stowed in his bag *two* extra pairs of golf shoes, whose metal cleats added another few pounds, as well as an extra box of balls. A slim, elegant woman I caddied for (who was known not only as a bad tipper, but also as a terrible player, and so I usually ended up with her, as in "You can have her") kept in her skinny Pepto-Bismol-colored bag the following: two pairs of shoes, a shirt, a pair of pants, a transistor radio, a box of balls, and her purse. Her bag probably outweighed her.

The bulk of caddying was silently lugging your bag and keeping up with your golfer, who was usually carrying nothing more than a club and chatting with his or her partner (not you), though the more experienced caddies and Super Loopers were more relied upon for their expertise. In other words, golfers new to the Cricket Club could be told what to avoid, how to angle a shot, and how the ground was either high or low near the green, and so on, by an experienced caddy. All things that were beyond me in the beginning.

When I returned from my first loop, not having done anything awful, Tommy said, "How'd it go, Sport?"

"Okay," I said.

"Good job!" he said, and clapped me on the back.

I ate lunch, chatting with the other caddies, many of whom were on the golf teams at their prep schools. They talked about their matches, their handicaps, when they would next play the Cricket Club's course, what the hardest hole was, what kind of clubs they liked the best, who their favorite players were, and so on. "Do you golf?" one said. "Not really," I said. "But I'd like to learn." They invited me to play with them after work, but I was embarrassed to tell them that I didn't own a set of clubs, so I made excuses.

I never felt like I fit in with the rest of the caddies because I didn't know much about golf so couldn't join in many of their golf-centered conversations. During the previous year, as a junior in high school, I'd enjoyed my classes immensely, had some great friends, and had even been elected Student Council president, so I was neither a shrinking violet nor a wallflower. High school was a social terra firma. By contrast, the Cricket Club, like many summer jobs, was terra incognita, and sometimes I found it difficult to engage in conversation, navigate the shifting loyalties, tease with ease, keep up with talk about pro golfers, and gauge the proper response to jokey comments from the older and more confident boys. And I began to wonder whether they resented me for Tommy's having arranged this gig for me without my knowing much about golf.

I was years away from living out an expression I heard in French class that year: comfortable in your own skin. *Boy, I would love that,* I thought when it came up in one of our little playlets: "*Il est bien dans sa peau.*" What would that be like? What would it be like to say to the older caddies, "Could you teach me how to use a driver?" Who knows whether they would turn up their noses? Most likely, they would be flattered to be asked. But I hadn't mastered the art of being honest, being myself, and certainly not being vulnerable. (Vulnerable was the last thing that a teenage boy wanted to be in those days.) I played it safe and spoke as little as necessary.

At lunch, most of the caddies, like me, opened a bagged lunch from home, supplemented by a soda from a machine in the caddy shack. Muttsy made hot dogs for us (at a price) in an adjoining room. We ate in the caddy shack, with its timbered roof and concrete floor. Some of the caddies played cards during their downtime, occasionally looking up to watch some golfer tee off at the first tee and critique his stroke and roll their eyes.

After lunch, Muttsy assigned me to a threesome. This time I was going to "cart-caddy." I noticed some of the other caddies raising their eyebrows.

"Have fun," one said darkly. The others chuckled and went back to playing cards.

Cart-caddying meant that three golfers rented a motorized golf cart designed for two people; two rode in the cart and one hitched a ride on the back, where two golf bags were stowed. That arrangement meant that the *third* bag couldn't fit on the cart and had to be carried by a caddy, that is, me. Consequently, the three golfers zipped ahead of me in their cart as I raced after them on the soft grass, sometimes actually running, while carrying the third golfer's bag.

They yelled, "Hurry up, caddy!" and laughed as I struggled to keep up, the third bag jostling on my shoulders. "Hahaha! He's gaining on us!"

I was caddying for three players, raking the sand traps after they had played, mending any grass divots (pieces of grass and earth their clubs had torn up), and removing and replacing the pin, or flag, when they were putting on the green. But most of the time I was running to keep up. I despised cart-caddying, though the tips were good.

By the end of the day, having done two loops, a single bag in the morning and the cart-caddy in the afternoon, I was exhausted, and beginning to foresee what the summer would be like. When I recently asked my sister if she remembered anything about that summer, she said, "Yes, you were always tired."

That night I drove home with less confidence than I had in the morning. As was often my pattern, rather than asking for help, I judged myself to be an idiot or a loser. Rita Coolidge was on the radio going home too, so I sang along with her.

Let it out, let it all begiiiiin.
Learn how to pretend.

Okay, I thought, *I'll learn how to pretend to be a caddy.*
When I got home on a still humid day, I flopped down on the sofa and said, "I hate it," before downing a cheese-filled Danish. How hard could it be? Very hard, it turned out.

My parents were sympathetic but also resolute about my working. "Well, you're not going to sit inside all summer," said my mom. Keep at it, they both said. Also, not having interviewed for any other jobs, and having put all my eggs in one basket, or golf balls into one bag, I was stuck being caddy that summer. I might as well try to do my best.

To make up for my lack of expertise, I read a few beginner's guidebooks on golf, asked Tommy questions on the phone, and one day played a round with the prep-school kids, one of whom kindly lent me an extra set of clubs. Wednesdays were "caddy day," when caddies could play for free. Compared with members of the prep-school golf teams, I was awful, something that kept me off the course for the remainder of the summer. Also, the last thing I wanted to do after walking around the course all week was to walk around the course on my morning off. I'd rather spend time on the tennis court. Or read about poltergeists. Or aliens. Or birds. Frankly, anything other than golf, which just reminded me of my ineptitude.

Another thing that discouraged me from playing was the crabby demeanors of a few golfers for whom I caddied. I had supposed golf to be a relaxing social sport, filled with friendly camaraderie and lighthearted banter and people saying, "Nice shot, Bill!"

But at the Cricket Club I found golf to be sometimes intensely, occasionally insanely competitive. The game seemed less like fun and more like work for the businessmen and attorneys and physicians who played with one another. It was a preview of the macho, intense, hypercompetitive environment I would sometimes encounter in my first job after college, at General Electric. Many golfers were teed off as soon as they teed off.

"*Damn* it!" they would say through clenched teeth as they sliced or hooked a shot, missed another putt, or hit a ball into a sand trap or water hazard. "*Damn* it!"

They were angry that they had sliced a shot and even angrier that they had done so in front of their golfing partners, who were often business associates. The men I caddied for seemed more uptight than the women, for whom it seemed more of a social occasion, and from whom I heard fewer "Damn its" and more laughs. Even though the other caddies disagreed with me, I preferred caddying for women because, although they were not as generous in tipping, they were more relaxed and often asked me my name and even engaged me in conversation. I realize that these comments sound sexist, but at sixteen this was how I saw it: In general, the male golfers were angrier than the female golfers; they were also better tippers. And the bigger the tip, the more the men made a show of it in front of their friends.

A single bag with a single golfer was my preferred loop, easier than double bags or cart-caddying. I also preferred not caddying with a threesome or foursome, which meant working with another caddy, which meant feeling embarrassed by my lack of knowledge. At times I tried to ask for advice, but the older caddies were more focused on their golfers, not on teaching a novice. At night I went back to my golf books to glean what I could. Then I got bored and went back to reading about poltergeists.

Sometimes I caddied for college or high school students, accompanying parents and the children, with the children delighted to have someone their age to order around, like a servant, saying, "Caddy, hurry up!" "Caddy, give me my nine iron!" Or, inevitably from the boys, "Caddy, wash my *balls*! Hahahaha!"

Alone, the male golfers felt freer to share their true feelings and curse more, using some creative and unfamiliar curse words that I stored up, ready to unleash them on unsuspecting friends.

Nonetheless, most of the golfers at the Cricket Club were polite, if aloof, occasionally asking where I went to school. That I wasn't at a prep school stopped a few conversations. Sometimes they would give me unsolicited and well-meaning advice on where to go to college and what to study: usually business, law, and sometimes medicine. Doctors were great tippers.

Often, though, I felt invisible. Occasionally only a few words would pass between me and my golfer: "Driver," "nine iron," "sand wedge" were sometimes the only things they would say over the course of four or five hours.

Strangely, I noticed that they would speak to me not only using different words than they used with one another, but sometimes with a different *accent*. I was once caddying for two women who spoke to me in conversational tones, with a Philly accent, which I retained until it was drummed out of me in college. But they addressed each other in more formal tones, with a clipped Main Line, almost mid-Atlantic accent, as if they were Katharine Hepburn in *The Philadelphia Story*.

The angriest person I caddied for was a middle-aged man golfing alone. Surly from the first tee, he stomped around the course frustrated by his slices, his landing in the rough several times, his terrible putting, and his overall lousy performance. I'm sure he was disappointed in his caddy too. "F—k!" he said over and over as we barreled through the front nine on a sunny day.

During these times I would try to distract myself by looking at the tall trees swaying in the wind, watching the shadows from the clouds pass swiftly over the grass, or listening to the birdsong that almost always accompanied me on the fairways.

At one point we were on a green overlooking a shallow, wooded ravine. He asked for his putter, which I gave him. Then I removed the pin and stood on the apron, as he began to putt.

Since Tommy had warned me, I was careful not to step between the golfer and the cup (or hole) when he was putting. I had inadvertently done that early in my time there, standing atop a damp green, and watched in horror as the ball went into the circular depression my footprint had made and circled right out of it, causing the ball to miss the cup by a wide mark. The golfer exploded and later complained to Muttsy. Tommy heard about it and simply said, plaintively, "Jimmyyyyy!" After that, I was vigilant about where I stood.

My golfer missed the cup. I moved the flag and stood out of his line of sight. Then he putted again and missed again. I moved again, being careful, as Tommy advised, always to stand either in front of him or behind him, never to his side.

He missed *ten* times (I was counting silently and I'm sure he knew it), his face reddening with each miss. I grew embarrassed for him, remembering how it felt to strike out in Little League. I tried to look nonchalant, but one of the problems for a caddy is that you can't pretend not to see how poorly your golfer is doing. You're *supposed* to be paying attention.

"F—k!" he said, turning purple. The heat and humidity didn't help his mood. Neither did the fact that his inexperienced teenage caddy was witnessing this. I thought he was going to have a heart attack. Would I still get paid?

Then he handed me his putter, which I assumed meant that we were finished on the green. We were not.

He asked for his driver and a tee. This was a cardinal sin: One uses a driver only when one tees off. And using a tee on a green was another no-no. I wondered what Tommy would say.

But the golfer was in charge, so I withdrew his driver from his big pro bag, unzipped the large pocket on the bag, and rooted around for a tee. I handed him both and stepped back. Sweating profusely, he leaned over, his face reddening. With one leg on the ground, the other in the air, his big stomach tightly encased in his polyester golf shirt and spilling over his belt, he pushed the tee deep into the soft manicured green.

He teed up his ball. I looked around, worried we were going to be arrested by the golf police.

Fueled by his putting rage, he faced the shallow ravine, addressed the ball, and smacked it as hard as I had seen anyone hit a ball. *Thwack!* Into the ravine sailed the little white ball, which became a tiny white dot and then disappeared, never to be seen again. My retrieving wand certainly wasn't going to reach it.

Then he strode over to me, silently reached into his bag, took his putter, snapped it over his bent knee, and angrily threw the two broken halves into the ravine with a grunt. The two halves turned over and over, silently somersaulting in the summer air, before disappearing. He did the same with his driver. Since Tommy told me never to criticize the golfers, I simply watched, mutely, though if I had said something it would have been along the lines of "Did you just break your driver and your putter? How much do those things cost?"

This was just the warm-up. To my shock, he strode up to me, sweaty and red-faced. *Was he going to hit me? I wondered. What did I do wrong?* (If something went wrong on the course, I would assume I had messed up, though in this case I was a good caddy.)

He said, "Gimme the bag."

The bag was standing on its own on the apron, as I stood beside it. I backed up a few paces. He grabbed the bag, carried it off the green, faced the ravine, hoisted it up to his chest, and then hurled it into the abyss, bellowing, "F—K THIS!"

Turning around, he looked at me and said, "We're *done*."

Too astonished to respond, I followed him across the course, bagless, drawing stares from the other golfers and caddies. When we reached the clubhouse, he gave me a twenty-dollar bill and said, "I'm sorry for that, but I couldn't take anymore. I'm *done* with this."

Muttsy emerged from the caddy shack and said to me, "Where's his bag?"

I looked imploringly at the man, who walked over to the caddy master, whispered something to him, and then left. Muttsy nodded and waved me over. A few minutes later I was out on the course again, this time for a full round with another man. Later I told the caddies what had happened, and they all had the same reaction: "Think how much those clubs cost! And wasn't he using a pro bag?" There was a brief discussion about retrieving his bag and perhaps salvaging the clubs, though I don't think that ever happened. For all I know they're still in that ravine at the Cricket Club.

Most days were not as eventful. Typically, I went out for one loop in the morning and another in the afternoon and made a good deal of money, much of it in tips. Golfers often pulled out a five-dollar bill and gave it to me with a flourish, in front of their friends. I was grateful for their vanity. I was also grateful to pour myself into the Gran Torino at the end of the day and turn up the radio, my shoulder sore but my wallet full. And as my sister noted, I was tired almost all the time, complained a lot, and was delighted whenever I woke up in the morning and it was pouring rain. *Rain*, I thought, *friend to lazy caddies*. I would just roll over and return to a guiltless sleep.

Usually, though, it was bright and cloudless (if humid). I was sunburned for most of my caddying career, which delighted me. In those days we thought that once you were burned then you could build a "base" for a "safe" tan. My dermatologist and a few skin cancer treatments have proved that to be largely incorrect.

Whenever my dermatologist discovers something, he'll say, "This is from fifty years ago," and I think of the Cricket Club.

That summer I also participated in one of the strangest weeks of my teenage life. Toward the end of my junior year I was somehow chosen (by submitting an essay? a nomination from a teacher? an application?) to participate in the "Tomorrow's Leaders" program, sponsored by the Rotary Club, an international humanitarian organization with a strong presence in my hometown.

Tomorrow's Leaders, a free, weeklong program designed to teach leadership skills, sounded like an amalgam of summer camp (which I liked) and summer school (which I didn't). Still, I was proud to be chosen along with another kid from my high school, my friend Paul. My guidance counselor and parents were also excited about the event, to be held at Cabrini College, a small Catholic school in suburban Philadelphia.

Cabrini was named after St. Frances Xavier Cabrini, aka Mother Cabrini, an Italian sister who worked with Italian immigrants in the late nineteenth and early twentieth centuries, mainly in New York. She founded the Missionary Sisters of the Sacred Heart of Jesus, the religious order that would start Cabrini College. She was also the first US citizen to be canonized a saint.

Many years later I would read her remarkable story, which included Pope Leo XIII sending her to New York, only to find that the local archbishop, Michael Corrigan, who initially supported her arrival, had decided that he no longer wanted her. She and a few sisters arrived on the docks of New York with no one to greet them. Eventually she found her way to Archbishop Corrigan, who curtly told her she was no longer needed. In her heavily accented English (I always imagined her sounding like my Sicilian grandmother), she said, "In America I stay!" I had zero idea of this when I signed up and was only dimly aware that Cabrini College was Catholic.

It was my first time staying alone away from home for an extended period, which I imagined would be good preparation for college the next year. As I packed, I wondered what I had gotten myself into. It was probably a good thing that I didn't know, or I might have opted for more caddying.

I still have the green brochure sent to me in May 1977, announcing my selection for the Tomorrow's Leaders Camp. The camp was a big enough deal for me to paste the brochure in my scrapbook alongside random photos, copies of articles I had written in the school newspaper, tickets to Phillies games, and autographs from various politicians.

The camp was founded in 1950 to give "carefully selected high school students" the chance to develop their "leadership potential." In 1977 that meant young men. The camp, which would be run by the "so-called Socratic method" (so-called?), would focus on three "interlocking aspects," described in language that was not only high-flown but maddeningly vague:

> An exposure to new, varied and stimulating values, concepts and philosophies.
>
> An opportunity for each participant to reassess and build on his own system of values, as a result of deeper understanding.
>
> Through first-hand leadership experience, an opportunity to test and strengthen both old and improved values and stereotypes.

I had no idea what any of that meant, but it sounded impressive! The brochure also added, rather sternly: "Attendance at all discussion sessions is mandatory." Why had I signed up for something that seemed like summer school?

In any event, one morning a Rotarian, a friendly and solicitous elderly gentleman, drove to our house, picked me up, and started me on my way to Cabrini College, my home for the next week. ("No leaving grounds without permission," said the brochure.) We stopped to pick up my friend Paul, and we eagerly chatted about the coming week.

After registering in the college's main building, we Leaders of Tomorrow made our way to our rooms in the college's dorms: simple, whitewashed, cinder-block affairs. My roommate, a friendly, skinny kid with impressively feathered blond hair, was enthusiastic: "This is gonna be a blast!"

After a dinner of college cafeteria fare—spaghetti and meatballs, garlic bread, and coconut cream pie—about a hundred of us gathered in a large room, where we were complimented on being selected, and were told the purpose of our week: to make us leaders.

What I remember chiefly about the week at Cabrini was the novel experience of sleeping a few feet from someone who snored quietly, the fluffy cream pies we had for dessert every night, and the oceans of free-flowing lemonade, which I guzzled in huge quantities, owing to the great heat. But what I remember most was what we were taught about leadership. And our lessons came from a surprising source.

You might think that a group of teenagers learning leadership skills in the 1970s from a charitable organization would be inculcated in values like charity, generosity, and compassion. Or, perhaps in a more practical vein, we would study the lives of famous leaders in business or politics. But you would be wrong. You might also think that, given that we were on a Catholic college campus, we might read the Gospels, meditate on the life of Jesus, learn about Christian values like love, mercy, and forgiveness, and talk about helping the poor. You might think that, but again you would be wrong. Instead, we spent the lion's share of our time studying the works of Ayn Rand.

At age sixteen, I had never heard of Ayn Rand, the twentieth-century Russian-born American writer and philosopher and founder of the school of thought she called Objectivism. I didn't even know how to pronounce her name when I saw it listed on our curriculum. ("It's 'Eye-n,'" we were told multiple times that first day.) Rand rejected religion, which didn't bother me as a desultory Catholic, but also altruism, which seemed odd even to someone not especially concerned about the poor. But that did not seem odd to Rand, whose approach was focused on selfishness and egoism as the most effective ways to get ahead.

At night, in our dorm rooms, we read several mimeographed essays in which Rand touted not only the values of capitalism (which I would hear touted even more forcefully at Wharton in another year), but also the evils of altruism, a virtue of the weak according to Objectivism. Many years later, in my Jesuit philosophy studies, I found echoes of her odes to selfishness in Friedrich Nietzsche's *On the Genealogy of Morals*, which suggests that Christianity is a religion for losers, duping people into thinking that things like asceticism, sacrifice, and charity are good, when, according to Nietzsche, they are unnatural for human beings and ultimately destructive.

For good measure, we also plowed through selections from *The Fountainhead*, Rand's turgid novel about a selfish but brilliant architect, Howard Roark, who, through force of will (and self-interest), claws his way to the top. It was in places unreadable, making me long for a Jean Shepherd story about a failed prom or a Brad Steiger tale about malevolent aliens. So it was that during our week at Cabrini, the primary model of leadership offered to us young and impressionable Leaders of Tomorrow was not George Washington or even President Carter, and far less Jesus, but Howard Roark, a man focused on himself and on making money.

Even at the time, knowing zero about philosophy or theology, and having a yet undeveloped sense of Catholic social teaching, the force-fed diet of Rotarian Objectivism struck me as bizarre and borderline cultish. But as a teenage boy wanting desperately to fit in (as I imagine the other boys did that week), I tried to follow along and participate and evince interest in Objectivism, between eating cream pies, playing basketball (I hadn't improved much since elementary school), and trying to sleep in our sweltering, un-air-conditioned, fanless, cinderblock rooms while my roommate snored and farted. I dutifully highlighted the mimeographed sheets of Ayn Rand articles so that I could hold my own in the daily sessions and tell everyone how important it was for all of us to be selfish and make money.

At the end of the camp, as the Rotarian drove me home, I wondered whether the week had equipped me to lead anything tomorrow. Most of all, I wondered why I had forfeited a week of work at the Cricket Club, where I suspected that not a few members agreed with the Objectivism that we were taught at Cabrini. Basically, I regretted giving up a week's worth of income. Then again, maybe Ayn Rand would have felt the same. So it was back to caddying.

One morning in August I woke up to a hot, damp, and cloudy day. My mom and dad took a dim view of malingering, or being too tired to work, and protests that it might rain fell on deaf ears. "Why do you think they call it work?" said my dad, not for the last time. Still, there was one thing my mom was worried about. "Be careful if there's an electrical storm!"

As I drove the familiar route, clouds gathered on the horizon. Philadelphia summers are often humid and sticky. "Close" was the term my mom used: "It's going to be close today." Summer thunderstorms broke the heat, but not without a cost: They were often quick, violent, and destructive. I enjoyed them when I was inside. Outdoors was another matter.

Nervously scanning the skies, I started off that morning with a single bag, a middle-aged businessman who told me that he hoped to get in nine holes before it started raining.

In the sixth grade I had written what I judged to be the world's most extensive report (five pages) on clouds and, having found the material fascinating, set my heart on being a meteorologist, though I wasn't sure how they earned a living. Did people pay you to know about clouds? The only meteorologists I knew were on TV, and there were only three in Philadelphia, on ABC, CBS, and NBC, so it seemed a limited professional field. Nonetheless, I was constantly scanning the skies to look for cirrus, stratus, and cumulus clouds and boring my friends with my knowledge. "Do you know what that cloud is called?" I once asked a friend during band practice as I looked up from my trumpet. "No, and I don't care," he said.

That morning at the Cricket Club I saw a dark cumulonimbus cloud, a sure sign of a storm, near the horizon. It would have been fun to see it in a book. Seeing it while standing a few feet away from a grove of tall trees was a different matter.

Muttsy was unconcernedly assigning other caddies, so I didn't feel that he wanted to hear a meteorology report from me. Deep down, I pretty much always wanted it to rain so I wouldn't have to caddy, but I was here so I might as well make some money. But it was starting to get darker. Maybe they'd tip me more for caddying in the rain.

In a few minutes I set out with my golfer. Early on, he hit the ball into a water hazard so I had to fish it out with his long metal retrieving wand. But it was old and I had a hard time collapsing it completely; it jammed and stuck out a foot or so from the bag.

After just a few holes, the sky grew alarmingly dark, almost green-black. The leaves on the trees slowly turned over, a sure sign of rain. Suddenly the daylight was all but blotted out and we heard a few heavy drops hit the leaves of the trees around us: *plop, plop, plop.*

Thanks to my sixth-grade report, I knew you could estimate how far away an electrical storm was by counting the seconds between the sight of the lightning and the sound of the thunder. Every five-second delay—essentially relying on the calculation of the speed of sound—was another mile.

Over the darkening horizon a bright bolt of lightning lit up the sky and zapped the ground, and one, two, three, four, five seconds later, a majestic clap of thunder rolled through the fetid summer air. The storm was only a mile away, almost on top of us.

It started to rain heavily, and both the golfer and I took shelter under a tall maple tree.

Suddenly, the golfer sprinted from the trees into the downpour and toward the clubhouse, his golf cleats making marks in the wet grass, and called over his shoulder, "This should be over soon! Stay *right there*!"

It started to pour. Loudly. "Don't let that bag get wet!" he shouted.

Then an immense bolt of lightning sizzled through the sky along with an instantaneous peal of the loudest thunder I had ever heard. *CRRRACK . . . BOOM!*

I realized that I was standing under a tall tree with a bag of metal rods and a long steel pole sticking out from the center. It was a place I had avoided my entire life, which was in danger of becoming short. I was standing next to a dozen lightning rods under a tree in a raging electrical storm.

Even though I knew Tommy and Muttsy would disapprove, I propped the bag against the tree and ran for the caddy shack as lightning crackled around me and the rain pelted down angrily. It went against every instinct in me to please, to follow directions, to not anger anyone. It took the threat of getting killed by lightning to overcome the fear of letting people down.

"Did you just leave my bag on the fairway?" said the golfer, as we huddled under an awning out of the rain. By now drenched, I nodded.

"Damn it!" he said. I muttered something about not wanting to get hit by lightning. Fifteen dollars did not cover the cost of getting electrocuted.

After about half an hour, when the storm had passed, we returned to the course. It was now too wet to play. Angry at my apparent dereliction of duty, he stiffed me with five dollars and no tip. Muttsy rolled his eyes and told me not to worry about it. "I've seen worse," he said. I drove home with wet sneakers.

On a recent trip home, I returned to the Cricket Club for the first time in more than forty years. Today the club manages three golf courses, a few miles from one another in the nicer suburbs of Philadelphia. Despite having worked there for a summer, I had a hard time figuring out from Google Maps at which course I had caddied. My first attempt to walk down memory lane took me to a country club that was wholly unfamiliar, with a clubhouse of recent vintage.

I asked a man crossing the parking lot, "Do you know where the original Philadelphia Cricket Club is?"

"Oh," he said confidently. "That would be the St. Martin's course."

I dutifully punched in the name and followed Google Maps, which took me into the Chestnut Hill section of Philadelphia, which, even given my poor sense of direction, I knew was incorrect. I pulled into the driveway of a huge house, the pro shop, and told a guy toting a golf bag that I was looking for the Cricket Club that I would have worked at in the 1970s.

"Oh yeah, that's our Wissahickon course," he said. "We're up on West Valley Green Road in Flourtown," names that instantly rang a bell. "Wissahickon!" he said again as I was leaving the shop.

As I pulled onto the driveway of the Wissahickon course, a tide of memories flowed into my heart: a certain nostalgia about the morning car rides with my new driver's license, but also the anxiety I felt at not measuring up as a caddy.

I walked down the driveway under the familiar bridge that

connected the two buildings, still clad in white-painted clapboard with a round clock in the center facing the still beautiful course. I couldn't believe how little it had changed. Hale, middle-aged, and elderly men, of the kind I would have caddied for, with deep tans, silver hair, and brilliant teeth, passed me. I realized that I was now much closer to their age than any of the caddies. I got a few suspicious looks since I wasn't as nattily dressed, until I said to one man, perhaps in his seventies, "I used to caddy here. Forty years ago."

"Oh, that's just *mah-velous*," he said, his face lighting up. "Welcome back!"

As I rounded the corner of the building, again largely unchanged in four decades, I came upon a golf pro: a pleasant, gray-haired, sunburned man named Chip, who, amazingly, had worked as a caddy a few summers before I did. We had gone to the same high school and he grew up not far from me, though I didn't know anyone in his family, which is unusual in Plymouth Meeting. I said that I was writing a book on growing up, prompting a quizzical but not unfriendly look.

I asked Chip if he knew Tommy or Ricky; he remembered neither. But he had been a teenager then, and I certainly couldn't remember the names of the other caddies. He didn't remember Muttsy's name either. But Chip laughed good-naturedly and said, "But he didn't know my name either. He called all of us *you*."

We reminisced about caddying in the 1970s, Chip telling me that he used to ride his bike over as early as possible, leaving his house at 6:30 to get here at 7:00. When I passed this along to Ricky, he reminded me that caddies wanted to get to the course as soon as possible but often ended up waiting for hours to be chosen. I had forgotten about the waiting.

Saturday afternoon at 3 p.m. was a busy time at the Cricket Club, with golfers and caddies carrying the bags off the course after their long, hot rounds. Chip pointed out the old caddy shack, now a storage room that is part of a larger (and nicer) series of buildings.

"When we were caddies, it was only a dirt or concrete floor, under a roof with exposed wooden beams," he said, as a golfer zoomed past us on his cart.

Chip saw me looking at the familiar course, a vivid green under the bright sun, and said, "It's a lot emptier than it used to be. When we were here, the course was filled with many more trees." Attrition, he said, had thinned them out.

"Storms too." I recalled that lightning storm.

"This I remember," I said, gazing at a site that had filled me with anxiety: the beginning of the course. It was where the golfers and caddies sized each other up and I would try to predict whether I would spend the next few hours with a good golfer or a bad one, a good person or a bad one, a good tipper or a bad one. It was also when I wondered whether I would screw up.

"You remember what?" he said.

"Uh, the first green," I said.

"You mean the first tee."

"Right," I said, "the first tee."

Then, as if I were sixteen again, I felt a lightning bolt of embarrassment, of not knowing as much as I should.

In the end, I was not a terrible caddy: strong enough to carry two bags for two loops, fast enough to cart-caddy, careful enough not to step between the cup and the golfer, attentive enough to rake up the sand traps and replace divots, and certainly polite. But I was not a good caddy, much less a great one: I rarely knew what clubs to use other than a driver, putter, and wedge; and I never grasped the intricacies of the game, certainly not with the love that Tommy had for it. His brother Ricky ended his caddying career the year before I started, and felt the same affection that his older brother had for the game. Ricky told me recently: "I loved it. When I was caddying for a guy and I was reading the green for him, and suggesting what club to use, and he used it and hit it well, I felt great for him. And I felt great about myself."

I didn't feel as great about myself: I never shook the feeling that I should have known much more about the game and probably got the job because of Tommy. But I was happy that the numbers on my bank book at Conshohocken Savings & Loan were getting larger. By the end of August, and the beginning of my senior year in high school, I knew that my caddying career would be a short one. "I'm tired of being outside," I told my parents.

I decided that I'd be back inside next summer, with a job that didn't require so much physical exertion. I suspected Tommy would be disappointed, but I wanted to move on. In the end, of course, Tommy understood. Golfing is not everyone's bag.

Today I treasure the memories of Tommy and am grateful for the time I spent with him and remember how generous he was with a younger cousin who knew nothing about the game he loved so much. Some twenty years later, at the age of forty-six, though in apparently perfect health, after playing golf with his son, Tommy died suddenly of a brain embolism, the day after my father died at age sixty-seven. Tommy's ashes were scattered on one of his favorite golf courses near his home. His son, Tom, Jr., is a great golfer too.

Since then, except for that brief return to the Cricket Club a few months ago, I've never set foot on a golf course, not out of any traumatic memories (though I still avoid standing under trees next to a bag of steel poles during lightning storms), much less any lingering resentment, but a lack of opportunity.

For the rest of high school, I stuck to tennis, bowling, street hockey, and running. During college I knew few people who golfed, other than guys in the more exclusive fraternities. After graduating and taking a job at General Electric in New York, I had several friends who golfed, but by that point, they were far better than I was, and I was too busy to take lessons. Finally, after entering the Jesuits at age twenty-seven, I started to live a vow of poverty, which precluded joining country clubs and put golf clubs out of financial reach.

Today, however, a few of my Jesuit brothers serve as presidents of middle schools, high schools, and colleges and run other Catholic charities and nonprofit organizations, and so they are required to do a good deal of fundraising. Sometimes this takes them to the golf course, as they court donors and mingle with alumni and parents of students. Occasionally they invite me to join them, and our exchanges are always the same, and end with a laugh.

"Do you want to come to our golfing fundraiser?" they'll ask.

I'll say that I don't golf that well, so I'd probably just slow them down.

"But," I always ask, "do you need a caddy?"

The Plymouth Meeting Mall, with its famous (at least for us) fountain, was the center of my social life in junior high school. Later on, for a few summers and winters, it was the center of my working life too.

After losing my reelection campaign as president, I stayed on in Student Council as a representative, like John Quincy Adams nobly remaining in Congress, I thought.

CHAPTER 5

How to Pop Corn for Ten Hours and Not Lose Your Mind

MY FAVORITE PLACE TO HANG OUT WITH FRIENDS ON Friday or Saturday nights during high school was at the movies. And the biggest social triumph was corralling my friends John or Gordon or Bob or Steven or Henry or Eugene, or Peggy or Barb or Pam or Jeanne or Sheila, in any sort of mix, or better yet all together, for a movie. If afterward we stopped by Friendly's Ice Cream for dessert, in the same complex as the aptly named Cinema on the Mall, even better.

Sometimes I'd persuade them to venture farther afield to the Ice Cream Inn, so that I could show off by saying loud hellos to Mr. Clare, bantering ostentatiously with Gladys, and instructing my friends about the intricacies of bussing tables and how the ice cream was made. In settings where I felt more knowledgeable than others, I was tempted to show off. It was an unhealthy habit, a reflexive response as I sought attention, approval, and admiration.

My friends showed polite interest but mainly wanted the free ice cream. They did, however, enjoy asking for wet nuts.

It was an easy time to love movies. Three summers before, *Jaws* had premiered at the Plymouth Cinema, a now-defunct theater in a shopping center a fifteen-minute bike ride from our house, across the street from the Ice Cream Inn. My parents took my sister and me to see the monster summer blockbuster, and as the film began to unspool, I knew that I had to see it again with my friends. On the way out, my dad playfully tried to embarrass us as we walked past the crowd lined up for the next showing. "Boy, how about that ending?" he said as people in the crowd covered their ears, and we remonstrated him: "Dad!"

The next weekend I was back in the air-conditioned comfort of the Plymouth Cinema. As soon as *Jaws* ended, we slunk down into our seats so we could see it again, undetected, though we already knew the heart-pounding ending. I thought there could never be another movie as remotely exciting as this and loved everything about it—the throbbing John Williams score, the lighthearted quips from Richard Dreyfuss, the cheesy-but-at-the-time-terrifying fake shark head chomping down on Robert Shaw's legs, even the portrayal of the seaside town, which seemed like a charming place to live, except for sharks eating you.

I had read the novel by Peter Benchley (which I pointed out to my friends to demonstrate my superior knowledge), and both book and movie left me, like millions of others, terrified to go swimming during our two-week vacation "down the shore," as Philadelphians say. That August in Ocean City, New Jersey, I scanned the glittering horizon carefully, seagulls reeling and squawking overhead. "There are no sharks in *Ocean City*!" my dad

How to Pop Corn for Ten Hours and Not Lose Your Mind

said when I peered warily at the water, like the residents of Amity in the movie. "Go in the water!"

Years later, I read a book called *Close to Shore: The Terrifying Shark Attacks of 1916*, which details a marauding shark that terrorized the South Jersey shore and went eleven miles *inland*, swimming up estuaries and streams to eat people. Had I read that in the summer of *Jaws*, I probably never would have taken a shower.

And just the summer before this one (it's now 1978, if you're keeping track), *Star Wars* had premiered, to packed audiences, mainly kids, most of whom I knew. In those pre–social media, pre-internet, pre-everything days, one saw "Coming Attractions"—that is, trailers—only in movie theaters. So as with *Jaws*, George Lucas's film remained largely a mystery, which made seeing it for the first time an overwhelming emotional experience. We were held rapt by the story and the CGI, and in the intervening fifty years, I've never heard a crowd applaud as loudly as when the Death Star was destroyed. (Sorry for the spoiler, but you haven't seen *Star Wars*?)

After the movies, the second most popular place to socialize was the Plymouth Meeting Mall, which held an outsize place in our lives.

For starters, the Mall was where most of my friends and I (read: our mothers) shopped for our clothes. In late August you could count on running into embarrassed, hunch-shouldered, eye-rolling classmates being led by their moms on clothes-buying missions at the Back-to-School Sales.

Few things equaled the discomfort of trying on stiff corduroy pants, a heavy woolen sweater, and a bulky winter coat when it was ninety degrees outside and somehow just as warm inside the plastic-laminated walls of the nominally air-conditioned dressing rooms, while your mom asked, in front of other mothers and, worse, your friends, "Are the pants too tight, Jimmy? Come out and show me. Oh, yeah, those pants are too tight. They're too short too. Did you grow again?"

As a Depression-era child, my mother delighted in finding bargains, so a reliable highlight of our lives was Clover Day, the every-few-months sales event at Strawbridge & Clothier, the venerable Philadelphia department store that anchored the Mall, along with Lit Brothers, another Philly stalwart.

Clover Day held as much prominence in our house as a minor liturgical feast. It certainly evoked more enthusiasm in my house than, say, the First Sunday of Advent, with my mom rousing my sister and me early in the morning: "Wake up! It's Clover Day! I don't want to be late, like we were last time." On Clover Days a scrum of moms hunted for the best sales and weren't shy about pushing or shoving to get them. Once, when my mom told my sister, then three years old, that they were going to Clover Day, my sister said, "Is that the place where everyone hits me in the face with their pocketbooks?"

A trifecta for my mom was finding something on sale for Clover Day, which had already been marked down, and then using a coupon (*KYEW-pon* in Philadelphia) for a further discount. Landing such a quarry was like Teddy Roosevelt bagging an elephant in Kenya. "Guess what I paid for *this*?" she'd say, pulling a dress or a blouse from her Strawbridge bag. "It was already marked down, then it was on sale for Clover Day, and I had an extra *KYEW-pon*. Ten dollars!" Quite impressive, even to me.

You went to the smaller Plymouth Square Shopping Center,

near our elementary school, and anchored by the A&P (where I briefly worked as a bagger), to buy groceries, to get your hair cut (at Gus Butera's Barber Shop; I went to school with Gus Jr.), to buy a wrench at the hardware store (run by Mr. Knoeller, whose son Jimmy I also went to school with), to get your dry cleaning done, to deposit money in the Conshohocken Savings & Loan, and to get poster board and paints at Woolworth's for school projects.

But the Mall was where you went for *important* things: birthday presents for my family at Strawbridge's or Lit's, new shoes at Florsheim, new eyeglasses at Wall & Ochs, and certainly Christmas presents. "Oooh, *Strawbridge's*," we'd say when we tore the wrapping paper from a package on Christmas morning and the box was revealed.

Speaking of Christmas, the Mall also featured the area's largest outdoor Christmas tree, erected on a forty-foot flagpole outside the main entrance to Strawbridge's. Long strips of thick green plastic garlands, with huge lights hung as ornaments, led to a massive white star, thus forming an immensely tall, perfectly conical, if not especially lifelike, tree. At night it was lit up, and it was a treat to be able to see it from my sister's bedroom window on clear and cold December nights. The leaves on the trees in the woods across the street had by then fallen off, which offered a clear view of the Mall, a few miles away.

You also went to the Mall to have your yearly photo taken with Santa Claus, who appeared the day after Thanksgiving, seated on his throne in a space near the Cinema on the Mall and Woolworth's and Waldenbooks.

When I was younger, there was some confusion about the

multiplicity of Santas who populated the nearby malls. A larger mall a few miles away, the King of Prussia Mall, had its own Santa, who was seated in a branch of Wanamaker's, the granddaddy of all Philadelphia department stores. "Ooooh! *Wanamaker's!*" we'd say with even more enthusiasm than over a Strawbridge box, when we opened a present sporting the distinctive swooping signature logo.

So where did the *real* Santa hang his red hat? Plymouth Meeting or King of Prussia? My parents had an elegant answer: The Santas at *neither* mall were real. They were elves who dressed up like him, missioned by Santa from the North Pole since, unlike God, he couldn't be everywhere at once. The real Santa was at Wanamaker's flagship store in Center City Philadelphia.

That made sense. After all, Wanamaker's had a special Christmas show that featured the famous Wanamaker organ pumping out Christmas carols, accompanied by geysers of water that shot up from marble balconies facing the atrium. Also, Santa's ornate throne in downtown Philly looked twice as large as the one in Plymouth Meeting. On the rare occasions I was taken to see the Wanamaker's Santa, it was like meeting God. But better, because of the presents. Santa was more reliable than God, I thought. If you asked Santa for something (a Matchbox car, a Rock 'Em Sock 'Em Robots set, a Silly Sand kit), you were more or less likely to get it. If you asked God for something (an A on a test, a home run, a puppy), you often didn't.

Growing up, though, I considered the Plymouth Meeting Mall if not the pinnacle of malls, then something to take pride in. On the first floor, outside Strawbridge's, was an immense circular fountain, with jets of water leaping up thirty feet or more. You could feel the spray even when you leaned over the metal railings on the second floor. During the Christmas season, the water was turned off and the fountain overlaid with a wire frame fashioned into a towering, tree-shaped display of red poinsettias.

At the entrance of the Mall was another impressive display. Behind glass was a five-foot-wide, cross-sectional slice of a massive tree dating from 1770 that had been felled to make room for the construction of the complex. Not long ago, I posted a photo of this display, which still hangs in the Mall, on a Facebook page for area residents. One responded that her father was an architectural engineer working with Mr. Strawbridge at the site and had asked the workers cutting the tree to cut a "slab" for him. Her father was planning to make a table out of it. But when Mr. Strawbridge asked whether it could be preserved, her father graciously offered it to him.

The tree slab fascinated me. Arrows pointing to the rings on the trunk highlight the progression of almost two hundred years of history, with special emphasis on local history. But in many cases local history is national history. The first entry comes six years after the tree's birth: the signing of the Declaration of Independence at the Pennsylvania State House, later known as Independence Hall. The second is the Revolutionary War battle at nearby Germantown in 1777. "Washington's Army encamped at Whitemarsh October 20th to December 11th," explains a card. The rings track the growth of Plymouth Meeting, with the opening of schools, libraries, post offices, iron mills, and canals, all the way up until the construction of the Pennsylvania Turnpike in 1940 and ending with the most important event of all: the opening of the Mall in 1966.

Five years old when the Mall opened, I vividly remember the

car ride with my mom and little sister, then two, to see the grand edifice. At the time, my father was on one of his many business trips to the Far East. A marketing executive for Wyeth, a large pharmaceutical firm, his work often required extensive trips, sometimes lasting weeks, to Pakistan, India, Indonesia, the Philippines, and Japan. His long absences were difficult for us, especially for my mom, although they added a certain exoticism to our home décor, our little split-level being filled with delicate Japanese porcelains, colorful Indonesian batiks, and intricate Pakistani wood carvings.

But despite the postcards, the foreign coins, and the other exotic gifts he brought home, my father's trips away were a source of sadness for my family.

Absent father or no, my mom wanted to be present at the Grand Opening of the Mall. At five, I had no clue what a big role it would play in my life.

Another reason to go to the Mall was to have our photos taken at Kinderfoto, a free-standing children's photo booth where we memorialized important events like First Holy Communion and Confirmation. A few days before First Holy Communion, I knelt on a platform covered in black felt in front of a white background and looked solemnly into the camera, while wearing a dark suit and white tie, hands folded piously. A few years later, my sister, in a white veil and dress, also was photographed, this time in color, in front of a sky-blue background. And while I have only a few grainy photos from the actual First Communion Mass, my Kinderfoto portrait is still as clear as the day we received it. All thanks to the Mall.

Peggy, a close friend from Plymouth Meeting, and with whom I went to both high school and college, told me recently that, like "countless girl classmates," she had her ears pierced at the Piercing Pagoda at the Mall. This was probably the only store I didn't frequent.

In junior high, my friend Steven and I spent hours at the Mall—not shopping, since neither of us had much money, but wandering through the patchouli-scented Spencer Gifts store to examine the black-light posters, the gag gifts, and the back section that featured "dirty" gifts like a board game with scantily clad women on the cover called Bumps and Grinds; Wee Three Records to review the Top 50 record lists; and Waldenbooks to see if a new edition of Mad Libs had been released.

Steven was a smart, funny, and kind friend, with whom I spent hours writing and recording on tape cassettes what we thought were hysterical plays and skits and comedy routines, which impress me today not for their humor, but for our nearly impenetrable Philadelphia accents.

So in the summer of 1978, hoping for an indoor job (again) after standing in the rain as a caddy the summer before, I thought the Mall seemed an obvious place to begin my search. The Magic Shop (where I spent too much of my allowance buying simple magic tricks) was hiring; so was Karmelkorn (which, if eating the stuff qualified me to work there, meant I should have been the CEO); and so was the Cinema on the Mall, where my high school classmate Mark had worked the year before.

The Cinema on the Mall featured two large theaters and was located inside the Mall, on the first floor. (Next to it was the aptly named Church on the Mall, a Presbyterian church where my friend Barb attended Sunday services with her family.) Jutting out into the Mall proper was the glassed-in ticket booth. A large, red-carpeted entranceway (how large I would discover when I had to sweep the floor with a hand sweeper—since vacuum cleaners were too noisy) led to the main lobby, with a candy counter and the usher's box, into which we tossed the customers' tickets that we tore in half as people entered the theaters. Cinemas I and II were to the left and right of the ticket station. Upstairs was a series of airless, smelly, cinder-block rooms, including the projection booth, a storage room, and a small room with an oversize metal tub on four legs, which was where popcorn was made.

A few weeks before the end of my senior year in high school, and before I started at the University of Pennsylvania, I was interviewed by the assistant manager, whom I'll call John, a pleasant man in his late twenties or thirties. In high school, anyone over twenty seemed old, so people's ages remained vague. For all I know, John could have been fifty.

The job was straightforward: tearing tickets, ushering people to their seats with flashlights after the film started, keeping order among the patrons, counting tickets at the end of the night, cleaning up the theaters after every show, mopping the bathroom floors, changing the outside marquee, and opening and closing the theater, which meant putting heavy chains and big padlocks on the exit doors and pulling down the vast chain fence in front of the large entrance in the Mall. Finally, ushers performed whatever odd jobs that John asked, which ranged from cleaning up vomit on the theater floors to hauling down boxes of candy and popped corn from the back room to asking people to stop talking during the films.

Working at the Cinema on the Mall seemed marginally glamorous. This was the largest theater in town, where I had seen *Star Wars* and other first-run shows, so it held some allure. Plus, I was sure to see my friends there. Maybe I could even get them in for free. I would not only be working in an exciting job, but also be *seen* to be working in an exciting job.

And, *How hard could it be?* Surely less work than bussing tables, washing dishes, or caddying, right? A child could tear a paper ticket in half.

My first day was just a few days after my high school graduation.

Despite occasional complaining with friends, I loved high school. I had my share of struggles and worries, but I had wonderful friends and great teachers, and was happy in a massive school that sprawled over several acres of suburban land. At the time some two thousand kids were enrolled. Plymouth–Whitemarsh Senior High School was so crowded with Baby Boomers that lunchtimes were staggered through four periods. One year, my lunch was at 10:20 a.m.

There were about eight hundred kids in my graduating class. For the next few decades whenever my mom ran into someone at the Mall, she would ask me, "Do you know Mrs. So-and-So?"

Invariably, I would answer, "No."

"You went to school with her daughter."

"Mom, there were eight hundred kids in my class."

"They live right down the street. You know them!"

"No I don't."

"Well, they know *you*!"

Maybe. I was more known than some kids in high school, probably because I had been elected Student Council president in my junior year, which was unusual, since the post usually went to a senior. My journal entry on the day the election results were announced includes a full page of scrawl shouting: "I WON! I WON. I'M PRESIDENT OF THE STUDENT COUNCIL!!! HOORAY!!!"

This was followed by: "Today Paul came into Science Class and said Congratulations and I said what for and he said he heard I had won! I was really excited but was nervous that I didn't! Then in Lunch Pam informed me since she counted votes! I was so happy! I told everyone and they were so glad that I won! Then last period it came over the announcements! Everyone congratulated me!"

I must have been insufferable. "I have so many great ideas and I'm bursting with new concepts and programs!!"

My joy was in part a fervent hope that the election results were proof of popularity. I had a nascent desire to do good, with "new concepts and programs" to help my fellow classmates, but altruism was not the cause of all those exclamation points. I wasn't an Ayn Rand trainee, lusting for power, but neither was I what Jesuits call a "person for others," someone whose life is directed toward service.

My classmates seemed genuinely happy for me. The next journal entry notes that people whistled "Hail to the Chief" all day whenever I walked into a class.

At a reunion a few years ago, I realized how lucky I was to have had so many generous high school friends, many of whom I'm still in touch with. At the time, I thought: *Peggy's nice. Steven's nice. Eugene's nice. Sheila's nice. Henry's nice. Barb's nice. Jeanne's nice.* But encountering them at the reunion as kind and generous adults made me realize that they had always been this way—kind and generous as teenagers—and reminded me how fortunate I had been. Are we ever fully aware how blessed we are by our friends?

Looking back, I wonder now if the post of Student Council president was considered so nerdy that few seniors wanted to run. I beat out another junior after an exhausting roundelay of plastering the school hallways with construction-paper and Magic-Marker posters with Steven, my campaign manager, and not embarrassing myself too much at an assembly where I laid out my presidential platform, which centered on, as did every high school election platform in those days, improving the cafeteria food, purchasing more vending machines, and giving us permission to smoke. (Smoking was important to roughly one-third of the student body.)

Despite our monthly Student Council meetings, however, the cafeteria food never improved (to be fair, it didn't get any worse), we got one more vending machine, and we still couldn't smoke. (At least legally: Entering the smoke-filled school bathrooms was like entering a Cheech & Chong movie, with a handful of kids lighting up by the sinks and chatting away.) In the end, the focus of my administration was an underattended Disco Dance, where people groaned when I requested "We're All Alone."

For my parents, and therefore for my sister and me, school was of paramount importance, more so than any extracurricular activities, though I was involved in too many after-school clubs, besides Student Council, which I stayed on the next year, post-presidency, like John Quincy Adams returning to the House of Representatives, and with no lack of hauteur. I had run for reelection senior year but lost to a friend in my "administration." So as I saw it, my main task during senior year as a Student Council representative was saying how much better I was as president or rolling my eyes ostentatiously when I would have done things differently.

My other activities that year were writing for the school newspaper, called *The Town Crier*, another nod to the area's colonial-era ties; Speech Club, which prepared us for several local contests, including one run by the marvelously named Optimist Club with the banal theme of "Tomorrow's Promise"; French Club; Future Business Leaders of America (there was no Future Jesuit Priests of America club); and the National Honor Society (which consisted mainly of organizing canned food drives). When not studying or attending club meetings, I burned off any extra energy with my friend Henry, who was on the track team, running laps on the school track or, when it was too cold during the winter, through the hallways of our school.

The lion's share of my after-school time during senior year, however, was working on the staff of the yearbook, called *The Milestone*, which meant we could hang out in the narrow, cramped yearbook office, which adjoined the classroom of our cool yearbook sponsor, Mr. Hummer, who was also our cool anthropology teacher, and who took adventuresome students on archeological digs at nearby Lenni-Lenape sites during the summers.

Hanging out in the yearbook office with the rest of the staff seemed almost unbearably cool, as if I had been admitted to some private club. I joined the yearbook as much for being privy to a secret space where we could talk, relax, and gossip, as for the actual writing. I was one of two copy editors. Unlike the current journalistic meaning of the term today (someone who edits someone else's writing), on the *Milestone* staff this meant that I was a writer.

Flipping through the yearbook, it seems that I was apparently the one responsible for the purplest prose, which I can barely read today. Here is the beginning of my take on swimming classes during the winter months: "December. The cottons have turned to corduroys, and the weather is cold. One thing stands in the way of winter comfort for the P-W student: the pool." (I go on to describe the water in the pool in the space of a few paragraphs as "murky," "uninviting," "forbidding," "tepid," and "unnaturally warm.")

I suppose I found the single word "December" at the beginning of the article a daring literary move: The end of the article reads less like a yearbook article and more like a bad novel:

> They emerge out of the water only to step onto the hard tiles which now seem even chillier. They walk through the cold air into the locker room for an icy shower. Swimming class is over.

Ask not for whom the pool tolls, high school student. It tolls for thee.

Despite the overripe writing, I did well in high school and was delighted to be accepted into the University of Pennsylvania's Wharton School of Business. My father had graduated from Penn, and Wharton was supposed to be the best undergraduate school of business in the country. In case there were any doubts, they told us that repeatedly after we arrived.

On my first visit to Penn the summer before, I fell in love with the campus, especially the freshman dorm, the Quadrangle, built in the Gothic Revival style popular in the 1800s. It breathed history and, as I excitedly pointed out to my parents, had *real ivy* on its walls. And if I could get a good business education at an Ivy League school (and not too far from home, which my parents liked), what could be better? Penn was also generous with its scholarship money.

During a visit to another college, the director of admissions was so enthusiastic that he offered me a free ride if I would sign up right there—while still in his office. "You'll most likely be accepted," he said to me. "No, you'll almost definitely be accepted, and we will give you a full scholarship." Then he paused. "The heck with it: You're *accepted*!" I blinked in surprise. I was happy to be accepted, but did I want to go there? He called my parents into his office and told them the good news and for good measure repeated his offer for a full scholarship.

I am grateful to my parents, who told me that they wanted me to go to the best school I could get into, and between their savings and my summer jobs, student loans, and a work-study job, we would make it work. Still, over the next few months, they kept referring to the college that had accepted me on the spot and offered a free ride: "Wasn't that a nice campus?" said my mom.

The other school I was considering was Princeton. That F. Scott Fitzgerald had gone there held some sway: We had read *The Great Gatsby* that year so the next closest Ivy held great appeal. One of our guidance counselors had given us a kind of mantra the year before: "When you are thinking of colleges, you should think, 'Harvard, Princeton, *Yale*. Harvard, Princeton, *Yale*. Harvard, Princeton, *Yale*.'" It was like one of those choosing rhymes for the games we used to play, though the stakes were higher. I didn't know anyone who had gone to any of them, but I was all for prestige. Harvard, in Cambridge, Massachusetts (where my sister ended up going), seemed too far away. And frankly I didn't even know where Yale was. Somewhere north. The college search process in the late 1970s, at least at my high school, was less rigorous than it is today.

As you may have guessed, the idea of attending a Catholic college or university never crossed my mind. Villanova was a fine school, nearby, and the alma mater of Marguerite, a cousin on my father's side. But my interest in any Catholic school lay not in its religious affiliation, or any desire to learn more about my faith, but whether a degree from that school would get me a good job. I didn't consider the idea that Catholic schools might provide a kind of moral framework through which to see the world—and to make moral decisions.

I applied to several schools, including Princeton, but a missing recommendation letter there made the application late. I found out later that a teacher had lied about sending it—he was busy and thought he'd get to it later and then forgot. Ultimately, it didn't matter. Penn was my first choice. For me, and my parents, getting a good job was the goal. My father scrunched up his nose when I wondered what Princeton would be like. "Too artsy," he said. "Besides, what would you study? English? You'll get a great job if you go to Wharton."

Between classes, yearbook, and college applications, I was also encouraged to try out for the school musical, *Bye Bye Birdie*, the story of an Elvis Presley–like pop star being inducted into the army. Many of my friends were in the school's successful marching band, and many of those musically inclined types were in the school musicals. I had never considered myself gifted musically, though I had sung in a few choirs in junior high school, but I thought, *How hard could it be?*

The part was Hugo F. Peabody, the clean-cut-but-callow love interest of the female lead. I was never sure whether the music teacher saying I was perfect for the part was a compliment or not. Nonetheless, I loved the experience and met kids I had never known. Where had they been all those years? It was fun to sing and dance onstage with my new friends and then to sit around afterward talking and talking while we removed our stage makeup and the room filled with the rosy aroma of Pond's Cold Cream Make-Up Remover. My parents and sister came to all three performances.

The next week in school people greeted me in the hall with a line from one of the songs from the musical: "Hiya, Hugo!" Plus I got to kiss Connie, by many accounts the most beautiful girl in the school, and the female lead. "Lucky duck!" said the guys. People even stopped me in the Mall! Was this what it was like to be famous? At least more famous than I had been as Student Council president. All those years trying to win acclaim and popularity— why hadn't I thought of the theater?

A few weeks before school ended came the pinnacle of the social year: the senior prom. I had gone to the junior prom with a friend named Cindy. That year I inadvertently locked the keys to my parents' car in the car when I was parked in Cindy's driveway, which meant they had to pick us up, which was mortifying. Also, as a sophomore, I was invited by a senior girl to go as *her* date, which was seen as a social coup. The senior prom was of a different magnitude. Attendance was imperative if you were to maintain any semblance of social standing. Also, it was something of an art to ask someone if you weren't going steady with them; I wasn't, though I had had my share of crushes and dates.

My friend Barb, whom I had known from French class in our freshman year ("*Ohhhhh, VRAIMENT?*"), seemed like the perfect senior prom date: friendly, pretty, and fun. It was 1978; my tuxedo would have to match Barb's dress, so I took the light blue cape that went with her gown and went to the Mall to rent my tuxedo. I picked out a light blue one along with a navy blue velour bow tie and a shirt with ruffles down the front. Barb and I had dinner at the Jefferson House Restaurant, the apex of dining in the area, a converted mansion set back from a busy road. When we entered the dining room, about twenty tables were occupied by kids from our high school; it was like going into French class. "*Bonjour, tout le monde!*" said Barb cheerfully to our fellow prom-goers.

The prom featured, as I would imagine they still do, loud music and, as I would imagine they no longer do, disco dancing. The prom committee had chosen for its theme "The Long and Winding Road," which seemed appropriate even though the Beatles song had been released eight years before. Still, it was an improvement over the theme chosen by a nearby high school, after a song by Kansas, "Dust in the Wind," which conjured up for me, but apparently not for the prom committee at our rival school, images of kids dancing in a Depression-era Dust Bowl farm.

The combination of being in the play, coming down from the prom-high, getting ready for college, and saying goodbye to my friends made for an emotional time at the end of senior year. I told a friend in class I was pretty sad (about the closest I got to being vulnerable), and he said, "Yeah, Martin, boo hoo!" But I saw tears in his eyes. My main memory of the graduation ceremony is sadness over leaving something I loved. We dressed up in our blue polyester graduation gowns on a hot and sticky June night and marched onto P-W's football field before our families. After I got home from a graduation party, I wept in my bedroom, finding it hard to sort out my emotions.

The questions seemed overwhelming: What would college be like? What was my newly assigned roommate, Brad, going to be like? Would I be able to sleep in the same room with someone? Was there air-conditioning, or would it be a sweat box like my room at Cabrini? Did I have the right clothes? And, most pressing of all: Would people like me? Untethered from high school, I could feel the bottom nearly dropping out from my emotional life: Would I be able to keep my friends from high school, and would I find new ones in college? I had no idea what Penn would bring.

But I knew what the summer would bring: work. And most days those questions took a back seat to my new job at the Cinema on the Mall, which began the day after graduation.

My first day started at 10 a.m. on another humid weekend. The first task was getting kitted out in a uniform. I was already wearing most of it: a white polyester, long-sleeved, button-down shirt; black polyester pants; and too-tight and unreasonably pointy black dress shoes—all purchased at Strawbridge's. Walking into the Mall, I desperately hoped none of my friends had seen me looking like an uber-nerd. The pointy black shoes were especially embarrassing.

In an airless cinder-block office, John, the assistant manager, noisily pushed around an assortment of electric blue polyester blazers on a metal coat rack. "This should fit," he said, sizing up

How to Pop Corn for Ten Hours and Not Lose Your Mind

my skinny frame. I slipped it on. It smelled like it had been dipped in popcorn butter.

"And this fits everyone," said John, handing me a clip-on black polyester bow tie that, since this was the 1970s, looked like an oversize butterfly. I clipped on the tie and slipped on the jacket. He sized me up again and said with a smile, "Now you're a GCC usher."

That was the regulation uniform for all ushers of the General Cinema Corporation, a nationwide chain of theaters in business from 1935 to 2002. GCC is perhaps best remembered today for the catchy theme music featured in the short "bumper," an animated logo that preceded every film. (You can find it today online.) Its snare-drum beat and plinking guitar music was fun the first few times you heard it, but after a few dozen times it grated. After several hundred times it drove you mad. Today the tune instantly conjures up the smell of sticky carpets covered with spilled soda, crushed popcorn, mashed candy, and hardened gum; trash cans filled with greasy, cold popcorn; and bathroom floors slippery with urine and other human excretions.

John introduced me to the rest of the staff on duty: the other usher (two or three high school boys worked on any one shift) and the young women who staffed the candy counter whom we called (sorry if this sounds sexist, but it was the 1970s) "candy girls." The candy girls also sold sodas and popcorn, which was advertised as "Freshly Popped!" but was assuredly not.

I enjoyed chatting with the candy girls when the movies were running, because not only were they fun to talk with, but they gave you free candy. The trick was not to let the patrons see you cadging any. Far worse would be for the manager or assistant manager to catch you.

The candy girls knew an ingenious way to hide pilfering. You couldn't simply just hand over a box of candy to an usher, even surreptitiously. That would ruin the inventory taken every night that had to be matched with the sales. Instead, a girl would secretly remove a box from behind the glass counter, carefully open it, and shake out a few Good & Plentys or Mike and Ikes into my hand. Then she would just as carefully close the box and return it to its home under the counter.

Problems arose only when a customer accidentally purchased one of the boxes that had been preopened. Once, a customer bought a carton of Good & Plentys only to find five candies lingering forlornly in the bottom of the box. He handed it back to the candy girl, furious.

In response, she looked at the package and read aloud, "Contents may have settled," and handed it back to him, stone faced.

Our candy counter featured popular candies—Milky Ways, Butterfingers, Baby Ruths, and the aforementioned Mike and Ikes and Good & Plentys—and also some candies made exclusively for the General Cinema Corporation. These were cheap knockoffs in crummy boxes with names and logos that aped the real thing. Customers rarely bought these sad candies, which were displayed in the rear of the counter behind the more popular ones, where they languished for months. The unpopularity of these knockoffs was a running joke with me and one of the candy girls. Once a customer bought one and the candy girl reached all the way to the back of the counter, held it up triumphantly, and shouted to me at the ticket box, "Hey, Jimmy! Someone *finally* bought the GCC candies! Hahaha!" The customer then asked for a refund.

How to Pop Corn for Ten Hours and Not Lose Your Mind

On many weekday mornings there was often only one usher. Just as often, you would be working with a man whom I'll call Stanley, a short, balding, stooped man, perhaps in his thirties or forties, who was forever pushing up the glasses that slid down the bridge of his nose. Looking back, I see now that Stanley was probably developmentally disabled, perhaps with a form of autism. It was never explained whether he was a friend of the manager or assistant manager, who were both kind to him, but I would guess that's how he was hired. Stanley was usually friendly unless you varied the procedures of the cinema: He didn't like you leaning on the ticket box, for example.

"Stanley was really good at collecting the tickets, but that was about it," my friend Mark remembered when I spoke to him recently. "And he liked to boss the younger guys around and tell them to use the carpet sweepers." Mark worked at the cinema the summer before I did.

Today I would be more solicitous of Stanley, who was, while occasionally difficult to work with, trying to earn a living. Did he live on his own? With his parents? Had he gone to school? Did he in fact have some kind of disability? I didn't know and I didn't ask.

As a teenager, I saw Stanley as just another part of the summer job landscape. Someone to work with and listen to, even though, as Mark reminded me recently, he let the younger ushers do all the physical labor: mopping the bathrooms, emptying the trash cans, cleaning the theaters between shows, pulling down the chain fence at night, and so on. I was never mean to Stanley, but I didn't go out of my way to engage him in conversation beyond pleasantries. As ever, I was more focused on earning people's approval, especially the other ushers and candy girls, and talking with Stanley did not increase your social standing.

Mark also remembers Stanley often asking for rides home. "He normally took the bus to work, but if it was raining, he would sweet-talk me into giving him a ride home. He was generally pretty nice to me, though he could be grouchy toward the rest of the ushers."

Mark's comments, shared over a phone call, embarrassed me, as I remember never having been generous enough to drive Stanley anywhere, much less to his home.

As an adolescent, I wasn't consciously mean to anyone, but neither was I the type of person I admired: the one who, not caring about the approval of others, was willing to spend time with those "on the margins," like Stanley. I knew a few kids like that, and they were a wonder to me. It was like they had some sort of superpower: not worrying about what others thought, knowing that it was not only okay but also important to be friendly to people who were seen as uncool. I admired them intensely but secretly. It would take years before I understood that being kind is a choice. And if you were the type of person for whom it was a value, it didn't matter whether others saw your acts of kindness or whether you were being kind to someone who was cool or uncool.

Overall, my approach was more Ayn Rand than Jesus. My goal was to get ahead and get people to like me. Mark and others were much kinder. They seemed both kind and comfortable in their own skins—a connection I did not recognize at the time.

My moral theology professor in graduate school, James F. Keenan, SJ, once talked about Jesus's notion of sin. Father Keenan suggested that Jesus didn't find sin in people who were "weak but trying," just as many of us fail in certain areas but keep making a conscious attempt to do better. For Jesus, sin was located where people were "strong but not bothering." In the Parable of the Good Samaritan, in Luke's Gospel, two religious men pass by a man who has just been beaten and is lying by the side of the road. They could help him, but they don't bother.

This, said Father Keenan, is where Jesus locates sin: *a failure to bother to love.* With Stanley, I just didn't bother. And I should have.

In a few weeks, I felt at home at the Cinema on the Mall, grateful for a summer job where I wasn't in danger of being killed by lightning, proud that I had been able to master the rather simple tasks of an usher, and relieved that I had more or less integrated myself into the social networks of ushers and candy girls, none of whom I had known before.

As expected, standing in front of a ticket box and tearing tickets and answering the same three questions over and over ("How long is the movie?" "When are you letting people in?" and "Is this movie any good?") was easier than caddying. The place was quiet once the movie had started, with people coming out occasionally for bathroom breaks or a soda refill.

That was not the case, however, when we had late-night showings of movies like *The Grateful Dead Movie* and especially Cheech & Chong's *Up in Smoke*, which attracted stoners the way the outdoor marquee lights drew bugs. Every pothead in the area seemed to come to that one, and they were forever leaving the theater to wander aimlessly around the lobby, consume vast amounts of popcorn, and ask questions like "Do you know how ugly your jacket is?" and "Where can we score some pot around here?" Frankly, they didn't have to; all you needed to do was stick your head inside the illegally smoke-filled theater to get high.

One weekday a group of giggling teenage girls begged me (literally: they fell to their knees on the sticky carpet) to let them into *Exorcist II: The Heretic*, which had opened the year before but which we would show if there was a gap between the end of one film's run and the arrival of the next film. They emerged from one theater during a break, bored with the more wholesome holdover from last year, *The Goodbye Girl*, and desperately wanting to see a more adult film.

Taking pity on them and also not really caring, I said, "Just don't tell anyone it was me if you get caught." Within five minutes, they came screaming out of the theater, "You didn't tell us it was that *scary*!" They retreated to the relative safety of the Richard Dreyfuss/Marsha Mason comedy, which I saw perhaps fifty times that summer.

We had to shepherd people out of the theater after the movie ended, saying the same thing over and over to the crowd. One afternoon in July, the golfing legend Jack Nicklaus was there, apparently taking a break from a tournament played at the nearby Whitemarsh Valley Country Club. I could barely wait to tell my dad. "That's great. What did you say to him?" he asked.

I paused to remember. "Exit to your left, please."

Between letting people in and moving them out, ushers were supposed to sweep the carpets, remove hardened gum from the carpets (by freezing it with an aerosol spray can filled with Freon and then prying it off with a screwdriver), fetch trash bags filled with popped popcorn from the storage room upstairs, and clean

How to Pop Corn for Ten Hours and Not Lose Your Mind

the bathrooms, both men's and women's, which were always filthy (Mark swears that the women's bathrooms were dirtier). Since there were no real janitors, we were forever mopping up any messes in the theaters, lobbies, and bathrooms, with messes in the bathroom including poop.

We also responded to patrons who stormed out of the theaters to complain that someone was talking. I sympathized: People talking during movies was a pet peeve of mine, a rudeness I could never fathom. You're in the theater, you know that people are trying to listen, and you still talk? As a cinema customer, I had always been too scared to say anything because I was afraid of getting punched.

But now my flashlight and uniform emboldened me. Doing it in the dark afforded even more bravado. So I could release my anger at movie talkers by silently walking down the aisle, shining a flashlight in their faces, and saying, "Hey! *Shut up!*" The assistant manager said, "Jimmy, next time, can you say, 'Would you mind not talking during the movie?'" I nodded but knew I would ignore him. "Shut up" was satisfying and also effective. This was one of the few things I really enjoyed doing at work. Other tasks were not as pleasant.

When a movie had finished its run, after the 9 or 10 p.m. show of a movie on its final night, ushers were responsible for changing the marquee, which I considered the worst part of the job.

A massive sign, perhaps thirty feet high, stood at the entrance of the Mall announcing the news to drivers on Germantown Pike. On the main part of the marquee next to the legend "Plymouth Meeting Mall" and the four-leaf clover logo were messages spelled out in one-foot-high, black plastic capital letters, like SANTA ARRIVES

THE DAY AFTER THANKSGIVING or CHECK OUT OUR BACK-TO-SCHOOL SALES and the biggest of all Mall-related events, CLOVER DAY!

At the bottom of the sign was a six-foot-high space dedicated to the Cinema on the Mall, divided into spaces for Cinemas I and II. It was up to the ushers to keep the marquee up-to-date.

Let's say *The Cat from Outer Space* (a wretched movie that played for several weeks) was ending that night and *The Goodbye Girl* was beginning the next day. Once the patrons for the final showing of *Cat* had taken their seats and started to spill their sodas and popcorn on the floor, you closed the doors and walked out of the Mall's entrance into the dark summer night. Rain or shine.

Then you walked through the parking lot, toward another first-floor entrance to the Mall, where you opened an unobtrusive gray metal door. Closing it behind you and switching on an overhead fluorescent light, you would find yourself in a small, airless room filled with spiders, moths, and beetles and shelves stacked with foot-high, black plastic letters, with metal clips on the back, neatly arranged alphabetically. We called this the Letters Room. The marquee was two-sided, so you needed to put up the movie info twice, which meant choosing two of every letter needed for the movie titles.

Leaving your GCC jacket in the room, you stacked the foot-high letters into an ancient shopping cart stored near the door, locked the door behind you, and pushed the clattering cart through the parking lot, careful to dodge the cars leaving the Mall in the dark. Letters would fall out at every bump and pothole.

At the marquee, you carried the letters and climbed a rusty metal ladder affixed to the side of the sign. The exposed ladder, only a few feet from the road, meant that teenagers from the neighborhood would, in the middle of the night, clamber onto the ledge and change the titles of the movies by borrowing letters from other movies or the main marquee, or deleting letters, so that "THE APPLE DUMPLING GANG" became "ANNIE GETS HUMPED AGAIN" and a few years later "CLASH OF THE TITANS" became, inevitably, "CLASH OF THE TITS." Once, some kids borrowed letters from another movie so that the film "SMILE" became "SMILE. YOU'RE ON LSD."

One day the assistant manager told me to change the marquee immediately, and when I walked out into the summer daylight, I saw that "THE CAT FROM OUTER SPACE" was now "CRAP FROM OUTER SPACE," which, to be fair, was a more accurate description of the film.

The main problem with changing the marquee in the dark was that you were perched on a narrow metal ledge a few inches away from a brilliantly lit sign. This meant that every gnat, fly, moth, beetle, mosquito, and katydid from the tristate area, along with pretty much every other nocturnal creature, flew and flapped and buzzed noisily around you as you snapped the letters on and off the marquee. Even during my two years in Kenya as a Jesuit, I never saw so many bugs in one place. I spent half the time on the marquee putting up the letters, and the other half swatting away flapping insects.

A person up on the marquee was a natural target for teenagers in passing cars. "Hey, *dickweed*! You missed a letter!" Or "Nice bow tie, *Poindexter*!" Or, once, "Hey, what kind of crappy summer job is *that*?" Then they would beep and drive off. Once, some friends of mine drove by, stopped their car, and shouted, "We're going to the movies! Do you want to come?" And I shouted back, "I'm already *at* the movies!"

Once, during a torrential summer storm, I walked to the Letters Room, pushed the shopping cart through puddles, changed the entire sign, as thunder rumbled, and ran while pushing the shopping cart back to the Letters Room, stored it, and ran to return to the theater, dried myself off in the bathroom, and returned to the ushers' box. When my manager saw me, he said, "You forgot the other side."

That was the most annoying task, but it was not the strangest one.

The biggest fiction of the Cinema on the Mall (besides the one about cats from outer space) was that our popcorn was "Freshly Popped!" as advertised in big yellow letters on a glass case at the candy counter. One could argue that at some point in history it was freshly popped, but by the time it was dumped into the display case, it was anything but. "Popped Last Month!" wouldn't have garnered many sales. But, like "Crap from Outer Space," it would have been more accurate.

The responsibility for popping corn was given to the ushers because we supposedly would be able to handle the heavy bags of corn and work the machinery. This was the 1970s, when the boys popped corn and the girls handled the supposedly lighter tasks of pouring sodas and selling candy.

Popping corn occupied an entire working day, a ten-hour shift. Each usher was assigned to pop corn only every other week. One of the few benefits of popping corn was that, owing to the messiness of the task, you could forgo the standard cinema uniform and wear anything you wanted, which usually meant a T-shirt and cut-off blue jeans.

How to Pop Corn for Ten Hours and Not Lose Your Mind

On the second floor, next to the projectionist's booth, was the Popcorn Room, a small and windowless space. Inside, a gray metal tub perched on metal legs stood four feet off the floor. The tub was about eight feet long, four feet wide, and a foot deep. At one end of the tub, mounted on a steel pole, was a circular pan, six inches deep, with a metal lid. On the floor of the pan was an arm that spun around like the second hand of a clock.

Here's how you made a lot of popcorn.

You arrived around 10 a.m., before the theater opened to the public. Then you made your way up to the Popcorn Room. Once there, you dragged a fifty-pound sack of popping corn from the corner of the room, where they were stored. Then you opened the circular metal pan, coated it with "butter" from a jug on a shelf nearby, and turned on the power, which made the small metal arm circle slowly around the pan. This spread the "butter" around and also kept the popcorn from clumping up. Then you tore open the bag, plunged in a metal scoop, and poured a few thousand kernels into the circular pan.

Once the corn was inside the pan, you poured in a few tablespoons of the secret ingredient, a potent powder called Savarol, which was, in essence, orange, butter-flavored salt. Popcorn by itself doesn't taste like anything. But the addition of Savarol gave it that "movie theater taste." Those few scoops of Savarol were approximately 10,000 percent of your recommended daily salt requirement. Also, to reveal some trade secrets, the "butter" it was popped in was a disgusting mixture of various animal fats. I read the labels on both the Savarol and the butter once, and that was enough to cure me of any desire for movie theater popcorn.

Then you closed the lid and waited for the corn, marinating

in the hot animal fat and Savarol, to pop. It popped in a few minutes, and then you overturned the circular pan into the metal tub and scooped the popped corn toward a six-inch circular hole in the bottom corner of the tub, making sure to pass the popcorn over a small grille with tiny holes. When you shepherded it over the grille, the larger fluffy popcorn passed over it, but the tiny unpopped kernels that could fracture a customer's molar would be strained into a metal receptacle.

The opening in the tub was connected to a large plastic trash bag, which was filled with the popped corn, closed with a twist tie, and then dated using a Magic Marker.

Until the bags were lugged downstairs to fill the display case, this was their final resting place for a few days. Or weeks. We popped corn every week, but how much we used and how quickly we used it depended on the demand. Our inventory might stretch a long way back, so when you brought down a bag marked "June 1" on July 1, you weren't supposed to let the customers see. One day I brought down the oldest bags, just so the candy girls could say, in front of the customers, "Jimmy, this bag's three weeks old!" I enjoyed a certain *delectatio morosa* seeing the customers' horrified responses.

During the first hour of my first shift, popping corn was interesting, even fun. Mainly because you could eat as much of the warm, freshly popped stuff as you wanted. But after downing handfuls of it, the novelty wore off, as did, over the summer, my taste for popcorn. Even today I can barely stomach the stuff. My appetite had a shelf date, even if the popcorn didn't.

Then reality set in: It was mind-numbing work in a stuffy room with no company but the noisy popcorn machine and the overpowering aroma of Savarol and animal fat. In an hour you were coated with orange salt and grease. Sometimes fellow ushers on their breaks would pop their heads in, ask after my welfare, and say, without fail, "God, I f—ing hate popping corn."

Fortunately, the ushers were allowed to bring one friend along with them: a transistor radio. You had to bring enough batteries to last the ten-hour shift, with breaks for lunch and dinner. Otherwise, you weren't supposed to show your face downstairs in your sweaty T-shirt and ratty cutoffs.

That summer one of the most popular songs burned into my mind like a tiny, burned popcorn pellet was Gerry Rafferty's "Baker Street," a catchy tune that, despite hearing it one million times between June and August, I never fathomed:

Winding your way down on Baker Street.
Light in your head, and dead on your feet.
Well another crazy day, you'll drink the night away.
And forget about everything.

I sang that tune over and over, leaning on the lyric

But you're cryin',
youuuu're cryin' now.

As with Rita Coolidge's lament, I had no idea what Gerry Rafferty was crying about, but being stuck popping corn for ten hours in an airless room seemed a good enough reason. "Baker Street" alternated on the radio that summer of 1978 with the soundtrack of *Grease*, which had just been released; Andy Gibb's "I Just Want to Be Your Everything"; and especially and endlessly Chuck Mangione's bouncy flügelhorn solo hit "Feels So Good." Today, when

I hear the first few notes of Mangione's hit I can smell the popcorn butter, or, more accurately, the animal fat, and remember how it felt to be coated with the orange, dusty salt, like some living, teenage snack.

Emerging for a meal break, you felt like a cloistered monk coming out of his cell. You bounced down the stairs and opened the door to the lobby and were confronted with hundreds of patrons pushing their way in to see *Corvette Summer*, having momentarily forgotten that you worked at a movie theater. Ushers nodded sympathetically at your enforced monasticism, and a candy girl might take pity on you and give you a Mike or an Ike and tell you about some customer who had yelled at her for putting too much ice in a drink.

But the half-hour breaks were for eating, not chatting, and the assistant manager was always watching. So I went directly to my favorite place to eat in the Mall: Roy Rogers, which, I am happy to say, is still in business (though not at the Mall) and still, I am even happier to say, carrying my meal of choice that summer: the Double R Bar Burger, which I considered the greatest burger ever invented—a hefty beef patty with cheese and ham on top. If I hadn't had my share of sodium in the popcorn room, this would have done it. Now older than sixty, I'm having to watch my blood pressure, and a summer of nonstop Double R Bar Burgers is probably part of the reason.

One day on my lunch break I was standing between two middle-aged women who had somehow gotten separated from each other in line. We were all staring at the choices on the display case in front of us, deciding what kind of burger we wanted, though I already knew.

One of the women sniffed the air theatrically. "Helen," she said, "do you smell *popcorn*?"

After two hours of popping, I was covered with Savarol and grease. My white T-shirt, emblazoned with the words "Hawaii 78," which my dad had brought me from one of his long trips, was now bright orange from the colored salt.

The other woman loudly sniffed the air, too, just a few inches from me. "Yes! I do smell popcorn. But the theater isn't near here, is it?"

I was mortified.

"No," said the first woman, sniffing the air more intently, like a hound dog on the trail of some quarry. "But it's so *strong*. Does Roy Rogers make popcorn? Now I think I want some!"

Helen asked the manager, "Do you sell popcorn here?" He shook his head.

"That's funny," said Helen. "The smell is so *strong*!"

I grabbed my Double R Bar Burger, returned to the theater, took my meal to the second floor, turned on the radio, and tried to figure out what Gerry Rafferty was so sad about on Baker Street.

The job at the Cinema on the Mall was one of the few summer gigs I didn't despise, though I could have done without ten hours of Savarol and animal fat and getting bug-bit while changing the marquee. Also, cleaning up human excrement was something to avoid, though I later put that skill to use as a Jesuit novice when I worked at a hospice for the sick and dying with Mother Teresa's Sisters in Kingston, Jamaica. My job was to help wash the old and infirm men (the Sisters cared for the women), shave and dress them, and sometimes clean up any "accidents." At one point the assistant novice director was visiting, and after I described having to clean up after one of the men, he said, "Well, I bet you've never done that before!"

And I said, "Oh yes, I have."

Ushering was mainly easy and I was a reliable employee. Other than stealing candy, eating too much popcorn (at least at first), and letting my friends in for free, I avoided committing any serious misdeeds. Mark confessed to me recently that he used to smoke pot behind the movie screen (we loved to watch the movies from behind the screen, seeing everything backward), but I wouldn't start smoking pot until a few months later, in college.

But I never got over being scared when I was the last person to lock up the theater. The candy girls closed up their counter before the film ended, and the manager would leave, but once the patrons were gone, one of us ushers had to lock up.

As soon as the final reel had run, the projectionist packed up and left. Now I had to pull down the great chain gate at the entrance to the Mall, and then go into the darkened movie theater to make sure the exit doors were locked and put chains and padlocks on them. Every time I had to lock up the theater, I feared that someone would lie in wait for me in the darkness, crouched down on a seat, waiting to pounce. I was always startled when I heard a noise, though usually it was my shoe stuck to a piece of candy on the floor. Only once did I find someone still asleep in the cinema, but he was snoring loudly so it wasn't terribly surprising. One of the ushers told me that he knew *for sure* that an usher had been stabbed at the GCC in Valley Forge, not far away. We both agreed that it was good to keep your flashlight in your pocket in case someone snuck up behind you.

At the end of the summer, having torn thousands of tickets,

filled innumerable trash bags with popcorn, changed a few marquees, but not having been stabbed, I left for college and started to feel wistful about leaving behind what had become a familiar environment. I would miss hanging out with the other ushers, bantering with the candy girls, letting my friends in for free, and even Stanley and my electric blue sports coat. I would go back to the Cinema on the Mall at Christmas break during my first year at Penn. I would also work there in the next year: the summer of three jobs.

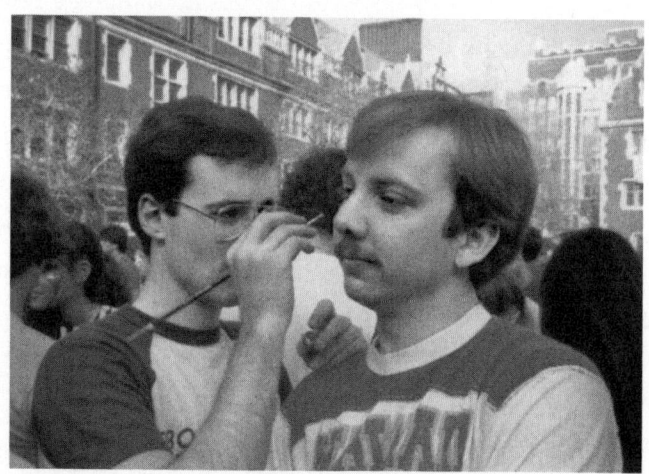

Spring Fling, 1979, painting my friend Gordon's face, after a few beers.

Freshman year at the University of Pennsylvania with my friend Peggy in her dorm room at the Quad. Still feeling guilty about the pope.

CHAPTER 6

How to Be a Man and Not a Mouse

I'M NOT SURE HOW I WORKED THREE JOBS AT ONCE THE next summer, but I know why: to pay for college, which in the summer of 1979 was well underway.

The University of Pennsylvania was more fun than expected. First, I enjoyed classes in the Wharton School, where I was, along with everyone else, majoring in economics, though "concentrating" in finance and accounting. The courses were fascinating, mainly because before college I had no idea what studying business would mean. My dad was a businessman, and one night at dinner I asked what he did at work. He said, "I go to meetings, talk on the phone, and write reports." This seemed both mysterious and dull. Years later, after I started at GE, my dad asked me what I did at work. I said, "I go to meetings, talk on the phone, and write reports."

Studies at Wharton opened up a new world for me: The stock market became less opaque as we learned how to value companies; international finance made more sense as we understood the flow of money among countries; and even macroeconomics seemed within grasp, after we were introduced to monetary and fiscal policies, which I had thought were the same thing (one has to do with interest rates and the supply of money regulated by central banks, and the other with government taxes and spending). One day in class, a student asked the professor, "Aren't fiscal policy and monetary policy the same thing?" Several people in the class swiveled their heads to look at this unfortunate young man. The professor paused, stared at him for a few seconds, and said, mournfully, "They are *not*."

Everyone laughed. He had forgotten the Wharton rule: Only ask questions that will make you look smart.

As much as I enjoyed academic life, I enjoyed social life even more: I fell in with a group of bright, talented, and funny friends in Speakman Hall in the Quad, the main dormitory for freshmen. We remain friends to this day. My college friends keep me humble (or at least humbler) and are refreshingly blasé about my being a Jesuit priest, an author, or anything else, which is a great blessing.

My freshman-year roommate, a charismatic native of Washington, DC, named Brad, taught me many crucial things in the first few days. First, the right way to dress: preppy. One of the first things I did in college was to ask my parents for money to buy a pair of khaki pants. As Brad explained, preppy meant "no unnatural fibers and no colors not found in nature."

A devotee of film history, Brad also introduced me to the world of international film and what we now call independent films. He would tell me about the latest Buñuel film that he had seen in class and then drag me to see it. Quite an education for a guy who, as I confessed to Brad, had seen *The Cat from Outer Space* multiple times. "At least you didn't enjoy it," he said.

Along with several of the other friends in Speakman, Brad also introduced me to pulling practical jokes (like having one's clothes stolen from the bathroom while one was showering), a dizzying variety of drinking games ("Zoom, Schwartz, Profigliano" was the most challenging), and smoking marijuana.

Pot was a mainstay of our social life, along with beer. But it was a novelty for me. I had never gotten drunk during high school and had grown up thinking that marijuana was something to be avoided at all costs. We had spent hours in health classes in elementary school talking about the dangers of marijuana, and incidentally learning about a dozen nicknames for it: pot, grass, weed, reefer, dope, Mary Jane, and so on, most terms past their expiration dates, like bags of popcorn on the shelf for too long. Also, those who smoked in my high school were generally considered to be "waste cases"—people who were not only "wasted" (high) but wasting their lives. I can still see the waste cases or stoners standing outside our high school, with their long, lank hair; Led Zeppelin T-shirts; black leather jackets; and flared, faded, ripped jeans, furtively taking a toke and looking disdainfully at anyone outside their tight group. My friends and I largely kept our distance.

So I was astonished when, in a hallmate's dorm room, my friend nonchalantly took a rolled joint from a plastic sandwich bag in his desk drawer, lit it up, and passed it around to my other new friends. Here were intelligent and motivated people doing something that I had associated with, well, waste cases. I resisted partaking until Spring Fling that year. One woman in our hallway who had counted on me to resist the pot peer pressure wept when she saw me with a joint in my lips. Until then we had been fellow members of the resistance.

From then on, smoking pot was a regular pastime, most often

on a Friday or Saturday night, always in a dorm room with friends. In my memory, Neil Young's song "After the Gold Rush" was always playing. Whenever I hear Neil's plaintive wail, I'm back in the Quad, crossed-legged on the floor, sampling the pleasantly earthy fragrance of the pot smoke, trying not to put my lips on the common joint but inhaling it through pinched fingers and enjoying if not entirely fathoming Neil's trippy apocalyptic anthem.

> There was a fanfare blowin' to the sun
> That was floating on the breeze
> Look at Mother Nature on the run in the nineteen seventies
> Look at Mother Nature on the run in the nineteen seventies...

As far as I could make out, Neil was singing about the end of the world, with selected earthlings being taken up into a spaceship to escape the ravaged environment. It seemed silly at the time, and the perfect song to get high to, but it now seems rather prescient (the environment part, not the spaceship part). As we passed around the joint, we'd sing, or rather caterwaul:

> All in a *dreeeeam*, all in a dream
> The loading had begun
> Flyin' Mother Nature's silver seed
> To a new home in the sun

If I temporarily resisted pot, I had no qualms about drinking. In those days, social life at Penn would have been nearly impossible without alcohol. This is not an argument for drinking in college, and certainly not for underage drinking; rather, it is more of a fact. Socializing meant drinking, at least at Penn in the late '70s and early '80s.

From almost the first weekend, I felt little aversion to getting drunk. But it took a while to develop a taste for beer. My parents drank a local beer called Rolling Rock. On many weekends, I would drive with my dad to the liquor store to pick up a case for him and my mom, but they never drank to excess, perhaps one beer with dinner on the weekends, and so a case of Rolling Rock lasted for a long time.

At home, I tried beer a few times and disliked it, finding it watery and bitter. But at Penn my palate slowly developed, perhaps motivated by my desire to fit in. Unfortunately, not having spent much time in bars, I had little tolerance for the stuff and so at first I was drunk quite often. In a few years, though, my tolerance was at its zenith.

In my first month of college, Catholics around the world were still getting acquainted with our new pope, who had been elected a few weeks before by the College of Cardinals. He had taken the name John Paul I, a nod to his two immediate predecessors, Popes John XXIII and Paul VI. The election of Albino Luciani, formerly the archbishop of Venice, followed the death of Pope Paul, who had been pope for much of my life. Paul reigned from 1963 to 1978. He was really the only pope I had known: an austere figure who looked a bit like my Sicilian grandfather, sans the dapper little mustache.

I knew Pope Paul wouldn't live forever, but it still was surprising to hear the priest invite the congregation during Mass to pray not for "Paul, our pope," but for "John Paul, our pope." Papa Luciani was soon nicknamed "the Smiling Pope," primarily because his predecessor seemed to do so little of that, at least publicly.

My hallmates were surprisingly interested in Catholicism in general and the new pope in particular. Many of my Penn friends were either Jewish or Protestant, and as far as I can remember, I was the only practicing Catholic among my friends in our hall. A fair number of questions were therefore lobbed in my direction during late-night discussions in our dorm rooms: "Do you have to do what the pope says?" (Not everything.) "Do you go to Mass every Sunday?" (Most of them.) "Do you really think Jews are going to hell?" (No.) I asked fewer questions of my Jewish friends because I had grown up in a neighborhood with many Jewish families, had attended many bar mitzvahs, knew some Hebrew and even some Yiddish, and also wanted to seem smarter than anyone else. I was happier to answer questions than ask them. Besides, I enjoyed being the token Catholic in the hall, despite knowing precious little about Catholic theology, church history, or the Bible. Most of all I liked being seen as the "expert."

One Thursday night in late September, a few weeks after I had started at Penn, we were at a local bar called Doc Watson's, now closed and then famous for their strombolis, a perfect bar food: a pizza folded in on itself, stuffed with various fillings—ground beef, sausage, or veggies. After one or two beers, I was buzzed. After a third or fourth, I was drunk. The conversation turned to Catholicism, and, my conscience submerged in beer, I started to tell jokes about Jesus.

As a college freshman, I found my Jesus jokes hysterical. My classmates enjoyed them even more. We were still telling them on the way back to the Quad, laughing along the way.

When I got back to my room and collapsed on the bed, one of my hallmates burst into my room and said, "Martin! The pope died!"

"You idiot," I said. "That happened a few weeks ago and there's a new one!"

How could anyone not know *that*?

"No," he said, "the *new* one died!"

We turned on a transistor radio, and sure enough, after only thirty-three days in office, Pope John Paul I had died. Instantly, I thought of all those jokes I had told.

My friend Andy had the same thought. "Martin," he said, "you *killed* him!" My drinking partners looked at me with a mix of horror and wonder.

"You told all those Jesus jokes—and now the pope is dead! You *killed* him!" said my friends, who were, I should point out, still drunk. As was I.

"That's ridiculous," I said.

Deep down, though, I felt awful about it, like when a friend finds out that you have been making fun of him, and it's true but you don't want to cop to it. Not only had I been telling Jesus jokes (bad enough), but I had been telling them (or so I thought) at the moment that the new pope had died. I tried to laugh it off, but I felt like the Worst Catholic Ever. Which at that moment might have been true. I wept in our hall's bathroom since I didn't want Brad or anyone else in our hall to see. I also liked Pope John Paul a lot. Years later, I would learn more about this simple and holy man, and read his beautiful book *Illustrissimi*, letters to people like Mark Twain, Charles Dickens, and St. Thérèse of Lisieux. But at the time I just felt guilty.

The next morning, I thought it would be over.

It was not.

"I heard you killed the pope!" said friends who had not been out with us the night before. Gradually, I got over the guilt (I had not in fact killed the pope), but my friends never let me forget it. The next year, Pope John Paul II visited Philadelphia and I skipped a class (a rarity) to attend the public Mass on the Benjamin Franklin Parkway. The following day, I skipped class again to see John Paul visit Children's Hospital of Philadelphia, where I stood a few feet from him as he blessed the children in wheelchairs who were brought before him. I found this moving. My friends found it deeply, almost irresistibly, amusing: "Did you tell him that he's pope because of you?"

Ten years later, when I gathered a few college friends at a restaurant in New York and told them that I was joining the Jesuits, my friend Andy immediately said, "Do they know you killed the pope?" The same thing happened *regularly* over the next few years of my Jesuit life: at my First Vows after the Jesuit novitiate; ten years later, at my ordination as deacon; a year after that, at my ordination as a priest; and then, ten years later, at my Final Vows as a Jesuit. In 2019, when I met Pope Francis for the first time, Andy said, "Did you tell him you killed that other pope?" My college friends keep me humble and enjoy reminding me that I wasn't always a Jesuit priest.

Occasionally I wrestle with some of my actions during my young adulthood, especially during college. Not that I was a terrible reprobate, beating people up, stealing from banks, or dealing drugs. (And I didn't kill the pope.) I don't think I ever broke the law, except for underage drinking, which was the norm for bars in a college town. And smoking pot was illegal then but seemed less so since so many of us did it. (I know that's not a convincing moral argument, but it's how I felt.) I think I was a fairly kind person then, as I try to be now. And I think God could forgive me for my jokes about Jesus, especially since I've regretted them for the past forty years.

Should one feel guilty for things one did at age seventeen—the incessant focus on money that began at Wharton and intensified while working in the corporate world, the almost nonexistent desire to help the poor, the self-satisfied pride that came with attending an Ivy League school, and the occasionally excessive use of drugs and alcohol? Or maybe the overweening ego that wanted to be liked so much that I couldn't be bothered with someone like Stanley at the movie theater?

Years later, I read Thomas Merton's autobiography *The Seven Storey Mountain*, the book that eventually led me to enter the Jesuits. Merton is severe about his college self during the 1930s. By his account, he led a rather debauched life as a young man, filled with drink and sex.

But you wouldn't know the whole story from his book. Some of his memoir was edited by the monastery censors for fear of offending the presumably delicate sensibilities of Catholics of the time. (That purportedly included reports of a mock crucifixion in which he participated while drunk, which left scars on his wrists.) This means that Merton's expressions of horror over his past sometimes don't make much sense to the reader. Still, he does include stories about his misadventures. Here he is describing his feelings after getting drunk with his fraternity friends at Columbia University and waiting in a bus station, weary: "The thing that depressed me most of all was the shame and despair that invaded my whole nature when the sun came up, and all the laborers were going to work: men healthy and awake and quiet, with their eyes clear, and some rational purpose before them. This humiliation and sense of my own misery and of the fruitlessness of what I had done was the nearest I could get to contrition."

My conscience was not as refined as Merton's. The day after that night at the bar, I was embarrassed by the jokes and sad about the pope's death but happy that I'd had fun with my new friends.

In general, I look at my younger self as I would look at any seventeen-year-old college student: a young person who has the responsibility to act morally but also deserves to be looked upon with a measure of compassion. I would hope that's how God looks upon me too. And on all of us. "Mercy within mercy within mercy" is how Merton describes God.

Other adults might feel the same. About twenty years ago, I wrote a book about entering the Jesuits and touched briefly on a few of these college escapades. The book was used by several Catholic high schools, and the principal of one contacted me to ask if I would write a letter to parents, saying that I disavowed the use of drugs and alcohol for teenagers. I wrote the letter, but months later the principal told me that it hadn't been needed. All the parents were of my generation and had apparently forgiven any misdeeds because they had done the same.

Most of the time, especially during my freshman year, I was not drunk or high or "killing popes." Instead, I was a "grind," spending the lion's share of my time on studies, even when hungover. To this day, I've never worked as hard as I did when I was a Wharton undergrad. The teachers were relentlessly demanding; they were also aware of the workload, as well as the difficulties of the exams and papers. "How long is the test?" we asked our Introduction to Accounting professor. "The test is four hours long," he said. "You have two hours to do it."

Alongside studies and social life, I had a work-study job, which helped to offset my college expenses. The agreement in our family was that my parents would foot the bill for tuition and I would pay for everything else: room and board and expenses such as books, meal plans, and weekend food. Beer too. Thanks to my summer job and some scholarship money from Penn, that worked out. But part of the financial aid package was a work-study job, which meant that I ended up working all four years.

My first work-study job was in Penn's Student Financial Aid office in Logan Hall, where I was a clerk, filing forms and applications and doing research for the financial aid officers. My dad used to joke about looking for extra money lying around the office, but I never found any.

Perhaps because I was so focused on studies and socializing, I never felt comfortable in the job and often felt like I didn't know what I was doing. I was intimidated by working in a real office. The stakes were higher than breaking a banana split glass or giving someone the wrong golf club. I also had an irrational fear that people in the office would contact the dean of Wharton and say, "How did this guy ever get into Wharton? He's an idiot." While it seemed okay to ask "How does this popcorn machine work?," I felt dumber asking "Where does this get filed?"

In class things were rosier and I did fairly well academically. Also, I could now drink almost a pitcher of beer without getting buzzed and knew the most efficient way to inhale when smoking a joint. Plus, I had made some wonderful friends. All in all, a good year.

By the end of freshman year, especially after seeing how much books and other necessities cost, it was time to return to a summer job hunt, which I did with vigor. I found three.

I knew that I would return to the movie theater; that was an easy choice. The Cinema on the Mall was happy to have a seasoned veteran back (the seasoning being Savarol). But that wouldn't be enough to cover all my college expenses.

So as soon as I moved back to my parents' home, I started looking for a second job. As ever, the Mall, whose place as the nexus of my social life had begun to wane now that my friends and I had access to our parents' cars, was still the best place to hunt for work. I found one at the Bakers Garden, a chain restaurant that centered around an in-store bakery and also served entrees in a groovy '70s décor: lots of rattan chairs, butcher-block tables, and macramé hangings.

Maybe thanks to my experience at the Ice Cream Inn, I got the job. It was a promotion from the Ice Cream Inn: No longer a dishwasher or busboy, I was a waiter. I was proud of my step up on the restaurant ladder, though I admitted to the manager that I had never actually waited on tables. Again I thought, *How hard could it be?*

Pretty hard. The first few days were an exercise in nerves: I was petrified that I would drop something on the floor, on the table, or into someone's lap. Much of the fare were croissants and other pastries, salads, burgers, and endless quiches. Load up two or three plates of quiche with sodas and bread dishes, and your tray was heavy. We were taught how to balance a tray with just one arm (jamming one end into your elbow and grabbing the other end with your hand). I never got the hang of it and always used two hands.

My favorite part of the Bakers Garden was the uniform, a big step up from the ratty smock from the Ice Cream Inn and the electric blue blazer of the Cinema on the Mall. In keeping with the formal design of the restaurant chain, waiters wore a muslin apron bearing the restaurant logo, with pockets in the front for your order pad or server pads. You wore that with jeans and sneakers to complete the casual late-1970s look. I was relieved to finally dress for work in attire that didn't embarrass me.

But waiting tables was scheduled work, not full time. My plan was to work as much as I could at the Cinema on the Mall, mainly at nights, and on the weekends work at the Bakers Garden, when they were busier. But that still left me wanting some full-time work.

That's where Kris came in, the only person among my high school friends I would call artsy. She was a talented artist who had drawn for the school newspaper and created the artwork for our Disco Dance. She was enormously enjoyable: fun, relaxed, breezy. Her mom, a Lithuanian immigrant, had worked at a nearby factory, and Kris got word that a local packaging plant, named Sharp Services, was hiring. From what I understood, they packaged pills in boxes. *How hard could it be?*

One day in May I drove a few miles for an interview. Sharp Services is still there and was recently the occasion for an in-depth, fact-finding visit for this book—that is, I drove there one weekend and peered through the windows. It still is a squat, functional, one-story brick building on Carland Road, sandwiched between two car dealerships on Ridge Pike, a main thoroughfare in Conshohocken.

In a few days, I got the phone call hiring me. "You're going to work on an assembly line?" said my mom. "Will it be dangerous?"

No idea. My only knowledge of assembly lines came from the episode of *I Love Lucy*, heavily in reruns, in which Lucy and Ethel fail to keep up with an assembly line of chocolate candies and resort to stuffing them in their mouths, and from history class when we studied the Industrial Revolution and saw a filmstrip about Ford Motor Company's giant car manufacturing plant in Dearborn, Michigan, that spat out cars.

I had no clue what I'd be doing. I hadn't seen the factory floor, had only the briefest interactions with the hiring manager, and didn't even know what we would be "assembling."

No longer working on shifts, I had snagged my first full-time job: 8 a.m. to 4 p.m. every weekday. And Sharp paid well. Also, it would be fun to work with Kris.

She picked me up on that first morning at 7:15 a.m. in her red Pinto. She did that every day that summer, and I came to look forward to our time together.

Until that summer, I hadn't known Kris well, other than working with her on the school newspaper and bumping into her in the halls of our high school. In a class of eight hundred kids, it was typical to know only a few of them well. But I knew Kris's house around the corner, from collecting for *The Recorder*, and that her parents were both immigrants from Lithuania. They always gave me money, which I appreciated.

When I spoke to Kris recently, it was after a forty-year hiatus. She moved to New York for graduate school in art, at Parsons School of Design, the same year I moved there after graduating from Penn. When I contacted her, we laughed when we realized that we hadn't spoken since a year after our college graduation. A few weeks later, over dinner at a Greek restaurant, we recounted for each other, essentially, our entire adult lives.

She told me about her family, about whom I had always wondered but was too incurious to ask about when we were driving to the factory. I knew her parents were Lithuanian-born, but there was much more to her story.

I'm amazed by how uninterested I was in other people's lives back then. So much of my life as a child and adolescent was focused on myself. The selfishness was perhaps natural for a young person, but it also meant that I missed a great deal around me.

Kris's parents met in college in Kaunas, Lithuania, where they helped found a Christian intellectual organization, her father a college professor and her mother a chemist and teacher. "During the Second World War," said Kris, "they were put into work camps, and after the war was over, they remained in displaced persons camps." They moved first to Canada and then to the United States, where they had three children and settled in Plymouth Meeting.

The kids all went to Lithuanian school on Saturday and Lithuanian Mass on Sundays, occasionally attending Mass at Epiphany of Our Lord, my family's parish. They planted bushes, fruit trees, and evergreens all over their property to remind them of their lives in rural Lithuania. I remembered how beautiful the front lawn of their house always looked when I was collecting for my paper route.

Then I asked her what she remembered about that summer when we worked at the factory together.

"Oh," she laughed, "you always smelled like smoke when you got into the car! I thought, *Jimmy doesn't look like a smoker!*"

Despite my collegiate habits, this was not because I was smoking pot in the morning. My parents were smokers and the aroma of Winstons and Kents pervaded the house, though I didn't notice it when I was at home. Only after I returned from winter break one year, opened the door to my dorm room, zipped open my duffel bag and wondered where the cigarette smell was coming from did I realize how much our house must have smelled.

Kris also remembers that her speediness as a driver alarmed me. "Red means stop," she remembers me saying as she sped through a traffic light. "You were so polite about it!" she said. Despite her race-car pace, I enjoyed the time we spent together. Kris had an artist's somewhat jaded approach to life and a mordant sense of humor that I found refreshingly adult.

It seemed that every time we drove (fast) out of our neighborhood, we were serenaded by Supertramp on Kris's car radio, singing "The Logical Song" from their new album *Breakfast in America*.

> When I was young, it seemed that life was so wonderful
> A miracle, oh, it was beautiful, magical
> And all the birds in the trees, well they'd be singing so happily
> Oh, joyfully, oh, playfully watching me
> But then they sent me away to teach me how to be sensible
> Logical, oh, responsible, practical
> And then they showed me a world where I could be so dependable
> Oh, clinical, oh, intellectual, cynical.

Our job at the factory was logical, responsible, and practical. It was also difficult. Kris and I belted out the last few verses as we sped to work in her Pinto:

> Please tell me what we've learned? (Can you hear me?)
> I know it sounds absurd (oh, won't you tell me)
> Please tell me who I am
> Who I am, who I am, who I *aaaaam*!

• • • •

Sharp's business was hard to describe. We called it a factory, but it didn't manufacture anything, like chocolates or cars. The company specialized in packing pills, which meant first inserting pills into "blister packs," which is what you usually see when you open a box of pills from the drugstore: plastic squares covered in thin foil with individual pills nestled in indentations, or "blisters." Today the company's website describes it as having more than "65 years of blistering experience." It elaborates: "Sharp Conshohocken specializes in controlled drug handling, low humidity and low oxygen capabilities to meet unique drug product requirements."

Pharmaceutical companies sent Sharp their pills in bulk, which were placed into blister packs, which were then inserted into small, personal-use-size boxes, which were then enclosed in cartons, which were finally placed into larger boxes to be shipped. Different pills required different rooms for packing: one for Unisom (one of the first over-the-counter sleeping pills, which had just come on the market) and another for Maalox, the antacid, and several more for nonpharmaceuticals, like the little chalky demineralization tablets used to clean a humidifier.

Since I was young and healthy, I hadn't heard of many of these pills, which amused the older employees.

"What's Maalox for?" I said to one man.

"Haha! You'll find out when you get old and fat like me!"

The days were a study in monotony. Kris picked me up at 7:15 a.m. so that we would arrive by 8:00. Sometimes we barely made it into the Sharp parking lot in time, despite Kris's breakneck driving. After we entered the building, we dropped our few things (including our bagged lunches) in our lockers and punched our time cards. For those too young to remember, you placed a card into a metal time clock, which made a satisfying *thunk* as it stamped on the card the exact time of your arrival. When you left for the day, you punched out, providing the company with an accurate record of your hours for payroll.

Then you donned your obligatory hairnet, which I hoped my friends would never see, and took your place in whatever room you were assigned that day. I asked Kris whether she remembered how we were assigned to the different stations. Did we volunteer? And for how long?

"Oh, I have no idea," she said. "I've blocked out most of that summer." Then she laughed. "But I do remember that we were never in a room together. I wish that we had been! At least we might have had some fun."

You started your day positioned next to one of the massive packing machines that disgorged hundreds of boxes of pills an hour. Sometimes you would be assigned to the blister pack station. In that case, you first had to check the tub of pills that the manufacturer had sent to see if any were broken or damaged. (One morning's highlight was someone finding a fly in one: "Hahaha! What do you think this cures?") Then someone would dump the barrel or tub of pills into a machine that would quickly insert the pills into the plastic sheets, until all the little indentations had pills in them. These were sent down a conveyor belt for us to inspect, making sure to fill any empty blisters. Then the inspected blister sheets would be covered with a thin strip of aluminum foil, heated, and stacked for later use.

But usually you were in a packing room, dominated by the room-size machines that hummed or whirred or buzzed or clunked all day. First, the machine inhaled the blister packs (fed into a long, upright metal chute by an employee who tore them into long strips). Then it swiftly inserted them into previously flattened boxes that came down another chute and were ingeniously opened by the machine. I was amazed by the way the machine expertly opened dozens of flattened boxes a minute, by inserting a thin metal arm precisely between the top and bottom of the little boxes, twisting them into an open position, stuffing them with blister packs, and then shutting them just as quickly.

Then the boxes filled with blister packs were sent down the conveyor belt, where they were inspected by employees. The finished boxes were spat out onto a table, where they would be gathered and stuffed into cartons containing eight or ten packs. Those boxes were then covered with shrink-wrap and packed by hand into large brown boxes for shipment.

So the assembly went: pills into blister packs, blister packs into small boxes, small boxes into cartons, cartons into packing boxes. It was like one of those Russian nesting dolls, little things in successively bigger containers, but not nearly as beautiful, and with sleeping pills.

Sometimes I would be at the top of the machine, tearing off the long strips of blister packs, which was mildly dangerous since the sharp metallic strips could slice open a finger. (We sometimes wore thin paper gloves, but the blister packs tore through them with frightening ease.)

Kris remembered that job well: "I didn't care that my fingers were bleeding," she said. "I wanted the world to see how much I was *suffering*!"

That was my least favorite position on the assembly line, since I didn't like getting my fingers sliced. Bloodied fingers prompted the inevitable comments from fellow employees: "You work at *Sharp*, remember? Hahaha."

Equally monotonous, and mildly dangerous, was standing in

front of the conveyor belt watching the small boxes whiz by with alarming speed, straightening them or adjusting them if they got out of place, and removing any that didn't have their quota of pills inside. You had to be careful not to stare too closely, and especially not too long, at the rapidly moving boxes, making sure, as we were told repeatedly on the very first day by both managers and employees, to look up every few minutes lest you get dizzy.

"DON'T STARE!" they said. "Look up EVERY FEW MINUTES!"

That summer I saw three or four people grow wobbly, lose their balance, and faint. "There goes another one!" someone would say as an employee swayed and grabbed onto the side of the machine for support. "Man overboard!" There was usually no lasting damage: People brushed themselves off, repositioned themselves in front of the belt, shook their heads, and continued with the day. This phenomenon was made worse if the person was hungover or high, as a few people were. Or just tired, which everyone seemed to be.

Speaking of dust, you had to take care not to inhale stray powder from the products, especially the sleeping pills. One day the machine jammed, and instead of the blister packs being inserted into the small boxes, the empty boxes got mangled at the top of the machine and stuck in one place, which meant the machine's little metal arm kept ramming the blister packs into one another, rather than into the little boxes.

Bangbangbangbangbangbangbangbangbang! Dozens of packs were crushed in an instant, sending white clouds of the pulverized sleeping-pill dust into the air. Though we tried to wave it away, people were coughing within a few seconds.

Someone hit the big red STOP button on the machine, and it hummed to a stop. But in a few minutes one of the men who had been near where the pills were atomized yawned. Then he simply lay down on the floor fast asleep and started snoring. We found that hilarious.

This was also the first job where I wasn't working with a primarily teenage labor force. Some Sharp employees were in their twenties, but most were adults, some my parents' age.

Much of the time, because of my age, I was asked to do the heavier work of putting the cartons into the bigger boxes after they came off the line. I stood at the end as the cartons were disgorged, ready for me to shrink-wrap them. That meant passing the cartons under a sealer that dispensed a clear plastic sheet. As you pulled the sheet off the roll, the sealer separated the one sheet into top and bottom sheets, making a plastic envelope for the box. Then you slid the carton into the envelope, under an open metal frame. When you brought down the frame, it would enfold the box with plastic wrap. Another machine heated the plastic, shrinking it tightly around the box. Once you got good at it, you could do it rapidly, though you had to be careful not to get burned by the glowing red wire that sealed the packages.

We stood there for hours, our hands doing the same motion over and over, mindless in its repetitiveness, inducing a near-trance state. I thought I would go out of my mind.

The next year at Wharton, we learned about time-motion studies, pioneered in the United States in the early 1900s by Frederick Winslow Taylor and Frank and Lillian Gilbreth (the latter two known better as the subjects of the lighthearted book on family life *Cheaper by the Dozen*, the basis for two movies of the same name). Taylor and the Gilbreths broke down physical work, primarily factory work, into a series of discrete tasks; timed them;

and then devised ways to maximize efficiency—that is, speed up the process. This was a boon for the bottom line, but not so great for the assembly line worker, condemned to do the same task repeatedly, as quickly as humanly possible, and for hours on end.

For me, this was a summer job; for many of the adults, this was the long-term job that put food on the table. There is dignity in all work, and perhaps some enjoyed it. But most complained bitterly about Sharp: the toll it took on their arms and legs, and hands and feet; the injuries they incurred (we didn't use the term yet, but many suffered from "repetitive strain injury"); and the unrelenting, unending, unrelieved boredom. And it was low paying: I was making the same hourly amount that they were, and while it helped with my college expenses, it didn't seem like a lot if you had a family.

Years later, I read Barbara Ehrenreich's book *Nickel and Dimed: On (Not) Getting by in America*, first published in 2001, now a classic of social commentary. Ehrenreich asks the question: How can anyone exist on minimum wage—much less support a family—in the United States? After working as a waitress and hotel maid, and at other low-wage jobs (sometimes two at a time), and living in residential motels and trailer parks, she finds that she is unable to make ends meet. It's an extraordinarily compassionate piece of writing.

Not surprisingly, Ehrenreich notes that many of these jobs are crushingly dull. This was one of the most salient lessons I learned at Sharp. There was no way around it: The work was mind-numbing and, as a result, mentally exhausting. It was no surprise that people were often sullen, that there was a lot of pot-smoking, complaining on the line, and asking when the day would be over. Ehrenreich also describes the effect that low-wage jobs often have on the workers: "When you enter the low-wage workplace—and many of the medium-wage workplaces as well—you check your civil liberties at the door, leave America and all it supposedly stands for behind, and learn to zip your lips for the duration of the shift."

Low-wage workers, because of the need to conform and follow rules to avoid losing their jobs, must, she writes, bow to environments that are "neither free nor in any way democratic." This has a psychological effect as well: "Any dictatorship takes a psychological toll on its subjects. If you are treated as an untrustworthy person—a potential slacker, drug addict, or thief—you may begin to feel less trustworthy yourself. If you are constantly reminded of your lowly position in the social hierarchy, whether by individual managers or by a plethora of impersonal rules, you begin to accept that unfortunate status."

Absolutely. And to "a plethora of impersonal rules," I would add a "plethora of impersonal tasks."

It bothered me to see people doing the impersonal tasks we did for hours on end. Of course they were done freely; the workers were getting paid, and the work did not take anything away from their dignity. But it disturbed me nonetheless to see human beings reduced to, in some ways, machines. Years later during my theology studies as a Jesuit, I read the papal encyclical *Laborem exercens*, written by St. John Paul II, which focuses on the dignity of labor and the rights of workers.

"It should be recognized," he wrote, "that the error of early capitalism can be repeated wherever man is in a way treated on the same level as the whole complex of the material means of production, as an instrument and not in accordance with the true dignity of his work—that is to say, where he is not treated as subject and maker, and for this very reason as the true purpose of the whole process of production."

When I read this in graduate school, I thought of my co-workers at Sharp.

For several days, I was on the Unisom line, next to a clattering machine packing millions of sleeping pills into little boxes. At the other end of the room, on the wall, was a large round clock, the kind that one used to find in classrooms. There was a running debate about whether it was better to see the clock or not. Half of the line (including me) didn't want to be reminded of the time, since it seemed to drag by, so we wanted the clock covered with an empty cardboard box, dozens of which were lying around. The other half of the line wanted to see exactly how much time had passed. So one guy would position a cardboard box on the clock until someone got frustrated and threw a pill box at it to knock it down.

"Put it BACK UP!" shouted the other half.

"No, leave it DOWN!" shouted the rest.

But everyone wanted the day to go quickly. We were united in that. There was friendship among people who had come to know one another, and lots of chatter on the floor. You quickly learned about people's lives as you stood next to them for hours on end with nothing to do but talk and not stare too intently at the boxes hurtling by.

Even with my underdeveloped conscience, I felt compassion for my fellow employees for whom life had not been easy. Some had done poorly in school, some were struggling with alcohol and drug addictions, some were held back by racism (many African Americans and members of other ethnic minorities worked on the line), some had health problems that limited their ability to succeed professionally. Not all of them had such difficulties—some seemed perfectly healthy, grateful for work, and cheerful on the line—but many did.

Even the cheerful ones complained about making ends meet: car payments, insurance payments, mortgage payments. Nearly all of them were kind to me, if occasionally impatient: "Hey, Jim! Hurry up with those boxes!" But I felt great compassion for the lives they led, at least from 8 a.m. to 4 p.m. So it was the first time I had worked not only with adults, but also with people I considered poor. And they worked hard. I realized how wrong Ayn Rand was: Hard work was no guarantor of success.

Often, they made light of their situation, especially when they found out I was in college. "I could barely get through high school!" "College? I'm too dumb for that!" Or, just as often, "Who needs it?" A few called me, sometimes with an edge, College Boy. So even though we talked about our lives as we stood there for hours, I didn't talk much about my life at Penn.

When I shared my experiences with my mother and father, they said, "It's good that you see how people have to work in jobs like that. And to know how lucky you are. It will make you work harder in college." At the same time, they said that I should leave my work problems at the door. There was no complaining about Sharp once I got home.

I had to clear my mind in some way from the almost stupefying dullness of the work. So I came up with a routine every day after Sharp and before heading off to work at the movie theater. After Kris dropped me off, I would race up the lawn, fling open the door, grab a slice of cake or some cookies from the kitchen, wolf them down, then go to my room, change out of my Sharp clothes, and pop the same eight-track into my stereo: Elvis Costello and the Attractions' album *This Year's Model*. I'd flip to "Pump It Up," which I would crank to top volume and dance to. Jumping up and down helped dispel the boredom that had settled into my bones like pill powder. It also gave me a boost for the next few hours at the theater.

> I've been on tenter*hooks*, ending in dirty looks
> Listening to the Mu*zak*, thinking 'bout this and *that*
> She said that's *that*, I don't wanna chitter-*chat*
> Turn it down a little bit or turn it down *flat*
> Pump it *up* when you don't really need it
> Pump it *up* until you can feel it!

I played it loud, sang it loud, and danced in my room, shaking Sharp out of my mind and body.

One day at Sharp, I was standing next to a woman probably in her late sixties, whose face I can still recall. She had blond hair going gray, whose wisps escaped from under her hairnet. Slim and upright with a lean face and high cheekbones and bright eyes behind eyeglasses. Looking back, I would say she resembled the Catholic activist Dorothy Day, whom I hadn't heard of then. My co-worker was taciturn to a fault. The few times I tried to chat with her, she seemed uninterested. She had a vaguely Eastern European accent, like Kris's mom.

I stood beside her as white-and-orange Unisom boxes sped by us on the conveyor belt. That day, the air-conditioning did nothing to relieve the Philadelphia humidity, which had seeped inside. She was wearing a white short-sleeved shirt. As I glanced down at the boxes speeding by, I noticed a tattoo on her forearm. It looked like a series of faded numbers or maybe letters.

"Oh," I said, pointing to her arm. "What's that mean?"

"Dachau," she said.

I didn't know what to say. As we stood over the conveyor belt, the machine whirring and clicking, I tried to imagine her life. For the next few hours, I felt a combination of pity, sadness, confusion, and discomfort, but mostly embarrassment over not knowing what to say.

I thought about the books we read, and especially the movies and filmstrips we saw about the Second World War during our history classes in school. In the 1970s, depending on how old they were, the second-to-last chapters of our illustrated history books covered World War II and the Korean War; the final chapters covered either the assassination of President Kennedy or the Civil Rights Movement. Vietnam was too recent to be considered history.

Our world history teacher in junior high school had an intense if morbid fascination with the Second World War. Once a year, to supplement his classes on that war, he festooned his class with Nazi flags and banners and displayed all manner of German Army paraphernalia: Helmets, pistols, knives, and pamphlets were laid out on desks and tables, and model airplanes hung from the acoustical-tile ceilings. Students from other history classes were encouraged to visit his classroom-cum-museum when his memorabilia were on display.

Recently I learned that a few parents protested but were rebuffed after complaining to the administration. Most students, as I recall, were more stunned by the sheer volume of items he owned and carted into school. My history teacher's annual display seemed to register no more alarm among most students than if he had brought in Revolutionary War artifacts, and for the record, he also collected US military memorabilia from that era. (He owned a US Army jeep.)

Looking back, it's hard to fathom this annual display, especially with so many Jewish classmates in school. On a Facebook page for those who lived in our neighborhood at the time, I asked whether people remembered this, and dozens weighed in, with a Jewish friend saying it "scared the stuffing out of me." Others disagreed, remembering him as a teacher committed to deepening his students' appreciation of history.

Because of my history teacher's interest in the Second World War, we spent several days studying the Holocaust. In English class we all read *The Diary of Anne Frank*, and toward the end of senior year we were assigned to watch the TV miniseries *Holocaust*. I also remember that during the many bar and bat mitzvahs I attended during junior high, there was at times an undertone of melancholy when grandparents would speak about relatives whom they wished were present. At one, a series of faded photos were passed around to the friends of the bar mitzvah boy, so that we would understand that the ceremony was more than a religious or coming-of-age event; it was also a continuation of a people.

Until that day at Sharp, I had never been close to someone who had suffered so much.

Pill boxes sped by us on the conveyor belt as I tried not to stare at her arm and struggled to think of what to say. In the end, I said nothing. I never mentioned it again, and neither did she.

The lives of my fellow employees seemed hard. Hers, I would suspect, was among the hardest. Yet despite the tedium, Sharp was not an unpleasant place to work: It was surprisingly noisy, with people shouting over the din of the machines, cracking jokes with one another, catching a smoke break, or eating together in the employee dining room, which featured a vending machine that stocked Rice Krispies Treats, which I consumed by the dozens that summer.

Even on an assembly line that mesmerized us into a stupefied silence with a plethora of impersonal tasks, there were funny moments.

As the low person on the organizational ladder, I often got stuck with the jobs that no one wanted. And if I ended up getting a cushier job, say, at an easier spot on the line, someone might say to me, "Oh, no, *I'm* doing that one, College Boy."

Almost every day I was called upon to clean up spilled boxes, soda, or food; wipe down the machines; or fetch supplies. I was also a convenient person to break things, for the common good.

Viz: Sometimes people decided that we all needed a break, even though lunch was still hours away. Time to stop the machine. The best way to do this was to throw a ruler, a hammer, or any available piece of hardware directly into the machine. And since no one else wanted to be caught, this was usually my job.

"Jimmy, we need a *break*!" someone would say. "Where's that ruler?"

Someone on the line would hand me a wooden ruler. I felt only mildly guilty doing this, my moral compass still underdeveloped. Yes, it was wrong to lie and also to do something that could damage an expensive machine. In my management class at Wharton, we occasionally (but not often enough) considered questions about experiencing peer pressure in a corporation to do something unethical, and while the moral arguments made sense, they were no match for the prospect of ten angry Sharp employees glaring at you for the rest of the shift because you didn't jam the machine and therefore denied them a break. In the moral calculus between doing the right thing or incurring the wrath of my coworkers, I always chose the ruler.

I made sure no managers were in sight before I casually tossed the ruler into the bowels of the machine. It made a horrible clattering noise and brought the machine to an immediate stop. Sometimes we'd use a wrench, but rulers were easier to locate. In a pinch, a big box that "accidentally" fell into the machine also did the trick.

Everyone would feign surprise. "Our machine is down again!" someone would say. Then they'd all stand back from their stations and relax, perch on a stool, or lean against the wall and start chatting.

Naturally it fell to me to report the problem. To do so, I had to use the "Terry phone." No one at Sharp, as far as I knew, was called Terry, but that's what we called the internal phone cum public address system: the Terry phone. Or maybe "terryphone." My deep research into the origin of this mysterious device—that is, I looked online—unearthed a description of terryphones as "mid-century intercom devices." All that summer, I thought it referred to a manager named Terry.

I picked up the Terry phone and called the manager. "Our machine is down again." A few minutes later he would appear and utter the same response: "I can't BELIEVE THIS! AGAIN! How many times is this F—ING machine going to break down? God DAMN IT!"

Then everyone relaxed and chatted until the repairman came by, cast us a justifiably accusatory look, and spent a good half hour trying to figure out what was wrong. He also said the same thing every time.

"How did this ruler get in here AGAIN?"

No one had a clue. Neither did College Boy. After the ruler was fished out and the machine started up again, we went back to our appointed tasks.

Sometimes I was called upon to fix actual problems with the machines, especially one that always seemed to have a metal gear that would slip out of place. Even without a ruler assist, the machines were forever jamming and needed someone to reach his (or her, but usually his) hand into the machine to force a cog back into place. The danger was that if the metal gears snapped back into place instantly, they tore a piece of skin off your finger if you weren't agile enough to avoid its hungry metal teeth.

One day when the machine ground to a halt, a woman whom I liked immensely for her boundless energy and wit yelled from the top of the line, "Jimmyyyy! Fix the machiiiine!"

"I'm not sticking my hand in there again," I said. "The last time I did that I almost lost a finger."

Then she good-naturedly shouted a question, which I can still hear today: "Jimmy! Is you a man? Or is you a MOUSE?"

Everyone laughed at her challenge. Clapping ensued.

Eager to prove that I was not a mouse, I reached into the guts of the machine and shifted a cog, losing only a little piece of my finger. The machine loudly snapped back into place.

"Jimmy, today you is a MAN!" she said, and clapped her hands.

During that seemingly endless summer, between packing pills at the factory, making popcorn at the theater, and serving quiche in the restaurant, I was wiped out. There was also less time to spend with my high school friends, except for the odd weekday night when I wasn't working. My social life suffered, a catastrophe for any teenager.

But I was richer. Between the three jobs, my bank account was bigger than ever. Which was a good thing, since I had to pay for textbooks (and beer) at Penn. Even so, I decided that three jobs was too much. I also had had enough of the mind-numbing work on the factory line. The next summer, I promised myself that I would get a "white-collar" job. If I could. Maybe in an office? That would be a lot easier.

How hard could it be to work in an office?

John and me on the beach near his family's house at Strathmere, New Jersey, during the summer of 1980. Proud of our creation, whom we named Sandy. Our hangovers made that seem the height of wit.

A (daytime) visit to Great Adventure in New Jersey, with (*from left*) Barb ("*Ohhhhh, VRAIMENT?*"), Peggy (my friend in junior high, high school, and college), and Pam (my junior-high prom date, who also beat me as Student Council president; Pam was a much better chief executive than I was).

CHAPTER 7

How Not to Sacrifice Your Life for a Summer Job

THE NEXT SUMMER, I KNEW TWO THINGS: I DIDN'T want to work in a factory, and I didn't want to hold down three jobs at once. And though I was still a young adult whose focus was on getting rich while getting people to like me, I had sufficient self-knowledge to know that the "inside one year, outside the next" pattern was futile. When I was inside, I wanted to work outside next time, and vice versa. Eventually I realized that I didn't want to be working *anywhere* in the summer. I'd rather play tennis, watch movies, or sit on our back porch and read.

It was also time to find a job that was at least marginally related to my studies. Maybe the business classes I had taken (I was about to start my junior year) would land me a decent job in an air-conditioned office rather than on an assembly line. Also, it was time to start building my résumé for the eventual job interviews during senior year. Studies at Wharton were geared toward one goal: getting a high-paying job. Penn's Career Planning and Placement office was superb and made searching for a job almost ridiculously easy. The early 1980s, the era of "Reaganomics" and a surging stock market, was a seller's market for recent college grads: By October 1982, *The Wall Street Journal* would call the market "exuberant."

But graduation was two years away, and I didn't have any contacts in the business world. I still had to hunt down a summer job.

Based on my studies, I had a dim idea that I might work in commercial banking. With its air of probity, stability, and dignity, banking appealed to me. One friend who worked as a bank teller suggested that as a possible summer position. In the spring of my sophomore year, I investigated some local banks.

Around that time, my uncle (my golf-pro-cousin Tommy's father) mentioned that a friend of his worked as a branch manager at Western Savings Bank, a local bank. Its name was pronounced by many Philadelphians as *Westren*. I'm not sure why this was a tongue twister, but it was.

Western was one of many small and medium-sized local banks that proliferated in the area during the 1970s and 1980s, before most were taken over by larger national banks. At the time, Western was flourishing, with branches throughout Philadelphia and the suburbs.

One afternoon in the springtime, I took the subway from Penn into Center City to apply at Western. A few days after I applied in the bank's main office downtown, I got a phone call telling me when to show up for "teller training."

Teller training would start after the semester ended at Penn. In a subsequent phone call, they told me to wear a suit and tie or at least a jacket and tie. Goodbye Sharp factory and your awful hairnet! Goodbye ridiculous bow tie and smelly blue jacket from the Cinema on the Mall! Goodbye rum-raisin-stained smock from the Ice Cream Inn! For that matter, goodbye T-shirt and shorts from my lawn-mowing, paperboy, and caddying days!

Goodbye to all that! I was now a *banker*. My mansion on the Main Line, closets filled with pin-striped suits and rivers of gin and tonics, awaited.

Now that I was home for the summer, getting downtown was more complicated. Living in the suburbs meant having to find transportation to Center City. My dad laughed when I asked if I could take the Gran Torino every day. "Are you kidding?" he said. "There's nowhere to park anyway."

"Take the A bus," said my mom brightly. I groaned. The A bus went from Lafayette Hill, a nearby town, all the way up Henry Avenue, through Roxborough, where my mom grew up and my cousins lived, across the Schuylkill (*SKOO-kul*) River, and then up the Schuylkill Expressway, and finally into town—a trip of more than an hour. Fortunately, my stop, in Lafayette Hill, was the first stop, so there were always seats. Still, I knew no one on the bus and missed my chats with Kris in her speedy red Pinto.

Western's main office was on Broad Street, the north-south axis in Philadelphia that went from the row homes in South Philly, past the elegant brick-and-brownstone Academy of Music, and then around the gorgeous French Renaissance Revival City Hall (which stands squarely in the middle of a busy intersection), past the beautiful Pennsylvania Academy of the Fine Arts, where Thomas Eakins had taught, past Temple University, and then through some of the poorer neighborhoods in North Philadelphia.

I felt prosperous just walking into the bank's main branch in the grand Real Estate Title & Trust Company building, described by David Brownlee, of the art history department at Penn, as "a lushly detailed brick and terracotta exercise in Venetian Renaissance classicism." My cousin Marguerite, who had recently graduated from Penn's law school, worked at a "white-shoe" law firm in the same building, a few floors up. Knowing that made me feel even more like an adult.

Teller training took about a week. And from start to finish I found it fascinating.

Before that week, had you asked me what a bank teller did, I would have said, "Give out cash and deposit cash." Tellers also cashed checks, wrote out bank orders, accepted payments for loans, sold and redeemed traveler's checks, opened and closed accounts, and fielded questions from customers about their accounts, including Vacation Club and Christmas Club accounts.

Cash wasn't the only thing dispensed: We also gave financial advice to our customers ("Can I use a torn twenty-dollar bill?" "Can you show me how to write a check?" "Can I cash a check that has been endorsed twice?"). And since our office was in Center City, we also answered questions from tourists on how to get to Independence Hall (not too far away), where to find the Liberty Bell (same), and where to get the best cheesesteak (which, depending on what establishment you recommended, would be contradicted by another teller).

Teller training was conducted in a small room with about a dozen new tellers of varying ages. The friendly and efficient instructors were committed to making sure we'd be ready for every possible contingency by the end of the week.

We started with the primary responsibility: giving and getting cash. For that we had to learn to count cash. Tellers are often presented with huge stacks of bills, of varying denominations, that must be added up *quickly*. This was also before the now-standard cash-counting machines, which in some banks have largely replaced counting by hand. We had one machine in our branch for large amounts, but for the most part we did it ourselves. And we were taught an ingenious and remarkably simple method, which I still use today, that enables you to count large sums of money with lightning speed. Our customers often asked us, "How did you do that so fast?" But it wasn't just for show: Speed was essential if you had a long line of customers waiting.

Here's how it works: You mentally remove the zero from each numbered bill so that, say, a $50 bill becomes a 5, a $20 bill becomes a 2, and a $10 bill, a 1. For each $5 bill you say "and" for every other one and then "one." Then you add the zeroes back and count out the remaining $1 bills.

That may sound confusing, so let's take an example.

If you're counting ten 50s, you'd say (silently), "5, 10, 15, 20, 25, 30, 35, 40, 45, 50." Then add a zero back when you are finished: 50 and a 0 = 500. That's easy: Counting bills in the same denomination is a breeze. But the method also works for mixed denominations. First, separate the bills into denominations, largest to smallest. Then mentally remove the zeros and count. A stack of seven 20s with six 10s, eight 5s, and three 1s, would be: 2, 4, 6, 8, 10, 12, 14 (seven 20s); then 15, 16, 17, 18, 19, 20 (six 10s); then "and 21," "and 22, "and 23," "and 24" (eight 5s). Now you're at 24. Then you add back the zero: 240. Then add the three 1s: 241, 242, 243. You've just counted $243 in a few seconds. To the untrained eye it looks like you're either a genius or a supercomputer.

We were also taught *never* to wet our fingers with our tongues to separate the bills when we were counting. "Cash is the dirtiest thing in the world," they told us. "Think of how many hundreds of people have touched it." In quantities, it also stank, giving off an earthy aroma, like a wet newspaper. Instead, to moisten our fingers, we were given little round dishes with sponges soaked in water. Many tellers preferred a gluey substance that came in small round containers.

A few weeks into the job, I got violently ill not by sticking my fingers in my mouth, but by failing to wash my hands after handling money and then eating a cheesesteak at lunch. It was the cash, not the cheesesteak. That was, I vowed, the last time that would happen. Before eating and before I left the bank, I would wash my hands, disinfecting them with alcohol if possible.

A good chunk of teller training was spent learning how to "settle" our cash drawers every night. You had to know how much cash you began the morning with, how much you took in and gave out (which meant toting up all the deposit slips and withdrawal slips, checks, and the like), and how much you ended up with. At day's end, you had to settle "to the penny." It was more difficult than balancing a checkbook but not as hard as some of the accounting assignments at Wharton, so I got the hang of it quickly. But I was still worried at the end of each day. Being "out of balance" was every teller's nightmare, incurring the wrath of the branch manager and pitying looks from fellow tellers.

Then came the most memorable part of teller training: what to do in case of a bank robbery.

A dozen or so baby tellers sat in our classroom as our teacher gently introduced the topic. "This is unlikely, of course," he said, "but sometimes we do get robbed."

This was a new wrinkle for my summer jobs. There weren't

How Not to Sacrifice Your Life for a Summer Job

many robberies at the Ice Cream Inn or the Cinema on the Mall, except for my own: stealing a spoonful of rum raisin ice cream from the storeroom or a few Good & Plentys from the candy display case, with the candy girls' collusion. But now I was working in a bank on a busy intersection in downtown Philly. I started to sweat. And what our teacher said next did not inspire confidence: "The first thing we want to say is this: If anyone has a gun, don't do anything stupid. We don't want anyone to get killed."

At the time, I wasn't especially religious and didn't want to be a martyr, though maybe, if I were feeling especially brave or holy, and with an extra helping of grace, I might sacrifice my life for God. But not for Western Savings Bank.

After the nervous laughter subsided, the instructor got down to specifics.

First, stay calm because few robberies end up violent, and the robbers are probably more frightened than you are. Ha! I had heard the last part about the dogs on my paper route, none of whom seemed the least afraid of me. And none of the dogs had a gun. I wasn't the only one who shifted in their seat nervously.

The second thing was to give the person all the cash they asked for and not put up a fight. I deemed that a good idea too.

"Whatever you do, don't panic," the instructor said. Then he told us about all the devices we would need to activate, presumably while we weren't panicking.

First was a small button at each teller station (what we called our window), underneath the counter on the right side. It looked like a doorbell and would alert the police when pushed. In addition, there was a pedal on the floor, which looked like the accelerator for a small car. Pushing that would also notify the police. "But don't do this if the robber is looking directly at you, in case he suspects something." Okay.

The most important thing was to give him (or her, I guess) the pack of "exploding 20s."

Now, I hope I'm not giving away trade secrets, but I'm going to assume that not many current or potential criminals are reading this book.

In each bank teller's drawer was a pack of "exploding 20s." This was a cleverly designed metal rectangle, the size of a pack of dollar bills, with a "dye pack" hidden inside. On the outside edges of the pack were paper ridges for verisimilitude. The top and bottom of the pack were covered with two real $20 bills, which were always included in your cash inventory. The exploding 20s were at the bottom of the $20 bills section of your drawer, where it sat on a metal plate. (Your drawer had slots for $50, $20, $10, $5, and $1 bills.)

When a robber asked (demanded) that you empty your drawer, you were supposed to surreptitiously include the exploding 20s. Removing the rectangle from the metal plate activated it. Then, when the thief passed under a sensor at the entrance to the bank, a timer would begin. A few minutes later, when the bank robber was presumably hightailing it down Market Street, purple dye would explode all over the bills, rendering them useless, and all over the robber, rendering him recognizable. We watched a fun film that showed just that.

Later an experienced teller at my branch told me that a robber once said to her, "And don't give me any of those exploding bills!" She wisely acceded to his wishes.

We also heard the story of a thief who sprinted out of a bank in Center City with a stack of bills in his hand and passed under the sensor. The pack burst, dousing the cash and him with the indelible purple dye. Realizing that the police would be able to identify him by his purple clothes, he stripped off his shirt and pants and ran down the street in his underwear. The police nabbed him quickly.

This was one of many boneheaded-but-true bank robber stories that we heard about in teller training. My other favorite was the thief who came into a Western branch and asked the teller to empty her drawer of all the $100 bills. She told him honestly that she was out of hundreds in her drawer and, not so honestly, that she had to ask the manager. Meanwhile, she pushed the alert button with her finger and the pedal with her foot. Then she went into the back office, where the safe was kept, and told the manager what was going on. For good measure, the manager phoned the police and, since the robber seemed to be in no hurry, told the teller to stall him.

"We're all out of hundreds," she lied.

"Then get me some fifties!" he shouted.

She returned to the back office and waited with the manager for a few minutes, letting the guy cool his heels at her window, waiting for her to find some fifties. By the time she returned, the police had entered the building. They drew their weapons and told the robber to drop his. He didn't have one after all, and they snapped on a pair of handcuffs.

As he left, the addled miscreant said to the police, "What kind of bank doesn't have $100 bills?"

When I related this to my dad, he told me that he once went to the dentist's office on Halloween and all the dental hygienists were dressed up as clowns for the day. Later they went to the bank to cash their paychecks; when the tellers saw them, they called the police.

I repeated the story of the addled robber to a teller who said,

"Yeah, I've heard that one. Bank robberies are funny until they happen to you." Several years before, a man had come to her window and pointed what looked like a gun, covered by a windbreaker, at her. Flustered, she thought it would be a clever idea to pretend to faint. So she pretended to swoon and collapsed to the floor. The man leaned over the counter, pulled out his very real gun, and said, "Get up or I'll blow your f—ing head off."

She stood up and filled the man's bag with money. "Stupidest thing I've ever done," she said, about pretending to faint. "He could have killed me."

The next Monday on the A bus, ready for my first day, I tried to remember all that I had been taught. I had the cash-counting method down but was worried about settling my window at night.

Happily, for the first few days I was apprenticed to another teller, a middle-aged woman with curly gray hair named Ethel, whom I liked immediately. There were two other tellers besides Ethel and me: Ellen and Tony.

For the first week, I shadowed Ethel, watching her greet customers, count cash, cash checks, check account balances, offer advice, sell traveler's checks, convert coins (or "coin" as we would say) to cash, and handle rude customers, while she offered a running commentary of what she was doing and, sometimes, thinking. After the doors closed, I watched Ethel settle her window, the most important of our daily tasks. At the time we had a simple computer that would give us the person's balance, but this was before the general inclusion of computers in the business world, so nearly everything else we did was unaided by computers: During the day and while settling our windows at the end of the day, we used an adding machine.

Western had recently installed brand-new ATMs outside, then called DAN machines (for Day and Night banking), which most of our customers didn't trust—or rather, found hard to believe—since ATMs were just being introduced. The banks had christened their new ATM systems with friendly names to make it seem like customers were dealing with a real person. Girard Bank introduced its George card, and Philadelphia National Bank (PNB) hit it big with its MAC (Money Access Card) machines, which grew into the first large-scale ATM network in the country. But at the time it was still a novelty. More than once, a customer would withdraw money from our DAN machine and then come into the bank, stand in line, and ask the teller to check the balance of their account. They couldn't believe that it worked.

The next Monday morning, I opened my window with butterflies in my stomach. Depositing a check to a wrong account was significantly more serious than breaking a banana split glass.

This fear of screwing up seemed to come from some primal part of me. And the fear usually hit me after I had been trained and was ready to start a job in earnest. Sometimes it was physical: My face flushed when I was confronted with something I didn't know how to do, or couldn't do, or was unable to do perfectly. It was like worrying about getting a strike in Little League or missing a layup in Bitty Basketball.

Part of this was healthy: I was a conscientious worker who wanted to do a good job. But part of it was a feeling that took years to shake: I was somehow not as smart, talented, or physically capable as other people. I was worried that I would shame myself by doing something stupid: striking out, as it were. It took me a while to realize that (1) on any new job, you have to be taught what to do; (2) making mistakes as a newbie is par for the course, to use some caddying terminology; (3) asking for help when you don't know something is not a crime; and (4) it takes time to master any task. And most of all, (5) no one's perfect.

But by that point in my life I needed a dose of humility. My ego, which expanded each semester at Wharton, was offended if I couldn't excel at every task put in front of me. It took me a while to recognize that you can't be good at every job, especially at the beginning. Learning, training, and practicing, even the flushed cheeks of embarrassment, are part of life. Ignorance is not a sin. And that initial embarrassment is part of the process. You'll get the hang of it, if you stick with it, ask questions, and push on.

"Don't worry," said Ethel. "You'll do fine."

Ethel stared at the large crowd gathered outside our branch, which faced onto 17th and Market Streets, a busy intersection in the middle of many office buildings, restaurants, and stores. Through the floor-to-ceiling windows you could see all the activity outside—the traffic, passersby, tourists, shoppers, food vendors, and the occasional homeless person.

The first day, just before the bank opened, as the crowd outside got more anxious and pulled on the locked door, Ethel leaned her elbows on her countertop, put her head in her hands, sighed heavily, peered over her eyeglasses, and uttered one of her favorite sayings: "The masses are asses."

She didn't mean it. At least not always. Most of the time she was a model teller: kind, friendly, efficient. But woe betide the person who tried to bend the rules. Or worse, who treated another teller rudely. Ethel, the senior teller, would come to your window and say, "Is there a problem?" and her baleful gaze always forced people to say, "No."

"I didn't think so," she would say.

My favorite habit was her running commentary on the days of the week, all gearing up to the weekend. On Monday morning, before the doors were open, she would sigh and say, "Is it Friday yet?" This continued every day of the week through Thursday: "Is it Friday yet?"

During my first week of apprenticeship, I wondered what would happen on Friday.

I had my answer Friday morning.

"Is it five o'clock yet?" she said as the doors opened. This continued throughout the day. Finally at five o'clock, the moment for which she had waited the entire week, she'd sigh and say, "It's almost Monday!" She did this every week, and it drove a few people crazy. I found it hilarious.

The first day went smoothly, thanks to the teller-training classes and the help from Ethel, Ellen, and Tony, the third of whom teased me good-naturedly about what he called my Ivy League outfit. Whenever I wore a striped button-down shirt, he'd say, "Yipes! Stripes!" At day's end, I settled to the penny, which pleased the manager. Most nights I was able to do this, and on the nights that I wasn't, I might be out only a few dollars. In the end, it was like balancing a checkbook (a lost art, I know). The most difficult part was not the balancing, but keeping enough cash in your drawer. At times, if you had too much cash in your drawer, you would put it in the safe and just remember when you toted up your balances at day's end.

In a few days, I was in the groove. Most of the customers were doing straightforward transactions: depositing paychecks, cashing Social Security checks and traveler's checks, withdrawing money, and checking their balances. Also, people would come from local businesses—restaurants and delis, pushcarts and souvenir shops, mainly—to deposit large amounts of cash and coins to their company accounts.

Mondays and Fridays were especially busy. Many customers would come on Fridays to cash paychecks and withdraw money for the weekend. And on Mondays, people who had forgotten to withdraw their money came to fill up their wallets with cash.

Ethel, Ellen, and Tony were fun to work with, as was the bank manager, who treated me like an adult. I was glad to be in a more professional space, rather than having to clean poop off bathroom floors, deal with annoyed golfers, or stick my hand into a clattering pill machine. Most of our customers were friendly, polite, and patient.

But not everyone. Chief among the challenges were impatient customers, who, no matter how fast you counted their cash or checked their balances, thought it was never fast enough. They let you know by sighing theatrically or noisily drumming their fingers on the marble countertop in front of my window. My relative youth made me an easy target.

Once, a man wanted to deposit a large amount for his business and simply plopped a huge canvas bag at my window, gave me the deposit slip, and then glared at me, as if daring me to go slowly. There were a few thousand dollars in twenties and tens and fives in the bag, which I dutifully started to count as fast as I could, which was pretty fast. At one point, though, I fumbled and, perhaps because of his glare, forgot where I was—a rarity.

"My God, are you starting over?" he shouted. "I'm in a *hurry!*"

Ethel calmly walked over from her window. I knew what was coming.

"Is there a problem?" she said.

"Yes!" said the man. "He's too *slow!*"

Ethel smiled and said to me, "Jim, remember for big deposits like that, you should count it at least three times." The man's face blanched. Needless to say, she was making all this up.

"Oh, right," I said. "Three times."

"And do it slowly," she said, smiling at him. "So you don't miscount."

"Right," I said. "Slowly." That effectively shut him up.

But this type of customer was the exception, not the rule.

Elderly customers sometimes needed more help. Many wanted their Social Security checks cashed but also craved conversation, lingering at the window for a few minutes after their transaction was completed. How happy they were when you spent some time talking with them. Even when there were impatient people behind a retiree, rolling their eyes as the person slowly pulled the check out of a purse or pocket, smoothed it out on my counter, and then slowly endorsed it, I tried to be patient.

I often wondered whether that visit to the bank was their one human interaction of the day. Who knows? For all I know, all those retirees may have had scads of friends and eaten out every night of the week. But usually they seemed lonely, so I tried to be extra attentive and polite, even chatty.

It was another reminder of how people in service jobs can brighten people's lives. How often since then have I been in a store or restaurant, having a bad day, when someone's "Have a good day!" or "Good to see you again!" lifted my spirit. It doesn't take much to be friendly, and you don't need a PhD to be kind. Much of the Christian life (and the spiritual life in general) is about being kind. It's not the entirety of Christianity, but it's a big part.

And it works both ways. My mom told me the story of

a checkout woman at her supermarket who was always dour. Rather than be put off, my mom made it her goal to be pleasant to the woman. Eventually, the woman softened and shared with my mom what a hard life she was leading. Afterward, the two became friends.

Sometimes the bank customers needed reassurance. One day a woman handed me a withdrawal slip for $100. I checked her account to make sure she had enough funds, and then I turned over the slip to stamp it, our usual practice. On the back of the slip were written the words: "THIS IS A HOLD UP! GIVE ME ALL YOUR MONEY!"

This was a common prank that kids would play. In the middle of the banking floor were long, waist-high desks with black marble counters. Atop the desks were cubby holes with paper slips for deposits, withdrawals, and money orders. Often kids would pull out a slip, write something threatening on the back and replace it. Then, when the customer reached the window, they would unknowingly hand the teller the slip, who would turn it over and, so the thinking went, panic. In reality, all the tellers knew the trick. Still, it was hard to resist some playfulness.

I held the fake hold-up note up for her to read. "Did you write this?"

She squinted, read, and recoiled. "No! I didn't write that! I promise!"

I explained it was probably just some kids playing a prank.

Then she laughed. "But if you want to give me all your money, I won't complain!"

A few years later, my sister worked as a teller in a bank near our house and had her own share of stories. One elderly woman was particularly worried about having her purse snatched after visiting the bank to cash her Social Security check. (In those pre-ATM, pre-direct-deposit days, banks on the first day of the month saw a flurry of activity, thanks to Social Security check mailings.) My sister was tasked with taking this woman into the vault so that she could, privately, pin the money into the woman's bra. "I was happy to do it," my sister told me recently, "but I did joke that it wasn't one of the advertised services in our 'full-service banking.'"

Her branch was located on an island of land located at the intersection of two busy roads. One afternoon, she returned from lunch to find that a car had veered off one of the roads and crashed through the side of the bank, flinging the assistant manager's desk across the lobby floor. The employees who witnessed it were terrified, and the assistant manager could have been killed had she not been out to lunch. (The driver wasn't badly injured.) But even in the midst of the damage, my sister said, "There were plenty of jokes about our 'drive-through bank.'"

At one point during the summer, my parents and my sister went "down the shore," for a week's vacation. I stayed home.

I wasn't cross about being left behind: You obviously didn't get "vacation time" for a summer job. Also, as a nineteen-year-old college student, I thought spending time with my family seemed uncool. Besides, it meant that I'd have the house to myself, which meant having friends over whenever I wanted and doing whatever I wanted.

One Wednesday night, my friends decided on a trip to Six Flags Great Adventure amusement park, in New Jersey, about an hour's drive. The distance and the prospect of a late night, for which my friends were notorious, made me less than enthusiastic. But I caved to the invitation rather than look weak or overcautious. Besides, I loved my friends.

We left around dinnertime, arrived at the park around 7 p.m., and made a beeline to Rolling Thunder, a terrifying roller coaster that had debuted in 1979 and, as the TV commercials trumpeted, took passengers not only upside down but "BACK-WARDS!" I despised roller coasters but rode it three times with my friends, because who wanted to look like a coward in front of his friends?

After the park closed we hung out in the parking lot drinking beer and smoking pot. As time passed, I checked my watch and grew increasingly worried about getting a decent amount of sleep ahead of a workday. "Come on, Martin! Live a little!" said my friend Gordon. We left the park at 2 a.m. Then, all of us either drunk or high, we stopped at Dascoli's, our preferred twenty-four-hour diner back home. In the diner parking lot, my friend Barb, high for the first time in her life, said, "You know what's amazing?" We all looked at her. "My hands aren't connected to my arms anymore!"

We pulled into my driveway at 4 a.m., because I pleaded that I had to go to work in two hours. A few minutes later, when I looked out the window of our living room, smoke was, like something in a Cheech & Chong movie, still pouring out of the open windows of the car. The song "Emotional Rescue," by the Rolling Stones, was blaring on the radio.

Two hours later, having unsuccessfully tried to sleep, I headed for the A bus.

It was the first time I had stayed up all night. Yet I was surprisingly alert. On the ride into town, I thought, *Wow! I feel fine! I stayed up all night and feel great!*

How Not to Sacrifice Your Life for a Summer Job

Upon my arrival at the bank, I told my fellow tellers that I had been at Great Adventure at 2 a.m. "Aren't you tired?" said Ethel.

"Nope! I'm not tired *at all!*"

Ethel rolled her eyes. The morning passed uneventfully.

For lunch I wolfed down a huge cheesesteak and a Coke and returned to my window. Suddenly an enormous torpor overwhelmed me, like an ocean wave. I rested my chin on my hands, wanting nothing more than to sleep. The next thing I heard was "Sir! Sir!"

I awoke with a start and saw long lines of customers at each of the other three windows, but only one man at mine. Apparently, I had fallen asleep so soundly that one after another customer stopped by my window and fruitlessly tried to wake me, gave up, and then sought service from the other tellers. I had been asleep for ten minutes.

"Nope!" said Ethel, laughing. "I'm not tired *at all!*"

Like Ethel, I lived for the weekends. And my favorite place to spend them was at my friend John's house "down the shore."

John grew up in a warm, large, and exuberant Polish-Italian family in Conshohocken, the town next to Plymouth Meeting. We had grown close during my last two years of high school, and I considered him one of my best friends. Growing up, I felt a constant pressure to call someone my best friend, and my candidates for the title shifted from year to year. I also hoped that I would be considered someone's best friend, but it seemed pathetic to ask, "Am I your best friend?" But in those days I would say that it was John. We're still close today.

A year behind me in high school, John was a saxophone player in our marching band, which was at the time nationally ranked and with some two hundred members played an outsize role in the social life of our high school. Seemingly all my high school friends were members. I'm not sure how we first met, perhaps through our mutual friend Gordon. With John and Gordon and another friend, Bob, all of them in the band, we made a frequent quartet. John was kind, extroverted, and funny. And still is forty years later.

One of the most unexpected joys of being friends with John was being invited into his family, which was more boisterous than mine—and this is meant as a compliment. My own family laughed a lot, but there were only four of us. John's family included two brothers and three sisters, plus a revolving door of cousins, aunts, and uncles. Over the years, I came to know his family well. Sometimes I was invited to join them for birthday parties or Christmas Eve celebrations, which were fueled by pasta and/or Polish *golumpkis*, a kind of cabbage roll stuffed with meat.

His mother was a lively, diminutive woman of Italian descent who always seemed to be happy. Often at the end of a funny story about someone in her family, she would say, "It was so funny. We *laughed*." John and I good-naturedly imitated her, often ending our own stories with "we *laughed*." For good measure, John borrowed a phrase from my mother, who called him Johnny Boy. He started calling me Jimmy Boy, and still does.

John's dad was a friendly, taciturn man with salt-and-pepper hair and a walrus mustache who worked at the Lee Tire Factory as a pipefitter. Mr. Olszewski (pronounced *Ole-SHEF-ski*), something of a handyman, was forever tinkering with something in their house, reinforcing something with a two-by-four, fixing a pipe, or hammering away somewhere. He was usually smoking on a pipe filled with Captain Black tobacco, which gave him, and his house,

How Not to Sacrifice Your Life for a Summer Job

a distinctive smell, especially when mixed with Mrs. Olszewski's cooking.

When I first met the Olszewskis, I was deep into Jean Shepherd's stories, one of which reminded me of John's family. In "The Star-Crossed Romance of Josephine Cosnowski," Shepherd tells the tale of puppy love for the Catholic girl in his neighborhood. While some Polish Americans might object to Shepherd's overly broad but obviously affectionate characterizations of their culture, which as a Midwestern Protestant he found "exotic," I found the ebullient Cosnowskis in sync with the Olszewskis. Shepherd is especially good when describing their cuisine. Here he is on his first taste of *golumpkis*: "Taking a deep breath, I took a bite. For a moment, the heady mixture of cabbage, spice and meat was a great, wet wad in my mouth, and then its haunting, incandescent succulence, inevitability and *rightness* hit me where I lived."

John's brothers and sisters would occasionally take John and me on their adventures, including roller skating, which, while not wildly popular at the time (more a vestige of the 1950s than the 1980s), was popular with the Olszewskis. Thanks to spending time with my neighbor Carol's Protestant youth group (I never darkened the door of our parish's Catholic Youth Organization but fell in with Carol's friendly Presbyterian, ice-cream-eating, field-trip-taking youth group), I knew how to ice-skate. I was happy to discover that the skill translated well into roller skating.

Along with our friends, John and I spent an inordinate amount of time drinking and smoking pot, sometimes at the same time. His bong (the long contraption that uses water to filter marijuana) was named Opel, in honor of his dilapidated Opel car. Most of my friend's bongs had names, including "Seven Up," which was made by stacking together five used soda cans. One day, Opel tipped over in the back seat of the Opel, spilling bong juice all over the car's already ratty carpets. The dank smell never left his car.

John's family, like my own, wasn't wealthy but had saved up enough money to purchase a house in Strathmere, a town on the Jersey Shore. It was a small house, on stilts, with just a two-lane highway between it and the beach, but to me it seemed like a small paradise. Often, I would drive down with John in the Opel on Friday night after finishing with Western and stay until Sunday night.

Most weekends the house was packed with John's ever-extending family: Lunches were usually cold-cuts on fresh rolls, and dinners were large pots of spaghetti and meatballs.

Crabs were a specialty of Mrs. Olszewski, steamed in a huge pot and cracked open at the kitchen table. They were fished from the bay behind the house, thanks to a small motorboat they owned. On board the boat was a sign that read, "A boat is a hole in the water that you fill with money."

I had never been crabbing before, but Mr. Olszewski was an avid fisherman and taught me how to fasten a fish's head on the bottom of a metal cage that was open on all four sides and attached to a rope. When you lowered the cage from the boat onto the bottom of the bay, the sides would open, allowing the crabs to nibble away at the fish heads. An hour or so later, you would return and pull up the cages, which would close the doors on the crabs, trapping them.

My first day on the boat Mr. Olszewski taught me how to bait the trap, set it down gently overboard, then wait till it plunked onto the bottom, as the boat bobbed in the relatively calm waters of the bay. A few hours later, under a sunny sky, after tanking up at a gas station located on a dock, we pulled up the traps, now swarming with crabs. We had to throw back any females that were pregnant, but the rest we kept.

But the crabs looked strange: a dull, greenish-gray color. Not at all like the bright red crabs that I had seen the few times I had eaten them in restaurants. I mentioned that to Mr. Olszewski and he chuckled. Later that day, I mentioned it to Mrs. Olszewski, and she laughed too. "You'll see."

A few hours later she called me to a steaming pot of crabs on the stove, lifted the lid, and amid the clouds of steam pulled out with tongs a bright red crab. "See?" she said. "They turn red when you boil them." For the next few months that was a running joke between us. "Did you catch any of those red crabs today?" she would say.

Our weekends down the shore followed a pattern, almost religiously. John and I would arrive Friday night and go drinking at a ratty, crowded bar called the Ocean Drive (which we called the Ocean Dive), either by ourselves, or with other friends who were joining us, or with John's older brothers or sisters; come home around midnight; smoke pot on the beach; and then collapse into bed. We'd rise around 10 or 11 a.m., have some sandwiches with fresh cold-cuts and Jersey tomatoes, then head to the beach, or out on the boat, then have dinner and start all over again. We stayed as late as we could on Sundays.

One Sunday, after foolishly falling asleep on the beach, I got a savage sunburn, mainly on the tops of my feet, which I had neglected to cover with sunscreen. (I've got a fair complexion or, as my Jesuit brothers whose last names begin with *O'* or *Mc'* say, "cheap Irish skin.") My feet started to burn along with the rest of my body around my third or fourth crab at dinner.

Mrs. Olszewski said, "Oh Jimmy, you're so *red*! You should take some aspirin."

"Aspirin?" I had never heard that before.

"Yes!" she said insistently. "Aspirin helps with sunburn."

I politely said that I would try it, but later I told John that I had never heard anything so dumb. Aspirin was for headaches, not sunburn.

That same day John needed to move a couch from the shore house to his off-campus digs. (John was also at Penn.) In the process of moving it from the house to the Opel, I scratched my leg on a rusty nail. During the two-hour-long drive home, I grew more concerned about the gash on my leg, which was dripping blood on the floor. John was his usual sanguine self: "Jimmy Boy, stop worrying! You'll be *fiiiine*!" Nonetheless, after we dropped off his couch, we stopped at Student Health at the Hospital of the University of Pennsylvania (which, since services were supposedly so slow you could die while waiting, we called Student Death).

By this point, I was scarlet. We wandered into the emergency room, and I sat on a gurney until a doctor saw us.

"Wow!" said the young doctor. "Are you here for that sunburn?" I pointed to my leg and told him about my run-in with the rusty nail.

He gave me a tetanus shot, bandaged up my leg, and said, "And as for the sunburn, you should take some aspirin."

John gave out one of his braying laughs. "Wait till I tell my mom!"

Indeed, she never forgot it, and would recount the story if I doubted anything she said. "Remember when I told you to use aspirin for your sunburn? That was funny. We *laughed*."

The next day my feet were so swollen I could barely fit them into my loafers. My mother was sympathetically horrified. She advised moisturizing lotion and said, "Take some aspirin too." Apparently, they had both learned this at Philadelphia Mothers School.

On the bus the next morning I was in a fair amount of pain. Having sunburn under a long-sleeved shirt and a tie and long pants is quite different from having it under shorts and a T-shirt. I could barely walk the few blocks from the bus stop downtown and made a great grimacing entrance into the bank, hoping for sympathy.

"Wow!" said Ethel. "Someone was down the shore this weekend!"

Gingerly I walked over to my window and opened it. "Ho hum," said Ethel. "Is it Friday yet?" In a few minutes the customers came in.

Behind the counter I realized that standing in my now too-tight shoes was quite painful. No way could I stand in them all day. I slipped them off and felt much better. A few minutes later, I had to do some work for a customer on the back table, so I left my window and walked a few steps back. He leaned over the counter and peered down at my feet.

"Tellers don't wear shoes?" he said. "Boy, you learn something new every day."

That summer of fish heads and sunburns did not mark the end of Western Savings Bank. During the winter break of my junior year, I worked at another branch, not far from home, in a shopping center in the West Oak Lane section of Philadelphia. This was a smaller branch, and though the other tellers were friendly, I missed my teller friends and the cheesesteak spots in Center City. All I remember is driving through the cold rain and snow to get there early in the morning, through an unfamiliar neighborhood, and that, owing to the time of year, it was dark outside when I returned home. I often felt a pang of regret that I wasn't working in sunny, humid, somewhat safer Center City.

Nor did that summer mark the end of partying. School breaks were still made for fun, and although I was not a wild kid, my birthday celebration that year was notably debauched.

John, Gordon, and another friend named Greg and I piled into John's Opel and drove the few miles into Philadelphia, across the Walt Whitman Bridge, and into New Jersey, because the drinking age there was nineteen—rather than twenty-one in Pennsylvania. The law was laughingly enforced at the bars near Penn, but my birthday came during the Christmas break when our favorite bars were closed. So off to New Jersey.

Across the Delaware River was a store called Roger Wilco, still there, which to a Pennsylvanian younger than twenty-one in search of alcohol seemed like Xanadu: endless aisles of liquor bottles, marshaled like little glass soldiers in colorful paper coats, lit up by fluorescent lights as if by the noonday sun.

Then we did the following, whose sequence I can remember for reasons that will become clear: We purchased a case of Foster's beer, drank that, drove to a nearby strip club, saw a "show," after which we downed a few rounds of kamikazes (a clear mixture of vodka, triple sec, and lime juice), drove back across the Walt Whitman Bridge, returned to Plymouth Meeting, ate stacks of pancakes at a local diner, went bowling for an hour, and returned to John's Opel and got high with the other Opel. Then, on the way home, when we felt the inevitable need to relieve ourselves, we passed the recently completed foundations for a group of homes still being built, got out of the car, figured out where bathrooms would be located, and urinated in the holes of the concrete foundations as we shouted to each other, "We're the first people to use their bathrooms!" Then John dropped us off, and I went to bed at 4 a.m.

The next day, actually my birthday, I awoke with the worst hangover before or since. By dinner time I felt mildly better. My parents were furious with me, since unlike at other times when I had been able to hide my hangover, this one was as clear as day. My mom had bought my favorite birthday cake—vanilla cake with vanilla icing and blue roses—from my favorite bakery a few miles away. But because I was so nauseated from the night before, I couldn't eat it.

As we were opening gifts at our kitchen table, my friend Bob called. "I heard from John what you did last night! I can't believe I wasn't there!" Since my parents and sister were listening, I tried, unsuccessfully, to play down what had happened.

"We have to go again!" he said.

"No way!" I said. But, desperate for people to like me, including Bob, I agreed.

I hung up the phone and told my parents, "I'm going out."

"*Jim*, you were just out last night!" said my dad. "Isn't that enough for one week?"

"You haven't even touched your cake and it's your favorite!" said my mom.

"Come on! It's *my* birthday!" I raced upstairs and called John and Gordon and Greg, and I left, to my parents' dismay, and we repeated the night, step by step, including the pee break at the new houses.

I share this story for a few reasons: It's outlandish, it represents what teenage boys considered fun in the 1980s, it's memorable for me, and it's one of the stories I tell when people ask me, "Did you live a real life before you entered the Jesuits?"

I also include this story because it shows that people are complex and can change and grow. Today I look back on that night with a mix of fondness (for my friends, with whom I'm still close), amazement (especially over Bob, who prevailed upon four hungover friends to repeat themselves), remorse (for disappointing my parents and my sister, who had tried to make a nice birthday for me, only to see me fly from the house selfishly after a phone call), embarrassment (that we twice visited a place called Live Nude Girls, which even then I found seedy and revolting), but most of all compassion for a teenager who was happy to know, on his birthday, that his friends loved him, even though he was more concerned about that than the love that his family showed him. I can still see that uneaten cake on our kitchen table and the disappointed faces on my mom and dad and sister.

This was far from the only debauched night of my youth. As one example among many, a few months after this bacchanal, we took my friend Peter, a friend from Penn, to the same strip club, which my Penn friends desperately wanted to see after hearing my story. In a bar afterward we ordered rounds of clear kamikazes for Peter, while we, in cahoots with the bartender, drank only shots of water. After five shots, Peter wondered why we weren't as drunk as he was. (An earlier version of this manuscript included many more such tales, including more escapades fueled by alcohol and pot, friends dragging me to X-rated movies, and so on. But I thought understatement might be best here.)

Nothing my friends and I did that night was criminal, except underage drinking and perhaps urinating on newly built foundations, which I suppose was trespassing. And one thing we did was immoral: I consider strip clubs exploitative of the people who work in them.

But it was what teenagers did. At least unreflective ones like me. So almost a half century later, as a Jesuit priest, when I meet people who regret something they did as a young adult, or even in the recent past, and feel a sense of shame, and then look at me, as people sometimes do, as if I am some kind of saint, or someone who never did anything untoward, or a person who doesn't know what it's like to have set a foot wrong, I often think back to that night, and I have compassion for them. And for myself.

The rest of my winter vacation was calmer, although it took a few days to recover from that two-night binge. Sometimes on my way home from Western Savings Bank from West Oak Lane on a snowy day, I would pass those houses being built and wonder whether we had been right about the placement of the bathrooms on the foundations. Eventually, they started framing the houses. In a few months, they were completed and occupied.

My mom and dad lived in Plymouth Meeting for many more years. So I would often return home to see them, my aunts and uncles and cousins, and friends like John and Gordon and Greg and Bob, often during the holidays. And from time to time I would pass that group of houses.

Today I often see those houses, now decades old, hidden behind tall trees, and remember that birthday with my friends all those years ago and all the conflicting emotions I felt, and still feel, about it. But mostly now I smile about that night, and whenever I spy one house in particular, I imagine knocking on the door and asking, "Can I use your bathroom again?"

3924 Spruce Street (on the left). Brad's room was on the first floor in the front.

In front of 3924 Spruce Street. The photographer snapped us as we were still arranging ourselves, which means that some of us are chatting and I'm jostling for position between Bruce and Peter. *Front row (from the left):* Gordon, Bruce, me, Peter, Andy, Rob. *Second row:* Brad, Michael, Mindy, George. *Third row:* Dave, Jacque, Eugene. *Last row:* Jean and Mark.

CHAPTER 8

How I Became a (Sort of) Stockbroker and, Then, an Adult

AS JUNIOR YEAR DREW TO A CLOSE, ALMOST EVERYONE in my class at Wharton started to look for a summer internship. The belief was that if you did well enough at your summer internship then you could effortlessly slide into a job at the same company after graduation.

This was decades before the advent of the now-common unpaid summer internship. In the 1980s, companies rightly paid college and high school students for their labor. Moreover, I would have considered the idea of working and not being paid, given my financial situation, to be insane. I didn't like it when I was delivering *The Recorder* either. If I wasn't going to get paid for something, I'd rather not get paid for sitting on our back porch reading.

Penn's Career Planning and Placement office, which would soon make it absurdly easy to apply for a job after graduation, was equally adept at finding us placements for the summer. As I recall (and it's strange to say that I can remember how much Savarol to use in making popcorn but not how I got this job) Career Planning put me in touch with The Pennsylvania Group, a discount stockbrokerage in Bala Cynwyd (pronounced *Bala KIN-wood*), Pennsylvania. The town was founded by Welsh Quakers in the 1680s, who eventually named it after two towns in Wales—Bala and Cynwyd.

We all have different gifts, and one of mine is that I can return in my mind to a scene from decades ago and more or less picture what it looked like: the back room at the Ice Cream Inn, the Letters Room at the Cinema on the Mall, the teller windows at Western Savings Bank—even though all these places are long gone. When I visited the Philadelphia Cricket Club forty years after working there, I was surprised at how the reality matched my memories. I also remember conversations, especially funny ones, because they imprint themselves on my mind and I often end up retelling them—maybe too often!

But I'm probably the least reliable when it comes to timing and sequences—when I started looking for work during that year, when I began a particular job, even how long I was there. Visuals stick with me; other things, less so.

My poor memory prompted me to see what I could find online about my manager from that summer, who was also the founder of the firm: Anthony Buford, whom everyone called Tony. A dapper, handsome, well-dressed man who reminded me of Cary Grant, he was almost impossibly preppy, having attended Deerfield Academy, the University of Virginia, and then Wharton for an MBA. I thought that it would be fun to email Tony and ask him for some memories of what I was like as an intern, and I was ready for the worst, since, like my experience in Penn's Student Financial Aid office, at The Pennsylvania Group I never shook the feeling that I wasn't sure of what I was doing. I was ready to hear him laugh and say, "You weren't our best employee!"

I found Tony all over the web and discovered on LinkedIn that The Pennsylvania Group had moved to Vero Beach, which instantly confirmed that I had the right guy. Vero Beach was a name I first heard from his lips that summer. I had no clue where it was, but it sounded posh.

But a few lines down from the LinkedIn listing, I saw this brief notice, published just a few weeks before I went online looking for him, from TCPalm, which carries news from the Palm Beach area: "Anthony A. Buford, Jr. of Vero Beach, Florida, passed away peacefully on February 1, 2023."

How sad that made me! How I would have liked to thank him for being gracious to me that summer. The obituary told a bit about the good-natured manager who hired me and the company I worked for: "After Business School, Tony joined the investment firm Drexel and Company and would become a Director, Executive Committee Member, Director of Corporate Planning, Chair of Drexel Funds, and President of Drexel Hedge Fund. In 1970, he co-founded the Pennsylvania Group, Inc., an investment and trading brokerage firm. A pioneer in the discount brokerage industry, The Pennsylvania Group was later sold to The Wilmington Trust Company."

Tony Buford could not have been more generous to a soon-to-be Wharton grad who, while having done well in his coursework, was not as interested as he could have been in the stock market. Many of my classmates were not only intelligent and hardworking (if occasionally cutthroat), but they also found reading *The Wall Street Journal* and *Fortune* and *Forbes* magazines fascinating, whereas I found them a chore. This was an early glimmer, or to use Evelyn Waugh's phrase in *Brideshead Revisited*, a "bat's squeak," of a message that perhaps the corporate world was not for me.

But in those days, I *wanted* it to be. And here is where I should have been more reflective as a college student and where Wharton disappointed me a bit.

Before Penn's alumni office takes offense, let me be clear: Wharton gave my classmates and me a superb undergraduate business education, perhaps the best in the country, maybe even the world. I can't imagine being better trained in accounting, economics, finance, management, and pretty much anything business-related. And in the years since, though I studied diligently during my Jesuit philosophy and theology studies, I've never worked as hard academically as I did at Wharton, where the amount of work required was often brutal. If I had to single out a specific course, I would say that I've never studied as hard as I did in Accounting 1A, Introduction to Accounting, which made my later philosophy and theology courses seem a breeze in comparison. So I'm grateful to Penn for a good education and for helping me make lifelong friends.

The big problem was that no one ever asked me what I wanted to do with my life.

As a high school senior, I was elated to be accepted into Wharton. That enthusiasm continued unabated for four years. I was proud—too proud—of being at Wharton and at an Ivy League school. Still, once you stepped onto Wharton's conveyor belt, which delivered you from Intro to Accounting to a high-paying job, few people asked you whether you were going in the right direction. Or whether you were on the right conveyor belt. Or even whether the belt itself made sense.

Business is a vocation for many people, including most of my classmates at Wharton. They enjoyed studying business, happily entered the business world, led fulfilling lives, and contributed to the common good. And after graduation, when I worked at General Electric, most of my colleagues there enjoyed their work. Some spent their entire careers with General Electric. They led happy, productive, and generous lives—marks of a vocation, a word that comes from the Latin *vocare*, to call. It was a calling for them.

But at no point did anyone at Wharton ask us, or at least me, "What kind of life would you like to lead?" "What is your calling?" or, more basically, "What kind of person do you want to become?" Maybe it was my fault for not asking these questions of myself, but as a young man I was largely incapable of that kind of self-reflection.

My parents didn't force me to study business. But as Depression-era children, they were intent on making sure that their children got good jobs. "Everyone has to work!" my parents would often say. The unspoken assumption was that our work would be in an office. Business seemed to be what everyone did: The fathers in our neighborhood "went to work," and that, I assumed, meant going to an office. And the best way to prepare for that, it seemed, was by studying business. And the best undergraduate business school, so we were told, was Wharton.

All roads seemed to lead to business. My high school career counselors were supportive of that path, even though the only course I took that was remotely related to business was typing.

So onto that conveyor belt I stepped.

Once you were at Wharton, no one challenged the wisdom of a business career. Why would they? No doubt they reasoned that if you applied to Wharton, had been accepted, and hadn't transferred to another major, then you wanted to be there. Who wouldn't want to be there? Hundreds of people would have taken our places if we had turned down our letters of admission.

But the focus on business to the exclusion of all else meant there were few opportunities to see whether you might be interested in anything else. Maybe things are different now, but at the time, no one asked those deeper questions of us.

Also, an unforeseen effect of my having taken a few Advanced Placement courses in high school was that I had "placed out" of a number of electives in the humanities. That meant that pretty much all my courses were in business.

Taking challenging courses outside of your business requirements was also a no-no at Wharton. Toward the end of one semester, I met with my faculty adviser, whose job was to ensure I was fulfilling the requirements for graduation. In the spring of freshman year, already deep into my business courses, I told him that I was thinking of registering for a course in American poetry. His eyes widened. "Why?" he said.

"Well," I said, "I thought it might be interesting." He rolled his eyes.

"I would strongly advise you against taking anything like that," he said. "It will only take time away from your real work. If you take a nonbusiness course, then at least take an easy one." He glanced at the syllabus for American Poetry and read aloud, "Walt Whitman, Emily Dickinson, T. S. Eliot . . ." He trailed off. "When interviewing time comes, no one will care how you did in a *poetry course*."

He let that sink in and said, "Can you imagine anyone at Goldman Sachs giving a damn about Emily Dickinson?"

Resisting my usual desire not to offend anyone, I ignored his well-meaning advice, took the course, and today remember more from American Poetry than from Real Estate Finance.

The other problem with my otherwise rigorous and marketable Wharton education was a lack of reflection on a topic I would later study as a Jesuit: business ethics.

In the early 1980s, the predominant, almost exclusive, economic approach taught at Wharton was called either "free-market capitalism" or "laissez-faire capitalism" (the basis of what is sometimes termed "neoliberalism"). Its champion was the University of Chicago economics professor and Nobel laureate Milton Friedman, who built on the work of classical economists like Adam Smith. The theory, in a nutshell, is that if everyone pursues their own economic interests (for example, opening a business in response to an economic need and closing it when the need dries up and the business is no longer profitable), the entire economy benefits. Smith called this the "Invisible Hand," a clever image of individual financial ambition untrammeled by intrusive governmental planning (which would never be able to keep up with constantly shifting market forces) almost magically (invisibly) creating the most productive economic system, and the most wealth, for all. In general, I agreed (and agree today) with the proposal that the most efficient markets are those with the least regulation.

The problem is that we were never asked about the visible people whom the Invisible Hand failed to provide for: the poor. Or, as one of my econ professors called them, the "transitional poor"—those who were poor only temporarily, until the market could lift them up, as it would, in time, presumably lift all boats in the rising tide of economic success. All you had to do was walk a few blocks away to West Philadelphia and see low-income families struggling to earn a living to know that the Invisible Hand didn't help everyone: The system was flawed. Clearly some regulation, some safety nets, some *compassion*, was needed. Besides, there were plenty of special non-free-market accommodations in the tax laws that tipped the scales toward the wealthy. All this seems obvious to me now. But at Wharton, acceptance of free-market capitalism was akin to a religious dogma; critiques were at best tolerated and at worst ridiculed.

The system could also lead to selfishness and greed. That result was depicted a few years later in the 1987 film *Wall Street*, in which Michael Douglas, as the financier Gordon Gekko, declared, "Greed, for lack of a better word, is good. Greed is right. Greed works." His quote was inspired by the real-life financier Ivan Boesky, who, the year before, was convicted, fined, and sentenced for his role in an insider-trading scheme. As part of his plea deal, Boesky implicated Michael Milken, who pioneered junk bonds, in securities fraud, which later led to Milken's indictment and imprisonment. Milken received his MBA from Wharton.

The fictional Gekko was right: Greed powers the economy. But without a sense of the common good, greed can lead simply to more greed, more selfishness, and finally more misery for those whom the market fails to provide for.

From my standpoint, all I was doing was learning what my professors were teaching me about economics and finance. It was a kind of values-free education (even though Penn's motto is *Leges Sine Moribus Vanae*: Laws without morals are useless). Besides, I hadn't cheated or defrauded anyone. And the poor didn't figure into my consciousness much if at all. Free-market capitalism seemed to work well, and so what if there were "transitional poor"? As for challenging the economic status quo, well, we were studying something that was simply there, like the weather. Critiquing it would have been like critiquing the rain at the Cricket Club.

It's perhaps also unfair to have expected my faculty adviser to ask me to reflect on my underlying vocation. He probably would have been fired if he said, "Ever think about the priesthood?" I was at Wharton, after all, not a seminary or a psychologist's office; and my parents and I were both paying a lot for the privilege of my being there. To that end, the question of how to pay off all those student loans also pointed to a job that paid a decent wage.

So I stayed on course, filled with pride for my Wharton credential, interested in my classes, committed to working hard, not bothered by any moral qualms, and excited about the money I would earn, but with a nagging, unspoken question: Will this make me happy? Or the question that every young person should be asked at least once: What would you do if you could do anything you wanted?

For the time being, I tabled those questions and stayed on the conveyor belt. Next stop: a summer job at a discount stockbrokerage, the proximate step to success on Wall Street. And I'd be lying if I said I wasn't excited. Even more than the teller job, where I came to know the actual scent of cash, this job smelled like money.

While my foray into commercial banking made me feel like I had grown up, it was the summer at The Pennsylvania Group that ushered me into the world of finance and made me know that I had left manual labor behind. There is absolutely no shame in those jobs: Most of the adults in those workplaces were decent people earning a living for themselves and their families. But manual labor wasn't what I wanted for a lifetime career. The Pennsylvania Group was more up my alley. A few days after junior year ended, I started at this discount stockbrokerage.

The Pennsylvania Group was located in a shopping center plaza in Bala Cynwyd next to a Saks Fifth Avenue store, a thirty-minute commute from our house. Since I now had a "real job," my parents let me use our Gran Torino. The ride took me from Plymouth Meeting through Roxborough, my mom's old neighborhood, down the hill into Manayunk and Wissahickon, the working-class sections of the city where my cousins Ricky and Tommy had lived (now trendy neighborhoods), across the Schuylkill River, past the sylvan West Laurel Hill Cemetery, and up Belmont Avenue (so called because of the commanding view of Philadelphia from the top of the hill) to the shopping center.

The first day at The Pennsylvania Group Tony spent an hour explaining what they did, some of which I knew from Wharton, but not all. A discount stockbrokerage caters mainly to individual investors and executes "buy-and-sell" orders on their behalf. Unlike a full-service brokerage, it generally does not provide investment advice, though the smart and friendly associates at The Pennsylvania Group often did in a more casual way with some long-term customers.

Discount stockbrokerages had burst into the financial world a few years before, after the Securities and Exchange Commission deregulated commissions on trading stocks. Before that, the high fees charged by full-service brokerages meant that only institutions and wealthier individuals could afford to buy and sell stocks. That changed with the SEC's deregulation in 1975. Deregulation substantially altered the costs of commissions, which were now regulated only by market forces and therefore dropped dramatically. This marked the advent of the discount brokerage boom. (Perhaps the most well-known discount stockbrokerages were Charles Schwab and TD Waterhouse.) In 1980, 13 percent of Americans owned stock, either directly or indirectly. By 1989 the figure had dramatically increased to 32 percent.

My job was to keep records of what was bought and sold during the day, as well as field questions and phone calls and direct people to the actual brokers in our firm, who themselves would speak with brokers on the floor of the New York Stock Exchange. I couldn't make the trades because I wasn't a registered representative, which required hours of study in order to pass the Series 7 exam. But I could still take down orders, fill out the paperwork needed to execute a trade, tell clients what prices their stocks were trading at—this was long before the internet, so it involved checking the newspapers, where the stock prices were listed; calling other brokers; and following an electronic stock ticker, which we had in the office—and answer any noninvestment questions. Even though I was filled with ideas about what to say to investors, based on a few years at Wharton, I was not allowed to. Nor should I have been.

Here's how I described it on my resumé the next year, which I found in a scrapbook: "Summer intern in discount stockbrokerage. Performed market research on low-activity accounts. Assisted in back office with duties including security quotation, mailing of open order and daily trade confirmations. Also served as replacement cashier, duties included maintenance and recording of securities, customer payments and trade proceeds."

Frankly, I can't remember what half of those terms mean now. It was a congenial place with a small staff who were unfailingly kind. No one asked me to stick my hand in a whirring machine, yelled at me for dropping a banana split glass, or ordered me to stand in a thunderstorm with their golf bag. And I wasn't cleaning up any vomit. So I was happy. The rest of the staff were traders who would execute the orders and then track the performance of the stocks for our clients. The Pennsylvania Group was the first job that I felt made use of what I was learning at Wharton. Sometimes Tony would ask whether I understood how what I had just done (a trade, offer a bit of advice) related to my courses at Wharton and whether I had any questions for him about the business. Tony and his small staff could not have been more helpful.

But I don't remember as much about that summer job as I do about others in this book. Maybe that's because working at a discount stockbrokerage meant that occasions for getting covered with popcorn flavoring, gumming up a machine with a ruler, or getting high were more limited. The stories aren't as memorable. What I chiefly remember are the car rides back and forth to Bala Cynwyd; Tony and the rest of his staff, especially Nancy and Dennis, two young brokers, tutoring me on the ins and outs of trading stocks; and a diner down the street called Mama's, which had the best cheesesteaks outside of Center City.

The other reason I don't remember much about that job is because the summer was dominated by something else.

On Saturday, May 30, 1981, I was on our back porch, barefoot, stretched out on a lounge chair, again plowing through *The Glory and the Dream,* by William Manchester. A doorstop of a book that I had started a few summers before, it was the kind of self-education project that I had liked to impose on myself: big, important, *impressive* books, because I felt that my Wharton classes weren't helping me in my quest to be more "well-rounded."

That summer I divided my reading time between Manchester's book and ones that I found more diverting: *Watership Down*, Richard Adams's book about a colony of rabbits trying to establish a new home (which sounds awful but was an engrossing social allegory), and Jack Higgins's novel *The Eagle Has Landed*, a World War II thriller about a plot to kidnap Winston Churchill. And my old standbys: Jean Shepherd on growing up in Depression-era Indiana and Brad Steiger on aliens, ghosts, and poltergeists.

The cicadas were buzzing on a humid day, the temperature in the eighties. My mom opened the metal porch door, which always screeched loudly. "Someone's on the phone for you," she said.

I put the book down and padded upstairs to my parents' bedroom, which had a separate phone line. Now twenty years old, I had discarded the custom of speaking on our main phone in the kitchen, because I preferred privacy.

It was Andy, one of my friends from Penn.

I had kept the same group of friends since freshman year in college. During our junior year, many of us banded together to rent an ornate but ratty Victorian row home in West Philadelphia with a big front porch and marvelous ornamentation outdoors and dark wainscoting indoors. Though technically off campus, 3924 Spruce Street was across the street from dorms and classroom buildings.

The house was the hub of my social life at Penn. Looking back, it prepared me for life in a Jesuit community: living in a house with a group of people from a variety of backgrounds who didn't always agree on everything. But unlike Jesuit community life, women lived with us as well. Also unlike Jesuit life, we frequently hosted themed dance parties, fueled by beer, wine, and grain alcohol, and accompanied by music from Blondie, the Police, the Cars, Bruce Springsteen, and especially the Go-Go's. In my mind we were forever singing and dancing to "We Got the Beat" in our crowded and overheated dining room with friends and strangers and jumping up and down in sweaty ecstasy. These parties, which packed our house several times a year, took me a few days to recover from.

Since most of my college friends did not live in the Philadelphia area, I saw them only rarely during the summer break, when I hung out with friends from high school. So it was nice to hear from Andy, probably the most sensible, rational-minded, and direct person in our group of college friends. In time he would become an attorney, and then an assistant US attorney.

"*Jim,*" he said over the phone.

"Hey, Andy," I said. "How are you?"

It's hard for me to remember exactly what Andy said, but I remember what I was doing: sitting on the floor, cross-legged, next to my parents' bed, atop their gold shag carpet.

Andy told me that my freshman-year roommate, Brad, had been killed in an automobile accident earlier that day. Driving the car was our housemate Michael. Michael's girlfriend, Mindy, was also killed. Suzy, Brad's girlfriend, had been seriously injured.

I could barely take it in. I burst into tears and raced downstairs to tell my parents. "Brad's dead!" My mother and father sought to comfort me. "Oh no!" said my mother with a look of horror on her face. "What happened?" said my dad. Brad had visited our house several times and had stayed over once during a holiday weekend. My parents were very fond of him.

My mom tried to hug me, but I ran into my bedroom, slammed the door, and knelt next to my bed and sobbed into the bedspread. I felt unmoored, violently separated from the adult way of being cool in the world, and reduced to my emotions. I cried like a baby and felt like a child. But of course this was my introduction into adulthood and the life of suffering. Nothing like this had ever happened to me. I didn't know how to take it in, to process it, even how to react.

"What happened?" my dad said to my mom. I could hear them through the door.

Many years later, Michael, who later became a physician, described what happened in a book he wrote on holistic health and healing.

> When I was twenty, a junior in college, I was spending the weekend away at my family's country home in upstate New York with one of my best friends, Brad, and his girlfriend, Suzy, as well as my first love, Mindy, the woman I believed would one day become my wife. While driving along a winding country road on a balmy summer day, our axle snapped, and the car flipped over numerous times. Mindy and Brad were killed instantly, and Suzy was horribly injured. Somehow, perhaps because I was the driver and had the steering wheel to hold on to, I walked away from the accident unscathed. However, the crash ripped my world apart. There I was one second with the windows down feeling the warm afternoon breeze beside the girl I loved, at the very height of my youth and hope—and one second later, it was all tumbling over the asphalt, landing in a heap of torn metal, glass, and the blood of the people I loved.

More than forty years later, I have a hard time conveying my shock. But perhaps you've had experiences like this yourself. In a datebook that I still have, May 30 is scratched out.

• • • •

Brad and I had been close as freshman-year roommates. A few years ago during an alumni reunion, I visited our room in the Quad and was stunned by its size. A cinder-block rectangle of maybe twenty by ten feet, it contained two small desks, two slim armoires, two modest bureaus, and two pull-out beds that doubled as sofas, which when pulled out were only a foot from each other. How did we live in such a cramped space? How had I even slept?

I enjoyed Brad's company immensely and envied him for his seeming effortless cool. A wrestler, film aficionado, and sometime poet, he was fun to be around. (Women seemed to agree: Brad had a string of girlfriends through college.) He seemed freer than me, and that included his chosen field of study at Penn. Brad would sometimes roll his eyes at my Wharton classes, not mocking them outright (at least not often) but finding them less captivating than his film studies at Penn's Annenberg School for Communication. His highest praise for a film was to call it interesting, or as he would say, "*inn*-arresting." Some Friday or Saturday nights he would drag me to a showing of a film by Hitchcock or Truffaut or Eisenstein somewhere on campus. Brad was a fun, smart, confident guy. In the summer after our freshman year I spent a weekend at his family's house outside of Washington, DC, with his parents and sisters, all of whom were equally smart and welcoming. And preppy.

During sophomore year, before our group moved off campus, Brad and I lived together in a high-rise dorm with another friend, Pete, from our hall, and a fourth person assigned to our trio. By then Brad had focused his future plans on combining music and video. I told him that I couldn't understand how he could possibly make a living with that, but he was adamant: video and music. I made fun of that and deemed it insane. Two months after his death, MTV debuted.

As I've mentioned, Brad was the one who taught me the right way to dress and introduced me to the New Wave music that defines that time for me. He loved listening to the Police, Blondie, the Clash, and, above all, Elvis Costello. He played Elvis Costello's "Alison" over and over on his cassette player till I knew all the lyrics. Brad couldn't sing that well but loved the last few lines of that somewhat dark song:

Alison, I know this world is killing you.
Oh, Alison, my aim is true.
My aim is true.

Brad was a direct guy, largely uninterested in what other people said about him. He tried to say what he meant and to do what he said he'd do. As I saw it, his aim was true.

He also tried to coax me out of what he saw as my square shell. During our first week at college, I told him about my high school activities: Student Council president, yearbook, the student newspaper, the musical, National Honor Society. His immediate comparison was to the uber-square comic-book character: "Oh my God," he said, "I'm living with Archie Andrews!"

He tried his best to loosen me up, sometimes with the practical jokes that became a staple of our freshman hall. One night, coming home late from drinking, Brad opened the door to our room and announced that he was too tired to go to the bathroom, which was at the other end of the hall.

"What?" I said, half awake.

"I'm too tired to go to the bathroom," he said. As I lay in my bed in the dark, I heard the unmistakable sound of jeans being unzipped and liquid streaming into a sink basin. I couldn't believe he was peeing in our sink!

"Hey!" I said, sitting bolt upright in bed. "What are you *doing*?" I flipped on the lights.

Brad was standing next to the sink, fully clothed, pants zipped up, with his hand on the faucet, as a thin stream of water emptied into the sink, making a trickling sound. He laughed his barking laugh. "Gotcha, Martin!"

Once, too poor to afford any food one Friday night, Brad and I saw a flyer for a reception at Penn's International House, the dormitory for international students. We had no connection to anyone in that dorm, and I was too narrow-minded to befriend any international students, but free food held enough appeal for us to walk twenty minutes under cloudy, threatening skies. We stuffed ourselves with free hors d'oeuvres and then split. On the way home, it began to drizzle, then rain, and then pour. In a few minutes, we were drenched, our shoes soaking wet.

Brad just laughed, looked up at the rain, let out a whoop, and took off his Top-Siders. He punched me in the arm and said over and over, "Take 'em off! Take 'em off! Take 'em off!" Practically allergic to getting rained on, I took off my sneakers and enjoyed the torrential rain. We walked barefoot on the flooded sidewalks, laughing the whole way. When we arrived at our dorm, our friends just stared at us. It was one of the first memories I have of not caring what other people thought. Brad was the one who got me there.

This was who had been killed. I couldn't stop thinking of the jeep rolling on top of him and his vibrant life ending in an instant.

The night before the funeral in Washington, DC, I drove to our house off campus to meet my friends who had driven down from New York City. I think it was the first time I had cried in front of people who were not my family. I remember wandering aimlessly around the house, ill equipped to handle this. What was I supposed to do?

All I felt was sadness and shock, and all I could do was cry. And I felt like whenever I opened my mouth, something stupid came out.

The movie *Ordinary People* had come out the year before, and I felt like the main character, Conrad Jarrett, a teenager overwhelmed with conflicting feelings about his older brother's accidental death. The film spoke to me on a visceral level, probably because it depicted the emotional life of a boy my age. In one scene Conrad's psychiatrist asks him how he felt on the day of his brother's death. Conrad doesn't know what to feel—or say. "I kept thinking what they say on TV," he says, "you know, stuff like: 'Oh, no, noo! Ooh, my God!'" I thought a lot about that scene in the days and weeks following the accident.

Brad's funeral service was on a hot day in Potomac, Maryland, at his family's Episcopal church. It was a simple building with a stark interior, its white pews trimmed with pine railings stained dark. Colonial. Dignified. Preppy, I thought stupidly, just like Brad.

Did we drive back home that night? I don't remember. I do remember that in the pew behind me was a former girlfriend of Brad's who placed her hand on my shoulder as I wept. I was so embarrassed for crying in front of my friends. Brad and I were close, but he wasn't my best friend. In fact, in recent months, we hadn't been as close as we were that first year of college. This I accepted sometimes with grace; other times, with jealousy toward those with whom he was closer. I felt small thinking about those things during his funeral: whether I was his "best friend" or not; whether he liked me as much as he liked others. I felt confused about what I was feeling, or should be feeling.

But there was something I wasn't confused about.

As the pastor spoke of God's love and mercy, and the gift that Brad had been, I felt something inside me shift. I didn't want to believe in God any longer. It was stupid.

My friend Peggy recently told me, "You seemed about as angry as I've ever seen you, though you didn't usually express anger in a straightforward way."

I've not spoken much about God in these pages. That's not because I didn't believe in God. I did. Rather, God didn't play a big role in my life during high school and college.

God didn't figure much into my summer jobs, the ostensible focus of this book, unless I was saying "Oh my God!" when standing in the lightning storm at the Cricket Club or "Jesus Christ!" when told that someone had vomited in the bathroom at the Cinema on the Mall.

My Catholic family went to Mass most Sundays. But we weren't the kind of family who said grace at every meal, prayed the Rosary together, or talked about God much, if at all. Neither my sister nor I went to a Catholic elementary school or Catholic high school, and Penn certainly was not a Catholic college. As a boy, I went to Sunday School (called CCD back then: Confraternity of Christian Doctrine) and "made" my First Holy Communion and was confirmed not long afterward. But my relationship to God was largely transactional: I prayed to God to ask for things. If I was a good boy, I would get certain favors, or at least have a better chance of getting them. And at the end of my life, if I had been good, I would get into heaven. That seemed fair.

Rereading my journal from 1976, however, brought me up short. There were more than a few references to going to church. I was surprised to read that during the Easter weekend, I had attended all three services of what is called the Triduum, though as recently as this year I told someone that the first time I went to these liturgies was after I joined the Jesuits.

"Since it was Holy Thursday, there were many rituals today," I wrote on April 15. "First we had a procession in church and then Latin songs, then we had our communion, dipped in wine." But those few lines paled in comparison to the day's big event: a visit to Philadelphia with my friend Carol, the details of which occupy two full pages.

The next day was Good Friday, when, by family tradition, we didn't watch TV or listen to the radio between noon and 3 p.m., the hours that Jesus hung on the Cross, according to tradition. "I went and there were a lot of people," I wrote. "We had a special ceremony like yesterday. There was the veneration of the cross & special songs. It was a very solemn mass. I came home and watched some TV and ate dinner. (Fish of course.)"

On Holy Saturday I played against my friend Eugene in tennis in ninety-four-degree heat and then came home and watched *The Greatest Story Ever Told*, the 1965 film on the life of Christ starring Max von Sydow as Jesus, filmed in Utah, Nevada, and California and featuring shots of nonexistent snow-covered mountains in Galilee. My in-depth review: "It was a really good program. I liked it." On Easter Sunday I describe in detail our Easter dinner (and our coconut Easter cake) but not as much about Mass: "In church we listened to many rejoicing hymns. Then we left."

Maybe I was more religious than I recall. Still, I was uneducated about things that most Catholic school kids took for granted. The next month I went to confession, which had been revamped after the Second Vatican Council. "Now it's 'reconciliation' or something like that."

During college, if you asked me about my image of God, I probably would have said that God existed, was more or less interested in me (mainly to spy on me to see if I was doing the right thing), heard my prayers in a way I couldn't describe (and sometimes didn't trust), and answered them far less often than I would have hoped. He (always he) was loving if distant, benign if unreliable, omnipresent if hard to find.

At Penn, I was one of a few practicing Catholics in my group of friends and so was often called upon to explain this or that Catholic belief, event, or person. (That is, when I wasn't making Jesus jokes or "killing the pope.") During the springtime of our junior year, for example, my Jewish housemates asked me about Lent. I explained that it came before Easter and you gave up things as a penance. They asked who decided what things you gave up.

"I do," I said.

"That's ridiculous," they said, averring that it was hardly a sacrifice if you decided on it. Far better would be for *them* to decide what I would give up. It was hard to disagree with their logic. So that year they decided that I would have to give up orange sodas and Snowballs, the insanely sweet round chocolate cakes with a buttercream center, wrapped in pink marshmallow and coconut. This was a much harder penance than I would have chosen. My housemates' communal penitential discernment continued into the following Lent as well, when they instructed me to give up jellybeans. After graduation, a few of my friends banded together and continued to assign me my annual Lenten penance. A few years later, my roommate Rob took over and has continued that tradition, now with his wife and son, for the past forty years. Every Ash Wednesday, I used to get a call with my prescribed Lenten penances. Now I get an email or a text. But I try to follow their penances to the letter, in addition to my own. The year I entered the Jesuits, my penance was to give up sex, which was redundant but still tough.

On some nights at Penn my friend George, an agnostic, and I would stay up into the wee hours arguing about religion: Does God exist? And if God does exist, why does he allow suffering? Is there a heaven? Hell? They were spirited discussions, but my main concern was convincing George that I was right. It was more of an intellectual pursuit than a spiritual one. We might as well have been arguing about the Invisible Hand, which I suppose was how I saw God: present and powerful but mysterious.

Religion was an obligation. I was interested in Jesus mainly as an example. And I hoped to get into heaven one day. But if you had asked me about my relationship with God, I might have said that I tried to be a good person, without understanding, much less believing, that I might be able to experience God's presence in any way.

It's hard to describe these feelings because they are so far from what I feel now. Maybe the best way to say it was that I believed in God, but I didn't know if God believed in me. God was, mostly, distant.

And hard to understand. God was everywhere and always

interested in our lives, but I didn't see many signs of that. Why didn't God reveal himself and tell me—or us—what to do? If God would just materialize every few years in my life, as a kind of vision, to say, "Do this and don't do that," I would have been happy to comply. Of course, I knew that God had already revealed himself as Jesus, and had already told everyone how to live, but that was two thousand years ago (more or less), and while that was nice for all the apostles and disciples (what was the difference between the two anyway?) and everyone in Judea and Galilee, what about us today? Why didn't God just pop by from time to time?

Since God apparently wasn't going to do that, I resigned myself to trying to be a good Christian out of obligation. Maybe when I died, God would take the measure of my life, like a teller settling his window at night, let me into heaven, and then answer all the questions that George asked but I couldn't answer.

There were a few moments when I had felt God's presence in an unmistakable way. Earlier in this book, I described riding my bike to elementary school on a warm spring morning, pausing in a meadow—filled with wildflowers and alive with the sound of birds and crickets—and experiencing an overwhelming sense of awe. I wanted the feeling to continue and wanted to know its source. I didn't have a vision, and I wasn't transported into some other realm. Rather, I felt the desire for union with God, though I would have said I was just enjoying nature. Not connecting those moments to God meant that the only signs of his presence in my life were when things worked out the way I wanted them to.

As I sat in the pew in that tasteful church in Potomac and thought about Brad and listened to the pastor, I thought, *Why should I believe in a God who did this?* It seemed obscenely unfair. Brad and

Mindy had been good people, and so was I and everyone else who had been touched by the accident. Why would God punish them, and their families, and all of us? And me?

I got angrier as the funeral service continued, and finally, when we gathered outside where Brad's ashes would be placed, I thought, *I'm done.*

For the next few months, I didn't believe in God. Why believe in a God like that? Why try to be a good boy, a good Christian, and a good Catholic, if God was going to *kill my friends*? So I stopped going to church. It made my Sundays freer, as I joked to my friends at the time. I could stay out later on Saturday nights at Doc Watson's.

I wore my newfound atheism proudly for a few months because I thought it was more intellectual not to believe in God. More adult. Cooler.

Around November, however, I was standing outside the Quad talking to my friend Jacque. Maybe it was after one of our Wharton classes, and we were getting a hot dog from one of the lunch trucks that lined Spruce Street and served all manner of unhealthy food. (My favorite selection was a chili dog from a greasy truck that we called Ptomaine Tony's.)

It was snowing lightly on the kind of damp, cold day that seemed to populate the winters during my college days.

Jacque was what we called a fundamentalist, though I don't think any of us knew what that meant. She was an active member of her family's church in a town outside of Chicago. And she took time to find the "right church" when she got to Philadelphia, a concept that struck me as novel: Like most Catholics, I just went to the nearest parish church whether I liked it or not. And she attended Bible study classes. But what should have tipped me off to her Christianity was this: She was one of the kindest people I knew. Unfailingly courteous, gracious, and sweet, she was also a hard worker and matched all of us in our Wharton classes.

As we stood outside the Quad, with the snow wetting our woolen hats and down parkas, Jacque asked whether I was still not going to church. I said yes and told her how angry I was at God, if God existed after all. I remember feeling superior to her—challenging her on her beliefs. Throwing down a spiritual gauntlet. My anger at God morphed into defiance toward Jacque, the most visible representative of God in my life. I told her that I didn't want to believe in a God who had killed Brad and Mindy. I supposed Jacque knew better than I did what I was doing: challenging God and challenging her for believing in him. Anyway, I was done with God. Maybe God was done with me too. I didn't really care anymore.

Jacque closed her eyes, opened them again, and said, "I've been spending the last few months thanking God for Brad's life."

Four decades later I can remember the subtle shift that happened in me right then. It was her way of saying, explicitly or implicitly, that you could believe in God even if you disagreed with God. Even if you were mad at God. You could even believe in a God who took your friends away. I don't think I had ever thought of being in a relationship with a God I didn't understand.

Her answer surprised me so much that I stood speechless in the snow. But she made sense.

So I started going back to church.

After the funeral, the rest of the summer passed uneventfully. I lived what was by now a normal summer: during the days working hard at The Pennsylvania Group and enjoying cheesesteaks at Mama's for lunch; at nights drinking and getting high with my friends; weekends going down the shore with John; and playing tennis, mowing the lawn, and reading books on poltergeists, aliens, and talking rabbits. But Brad was almost always on my mind.

I felt different, more serious somehow.

An adult, I guess. Or at least not a kid.

Graduation day, 3924 Spruce Street. The *M* on a few of our caps was a nod to the Capital Asset Pricing Model some of us had studied at Wharton, commonly called the "Cap-M."

After camping out overnight to purchase season tickets for Penn basketball, my housemates and I re-created da Vinci's *Last Supper*. Our friend Jacque (off camera), the most Christian person in our group of friends, directed us.

CHAPTER 9

How I Graduated from College and Almost Met Grace Kelly

L ET ME CLARIFY SOMETHING ABOUT MY TEENAGE WORK-ing life. It's not entirely accurate to say that I made money only during the summers. I also worked during winter breaks, as a teller at the bank or as an usher at the movie theater. That continued throughout my college years. That was not unusual, but neither was it the norm.

Most of my friends at Penn came from middle-class backgrounds. Few, as far as I knew, were poor. But some were wealthy and a few were fabulously wealthy, with parents who owned multiple houses and had established trust funds for them.

Freshman year was the first time I encountered wealth of this sort. In high school, nearly all my friends came from middle-class families, and the few who lived in houses that were slightly larger than mine were deemed rich. Sometimes my parents would have occasion to drive my sister and me through the wealthy neighborhoods of the Main Line of Philadelphia, on the other side of the Schuylkill River. Remember the line from Paul Fussell, the social critic (and at the time Penn professor), who described the top of the economic ladder as the "top out-of-sight"? We could barely see their lawns, let alone their houses.

Even the home of the most well-known person in our area, the boxing legend Joe Frazier, whose affable kids Jacqui and Marvis went to our high school, was modest: a decent-size but not ostentatious house in Whitemarsh. The wealth that one sometimes encountered at Penn was, however, on a different scale, and the disparity between the haves and have-nots was far greater than what I could have imagined in high school. The chasm between the trust-fund kids and the work-study kids was simply accepted, much as you accepted Philly's humid summers and slushy winters. I was also too embarrassed to talk about it because I knew that my family wasn't rich, and my rich classmates didn't seem to want to be reminded of their wealth.

Delta Psi, a fraternity called "St. Anthony Hall" or "St. A's," attracted wealthy prep-school kids. (The nickname comes not from any religious provenance, but because it was founded at Columbia University on the Feast of St. Anthony.) The most durable rumor about St. A's was that it required members to pledge 1 percent of their lifetime incomes to the fraternity. We were never sure whether it was true, but it sure looked that way: When I was invited to a party at their handsome stone building, white-gloved waiters served us mixed drinks on silver trays.

As a freshman, I was surprised to learn that people had multiple houses or a pied-à-terre in New York for times when their parents felt like staying in "the City." (Gratingly, even when living in Philadelphia, when New Yorkers referred to "the City" they meant the one farther north.) When someone in my econ class asked me where my family "wintered," I hadn't a clue what he was talking about. He explained that during winter vacations (still universally called "Christmas vacation"), his family went to "the Islands." I didn't know what that meant. "Which islands?" I asked. He "wintered" in the Bahamas, he explained.

I don't mean to say that I hadn't read about wealthy people or was unaware of the "top out-of-sight," but I was still confused: *Why would you take a vacation during the winter? That's for the summer.* After we returned from the Christmas break of my freshman year, I was likewise amazed to see students with golden tans. Years later, I read Fran Lebowitz's mordant observation: "Generally speaking, the poorer person summers where he winters."

At one point, I took a fascinating elective course called Social Stratification with one of the stars of Penn's faculty, a sociologist with the impressive name of E. Digby Baltzell, who was famous for coining the term WASP (White, Anglo-Saxon, Protestant). A WASP himself, always resplendent in khaki pants, Harris tweed jackets with leather patches sewn over the elbows, buttoned-down striped shirts, and polka-dotted bow ties, Professor Baltzell steered us through the varieties of class and what he called the "hegemony" of the WASPs, as outlined in his book *The Protestant Establishment: Aristocracy & Caste in America*, first published in 1964.

The thesis of his now-classic study was that WASPs had maintained their social and cultural hegemony (he used that word a lot) in the United States for so long mainly because as other groups assimilated into American life, they sought to gain entrance into the

WASP-dominated world of white-shoe law firms, investment banks and corporations, private clubs, and the "right" neighborhoods. Baltzell correctly predicted that their social dominance would wane as newer groups increasingly rejected the mores of the "Protestant establishment." That is, people stopped wanting to be like them. Overall, Baltzell's class was not only one of the best classes I've ever taken, but it also helped me understand Penn, St. A's, and all the students who "wintered."

Over my Christmas vacation, I wintered at Western Savings Bank and at a series of jobs found by a nearby temp agency, where I had found work at odd times ever since high school. Peak Personnel sent me into nearby offices where I did light accounting work, while telling everyone how much accounting I was studying at Wharton. I'm sure I was insufferable.

During senior year, I stumbled upon a better job than working in Penn's Student Financial Aid office, where I felt addled most of the time. My housemate Bruce, also in need of cash, had a job at the box office of the Annenberg Center for the Performing Arts at Penn. Even though he worked in the box office, selling tickets, Bruce's job sounded positively glamorous.

Another friend from the DC area and a year behind me, Bruce was one of the wittiest people I had (and have) ever met. I was forever stealing his jokes and repeating his sardonic observations. Bruce was also one of the few practicing Catholics in our circle, a graduate of a prestigious Jesuit high school in DC called Gonzaga College High School.

At the time, I had only a vague notion of who the Jesuits were. I knew they were Catholic priests and brothers and was dimly aware that they ran high schools and colleges. Perhaps, I thought, a Jesuit held an academic degree that made him a Jesuit. Something about the way Bruce spoke, though, suggested that a Jesuit education made you pretty sophisticated. Six years after I graduated from Penn, Bruce would be the first person I told, even before my family, that I was entering the Jesuits. At the time I was dithering about the decision. "Trust me, you're a Jesuit," he said. "You even dress like one."

Bruce also introduced me to a memorable way of making money.

One day I saw on Bruce's forearm a series of small metal disks, no bigger than nickels, affixed to his skin with white surgical tape. "What's that?" I asked.

"Medical tests!" he said happily. "Five dollars a disk! You should try it."

Bruce had spotted signs on campus kiosks looking for student volunteers for medical tests, this one from the dermatology department at the Hospital of the University of Pennsylvania (or HUP). He was happy to rent out his arm to HUP for a few dollars a disk. Other experiments included being infected with a cold virus and sequestered in a hotel room for a few days, requiring him to blow his nose into tissues and collect them in plastic bags.

I wasn't sure that I wanted to get a cold on demand, but I was eager to be a guinea pig for Penn's Department of Psychology, something else Bruce discovered to earn extra cash. The psych building was not far from the high-rise dorm where I was living during sophomore year, and our off-campus house during junior and senior years, so I went several times to be "tested."

At the time I was unaware that many of these tests were focused not on what seemed to be the topic (an intelligence test, a spatial-relations test, a fill-in-the-blank test), but on what was happening *around* the test. Once, before a test requiring the subject to assemble a building from children's wooden blocks, I was made to wait for an hour in a stuffy waiting room. My suspicion was that the psychologists were more curious about how I dealt with delays than how well I arranged colored blocks. Another test involved looking at drawings of animals on small white cards, which a grad student moved in and out of your field of vision, while your head remained immobile. I still have no clue what they were testing—maybe how fast people get headaches. Each test paid twenty-five dollars, a significant amount of money for me as an undergraduate, enough to buy a textbook, a night out at Doc Watson's, or a week's worth of chili dogs at Ptomaine Tony's.

One test ended up being unintentionally useful. During one exam, which we took on separate occasions, Bruce and I were asked random general intelligence questions: How far is it from New York to Los Angeles? Where does rubber come from? And, memorably, when was Johann Wolfgang von Goethe born? I knew the answers to none of these.

Out of curiosity, Bruce and I looked up the answers afterward. This was long before the web, so it took some doing. So: twenty-five hundred miles by plane, from a tree, and 1749.

Almost a decade later, when I was taking psychology tests as a requirement to enter the Jesuits, the psychologist examining me pulled out a sheet of paper. "Now I'm going to ask you some general intelligence questions," he said. I smiled.

"When was Johann Wolfgang von Goethe born?" I answered all the questions, thanks to my need for cash in college. My examiner was surprised when I practically shouted out "1749!"

Bruce's main source of income was a work-study job at the Annenberg Center box office, a gig I desperately wanted. So in September of my senior year, I filled out an application and was accepted. As with my job at the Financial Aid office, this was part of Penn's work-study program. Certain jobs on campus were available to students who were invited to participate in the program. (This was specified on your financial aid package at admission: We're giving you this much in scholarship, and out of that, you have to earn this much through work-study.) We were allowed to work no more than twenty hours a week.

The Annenberg Center box office was a cozy workplace, in the middle of the large theater complex. Brad had studied at the Annenberg School for Communication, which was directly across Locust Walk, Penn's cobblestoned main thoroughfare, from the Wharton School's main classroom building, so I knew it well. Brad and I had seen several films there.

But the Annenberg Center was, strictly speaking, not part of the school; rather, it was a sprawling entertainment complex that included, at the time, four theaters. The Zellerbach Theatre, the main theater, seated almost a thousand people. The Harold Prince Theatre was a black-box theater that seated roughly two hundred people; and the smaller Studio Theatre, now named the Bruce Montgomery Theatre, could fit 115 people. Another theater was located in the Annenberg School building, that is, where Brad took his classes.

With its many stages, Annenberg was a major performing arts center in the city. And as Bruce reminded me recently, the Annenberg Center did not focus on student productions but professional ones, usually chosen from whatever was on tour. It was an important part of the Philadelphia theater scene.

During my stint there, Annenberg produced some marvelous shows, including a play by the South African playwright Athol Fugard, called *"Master Harold" . . . and the Boys*, about the relationship between a young white teenager and the two Black workers in the boy's family's tea shop. In the play, staged at Annenberg before its Broadway run, the boy (played by Željko Ivanek) moves from friendship with the two older men (Danny Glover and Zakes Mokae) to casual bigotry. After one performance, Mr. Fugard himself spoke to the audience, which I attended and found fascinating, primarily because I had never seen a playwright in person.

Very occasionally, we ran into well-known actors. Bruce rode in an elevator once with Rex Harrison and Claudette Colbert, who were starring in Noël Coward's *Private Lives*. We had been told not to pester the actors (or playwrights or directors), but Bruce told me recently that even if he hadn't been warned, he wouldn't have spoken to them because they seemed "too formidable." He also saw William Marshall, who appeared in Henrik Ibsen's *An Enemy of the People*. Mr. Marshall was perhaps better known as Blacula.

As part of the celebration of its three hundredth anniversary in 1982, just a few months before I graduated, the City of Philadelphia decided to honor a local movie star: Her Serene Highness Princess Grace of Monaco, aka Grace Kelly. Also part of the celebrations was another visiting royal: Queen Elizabeth II. The ship, that is. The actual queen had visited Philadelphia a few years earlier, during the Bicentennial, but sadly, she did not participate in the Bicentennial Wagon Train. It would have been fun to see Her Majesty ride by the Ice Cream Inn in a Conestoga wagon.

Grace Kelly grew up in the East Falls section of Philadelphia, and every time we passed St. Bridget's Church, one or both of my parents would say, "You know, this was Grace Kelly's church!" One summer, "down the shore" in Ocean City, I saw her in the Acme Supermarket, wearing a turban and huge sunglasses. But she was more than a local movie star; she was a local avatar. My sister told me recently that our mom would often say to her, "If you don't know what to do in a social situation, ask yourself, 'What would Grace Kelly do?'" My sister continued, "If I said something even the slightest bit off-color or crude, Mom would say, 'Really, Carolyn? Is that something Grace Kelly would say?' Her influence on women and girls from the 1950s to 1980s cannot be overstated."

The entire Kelly family enjoyed outsize influence in Philadelphia. On the East River Drive, now called Kelly Drive, which runs along the Schuylkill River roughly from Manayunk through Fairmount Park to Center City, a striking bronze statue of Jack Kelly, Grace's father, was installed in 1967. Whenever we drove past that statue, my father would tell me the story of Jack Kelly.

He was the son of an Irish immigrant, war veteran, and bricklayer who founded a still-thriving brick company known in Philly for its slogan, seen on countless T-shirts: "Kelly for Brickwork." Jack Kelly was a champion rower but was rejected in 1920 from the prestigious Henley Royal Regatta in England because, as my father told me, "he worked with his hands." But a few months later at the Olympic Games in Belgium, Kelly beat the British sculler Jack Beresford and won the gold medal for the US team. He reportedly sent his racing cap to King George V for having been snubbed at Henley with a note saying, "Greetings from a bricklayer."

Grace Kelly's father won two gold medals at the 1920 Olympics and another one four years later in Paris. The sculpture of Jack Sr. rowing is situated at the end of the Schuylkill River rowing course, near the Penn Boathouse on Kelly Drive. But Kelly Drive is actually named after his son Jack Jr., another Olympic rower, who, in 1947, avenged his father's snub by winning the Diamond Challenge Sculls event at the Henley Regatta. That was my dad's favorite part of the story.

So Grace was not the only well-known Kelly in Philadelphia.

Still, Jack's sister and my sister's avatar was the main attraction at the gala that the Annenberg Center was hosting on behalf of Philadelphia, emceed by Bob Hope. Afterward came a four-day Grace Kelly film festival at Annenberg, including showings of *The Country Girl* and *The Swan.* At a press conference before the event, Princess Grace said, "It's a great thing for me to come back to Philadelphia and be received in this wonderful way."

The Philadelphia Inquirer gushed over her appearance: "She was dressed in soft pink, with ruffles framing a face that seemed unchanged since her last film, made in 1956. Her hair was in a braid worn like a gold crown."

Bruce was unable to go because employees were supposed to purchase a tuxedo, which he couldn't afford. Luckily, I was working at the box office that day and saw, through the tiny window, some of the stars enter the lobby. In quick succession came Jimmy Stewart, Frank Sinatra, Farley Granger (someone had to tell me who he was), and finally Her Serene Highness. She passed near the box office window on her way to the event, and she was beautiful: by this point a more mature woman than the slim movie star of *Rear Window* but still drop-dead gorgeous in a gold lamé dress with her golden coronet of hair.

The rest of my time at Annenberg was less glamorous. I spent most days answering the phone and taking ticket orders in the cluttered, musty office; selling tickets at the window for future shows; and giving out tickets for afternoon and evening shows that day and evening. The box office was open from noon to the last intermission of whatever show was playing.

We sold season and series tickets, and in the spring, once the shows were chosen for the next fall and winter, we would call existing members to see whether they'd like to renew. The job involved a lot of looking up of names, calling people on the phone, taking credit card information, and filling out renewal forms. The box office manager, a relaxed, bohemian woman who lived with her husband in nearby Powelton Village and made pottery on the side, was chill and fun to work with. The only busy times were when the crowds came in for a show, so the rest of the time in that cramped little office was pleasant enough and an easy way to make some money. It was also rather exciting to work in "the legitimate *thea-tuh*" as one of the other work-study students used to say. More glamorous than the Cinema on the Mall. But no free candy.

Once I graduated from Penn, the summer jobs would end. From then on, my summer job would be my spring, fall, and winter job too.

But I had to find one. And now, during senior year, the job hunt, not our classes, was the unrivaled focus for Wharton seniors. Even though we would all graduate with a bachelor's degree in economics, our time was designed not so much to help us solve the world's economic problems, as it was to get the highest-paying job we could.

As graduation neared, I grew addled about the future. I had spent the previous four years studying business and had enjoyed my time at The Pennsylvania Group as a sort-of stockbroker, and even at Western as a teller, but did I want to spend the rest of my life in business? Was business a good use of my life?

But at that point, what else could I do? A few friends were applying to law school, and though I had enjoyed my course in business law, I didn't enjoy it enough to commit to law school. Graduate school in general was out: Even though I had worked constantly through my high school and college years, I didn't have enough money for grad school and already had a sizable amount of student loans to pay off: two hundred dollars a month.

When I shared my trepidation, my friends usually shrugged and said, "Why did you go to Wharton if you didn't want to go into business?"

Good question. Everyone told me how lucky I was even to *be* at Wharton, a guarantee of the "fast track" to success. Some of the firms that came to campus to interview, we heard, were paying upward of $25,000 a year, some even $30,000, the equivalent of roughly $80,000 and $100,000 today. How could you not want that? It seemed ungrateful, ungracious even. And those numbers allured me. So like all the other Wharton students, once the fall came, I signed up for interviews.

Penn's Career Planning and Placement office made finding a job easy. And early that year, until August in fact, the stock market and the economy overall were booming. All you had to do was write up a résumé, get a few hundred copies printed, and then go to the Career Planning office, which had set up a wooden wall punctuated with dozens of slots. Each slot represented a different job offer—some companies were offering multiple jobs—and next to the slot was a three-by-five-inch card describing the position: Investment Banker: Lehman Brothers; Corporate Financial Analyst: IBM; Auditor: Arthur Andersen.

You slid your résumé into the slot, and if the company was interested, you received an invitation to interview a few weeks later, as if by magic. No cover letters and no follow-up phone calls necessary.

Interviewing season had its own rhythm. The Big Eight public-accounting firms arrived first, which mirrored what I imagined to be their preternatural efficiency, to skim off the cream of the accounting students. Suddenly accounting classes suffered a precipitous drop in attendance as students who had accepted job offers became more interested in finding a new apartment than studying for an exam that wouldn't make a difference anyway.

Next came the investment house banks and brokerage firms, some now defunct but whose names caused Wharton students to salivate: Salomon Brothers, Lehman Brothers, Goldman Sachs, Smith Barney, Merrill Lynch—all on the hunt for the top finance majors. It's hard to describe how prominently those names figured into our consciousness. Getting a job with any of them was like winning the lottery. Or an Oscar. We used to joke that the answer to the common interviewer's question "Why do you want to work for Salomon Brothers?" was (given its reputation for huge salaries) "Because you're hiring."

Finally, in a flurry of activity in mid-November came the big commercial "money-center" banks: Chase Manhattan, Citibank, Manufacturers Hanover; large industrial corporations like IBM, GE, and AT&T; and elite consulting firms like Booz

Allen, McKinsey, and the Boston Consulting Group. Besides investment banks, the consulting firms were considered the most desirable of the companies that came.

Overall, I enjoyed interviewing. Again, the money was a draw. I couldn't wait to see those big paychecks. And I was dazzled by the well-dressed men and women who came to interview us. At the time, the women wore outfits that were nearly identical to what the men wore, and in the same colors—blue and gray—except with a skirt and a floppy foulard bow decorated with a tasteful pattern. "Dress for success" was the rage, with a few students paying on the side for courses in what to wear. Some of the larger companies, especially the Big Eight accounting firms, even offered late-afternoon cocktail parties at hotels near campus. Free food!

It's one thing to wander into the Ice Cream Inn in a T-shirt and jeans, ask to see the assistant manager, sit down at a table that still has plates of half-eaten dinners on it, fill out a two-page application, and hope that they called you back; it's another to don a Jos. A. Bank suit, button-down shirt, and silk tie and sit across from an even better dressed interviewer from Salomon Brothers who is wearing Brooks Brothers and asks you questions about security analysis and macroeconomics. Or in my case, *two* interviewers from Salomon Brothers, in the most nerve-racking of all my interviews.

The first interviewer was tall, blond, and immaculately dressed and asked, after dispensing with a few awkward pleasantries, where else I was interviewing. I offered a generic answer: other investment banks. I named a few and he nodded noncommittally. Also, I added, "First Pennsylvania, Chase Manhattan..."

"*Commercial* banks?" he said, as if I had mentioned a job with a circus—not Salomon Brothers but Ringling Brothers.

"Yes," I said, my voice suddenly breaking. Why did I feel so dumb already?

"Do you know the difference between an investment bank like Salomon Brothers and a commercial bank?" He sniffed. "I certainly hope you do. *Do* you?" He leaned back in his chair in one of the tiny generic office spaces that Career Planning had provided for interviews.

Asking a business student that question is akin to asking a baseball player whether he knows the difference between a ball and a bat. So why did I still feel so nervous? "Yes, I know the difference." My voice cracked and I felt like a teenager applying for a summer job all over again. I offered an explanation, as my face flushed.

Then, without a knock, another tall, blond-haired fellow strode into the room. For a moment I thought he had stumbled into the wrong room. But this was known in the trade as a "high-pressure" interview, where they would see how well you did under stress. Now there were two tall, immaculately dressed investment bankers ready to grill me.

"Bill, Jim was just telling me that he's interviewing with commercial banks."

"*Commercial* banks?" said WASP #2, horrified.

I flashed back to my time at the Ice Cream Inn, having mistakenly bussed those tables during the Bicentennial Wagon Train. I knew that I had done something dumb but didn't know what it was. I tried to explain that I thought commercial banking was an important and dignified profession. They both pursed their lips.

This was a lesson I had to learn over and over. Just because someone is trying to make you feel dumb does not mean that you are dumb. At the time, though, I felt humiliated.

From there, the interview went downhill. When I spoke to some fellow students, they laughed and then told me what I should have said: "Ever since the first moments of my consciousness as a human being, indeed the very moment of my conception, I have only ever wanted to work with one company: Salomon Brothers." (The company's cutthroat corporate culture would be skewered in Michael Lewis's excellent—and surprisingly entertaining—book *Liar's Poker*.) In a few days I received a rejection letter.

I'd like to say that having seen how snotty those two men were, I decided I wouldn't want to work there anyway. But that would be a lie. I desperately wanted to work there. For the money. And the prestige. I added it to my rejection letters that I had pasted on the door of my bedroom in our off-campus house. Eventually I took to throwing darts at them.

In the end, my decision came down to three offers. Wachovia Bank, a large regional bank based in North Carolina (and later acquired by Wells Fargo), had a friendly and welcoming vibe. The interviewer actually *laughed* during our interview on campus, and they flew me down to Winston-Salem, for a job as a security analyst, selecting stocks for the bank's investment portfolio. That sounded fun, plus Winston-Salem (a town founded, as the name suggests, on tobacco money) was charming—and inexpensive. My dad smoked Winstons and jokingly asked if I could bring him a few packs from my visit. Next came Arthur Andersen, one of the Big Eight that had a management consulting program based in either Chicago or Washington, DC.

Finally, General Electric, at the time an immensely influential company, was offering a spot in its Financial Management Program, a two-year training program said (by them) to be the equivalent of an MBA. I flew to Boston and found my way to a colossal plant in Lynn, Massachusetts, one of the two main facilities for GE Aircraft Engines. I was ushered through an immense factory floor where massive pieces of equipment were being assembled, and afterward was interviewed in a green cinder-block office that had all the charm of a penitentiary. "I bet you've never worked in a factory!" said one of the interviewers. I had, I said, but nothing like this one.

Even if I didn't want to live in Lynn ("Lynn, Lynn, the City of Sin, you never come out the way you went in," went the doggerel based on its colonial-era reputation as a hotbed of vice), there were other possibilities for a job at GE. "You could work in New York at our International Finance and Accounting office," they told me in Lynn.

I was getting letters and phone calls from each of these three suitors—GE, Wachovia, and Arthur Andersen—almost weekly. The representative from Wachovia was especially alluring, offering all sorts of bonuses and emoluments if I worked there. But I didn't think I wanted to move to Winston-Salem, which, while charming, seemed sleepy. So it came down to GE and Arthur Andersen. What sealed the deal was a conversation with another interviewer at GE, as I was getting close to deciding. I remember him saying this to me in person, though I forget where this was.

"Arthur *Andersen*?" he said, virtually spitting out the words. The way that some of the interviewers talked about competing firms was akin to the way a Red Sox fan talks about the Yankees.

"Yeah," I said, fearing another put-down à la Salomon Brothers and commercial banks. But what he said was more effective.

"You know what they'll put on your tombstone if you work for Arthur Andersen?"

This was not the kind of question I was asked at the Cinema on the Mall.

I shook my head.

"Here lies Jim Martin. He worked for Arthur Andersen. PERIOD!" He paused for dramatic effect. "Because that's *all* you'll have time for!"

Well, I certainly didn't want that.

Moving to New York for GE was growing in appeal. Despite my proximity to "the City," I could count on one hand the number of times I had been there, mainly as a child, along with my sister and parents, once visiting the Empire State Building and the United Nations and having a wretched dinner at Mama Leone's, a notorious tourist trap, whose gloppy Italian food compared unfavorably to my mother's cooking. We had also seen the Statue of Liberty, Radio City Music Hall, and St. Patrick's Cathedral. That's all I knew about New York, other than, in the early 1980s, it was big, loud, dirty, crowded, and dangerous. But New York also betokened fun, excitement, and money to my twenty-one-year-old self.

When my housemate Rob told me that he had accepted a job in New York and was looking for a roommate, GE started to seem like the perfect fit. A great company and a good training program and a fun and easygoing friend to live with. But what really convinced me was the starting salary: $20,000, at the time a princely sum. I would be making much more than I ever had, even at the stockbrokerage. I said yes to GE, and a few weeks after graduation from Penn, a low-key affair livened up by one final party at our house, where we danced till the wee hours to the Go-Go's, I packed up my things and prepared to move to the City.

The exterior clock of 570 Lexington Avenue, the art deco structure then known as the GE Building, with the Chrysler Building in the distance (*left*). And the tower of 570 Lex (*right*). GE's CEO Jack Welch had an office on the top floor, which he rarely used. But the rest of us did, sitting in his chair and putting our feet up on his desk. *(Photos by Howard Sherman)*

Rob was nearly the perfect roommate. (He'd say the perfect one.) Here he is pointing to Jesus, whose Society I would enter a few years later.

CHAPTER 10

How My Last Summer Job Turned Out

SINCE I STARTED WORKING IN AUGUST, I SUPPOSE YOU could say that GE counts as a summer job. But it lasted considerably longer than any of my prior summer jobs: six years versus three months.

Before meeting up with Rob to search for an apartment in New York, I spent a month with a high school friend, Jeanne, backpacking through Europe on a Eurail Pass, a flat-fee train ticket (around $250 back then) that gave you access to dozens of trains, and therefore dozens of cities, in Europe. Our junior-high-school French came in handy, and since I didn't run into anyone from Quebec, I was never tempted to say, "*Ohhhhh, VRAIMENT?*"

But I felt like an idiot for not knowing how to pronounce the name of a place I hoped to visit: the town where Joan of Arc saw King Charles VII crowned. Reims, in northern France, is not pronounced *Reem* or *Rem*, as I thought, after several years of French.

I stood at the window of the Gare du Nord station in Paris and twice asked for a ticket to this town, as the man behind the counter stared impassively at me. "*Où?*" he said. Where?

I tried again, wondering how Margot or Mon Oncle would say it.

He stared at me.

"*Éppele-le,*" he said. Spell it.

I did, *en français*, mortified and sweating: *Err, uh, ee, em, ess.*

He rolled his eyes theatrically and said, "*Rrrrrrance,*" with an impressive guttural *R* and infinite Gallic contempt. I have never heard so much disdain packed into one word.

We visited our friend Peggy, who was studying at King's College in London, and worked our way through most of the sites that a college-age tourist wanted to see: The trip was equal parts churches, museums, restaurants, and bars.

With embarrassment I remember being told that we could not enter the Duomo, the grand cathedral-basilica of Florence (technically the Cattedrale di Santa Maria del Fiore), because Jeanne and I were wearing shorts and T-shirts. I told Jeanne pompously that it was my right as a Catholic to enter. "*Io sono Cattolico!*" I said to the guard at the door. "So is everyone else here," he said in English, sizing up my cutoff jeans with only a little less disdain for me than the ticket master in Paris had shown. "And they are dressed *correctly*."

By this point, even though I was going to church again, my Catholicism was still along the lines of what you might call the "duty model." I attended Mass mainly out of duty and to ensure that I was in good graces with God, so that I could (1) get what I wanted when I asked or (2) get into heaven when I died. The duty model was close to the "transactional model," wherein if I did the right thing, God would reward me. Such "rewarding" happened less often than I would have hoped, but I still tried to please God, or at least not annoy him. Or Him. I hoped my drinking and smoking would be forgiven.

But I still knew little about Catholic history, traditions, and culture, other than whatever I had picked up in world history classes in high school and my parish's religious education classes before First Holy Communion and Confirmation. I ceased my religious education after Confirmation, that is, around sixth grade, figuring I had gotten what I came for so why prolong courses in something I wasn't interested in? My parents didn't see much need to continue either.

My main source of information about Jesus was the 1977 Franco Zeffirelli miniseries *Jesus of Nazareth*, which aired for a few years around Easter and Christmas, the highlight being the raising of Lazarus. This was my introduction to the New Testament.

Sometimes when I would hear a quote from Jesus, I caught myself thinking, *That came from* Jesus of Nazareth. I had to remind myself, *That came from the Gospels*. For many years, my mental image of Jesus was of the British actor Robert Powell, who declaimed Jesus's lines with a plummy Oxbridge accent: "Lazarus, come *fawth*!" Sometimes I wonder if, when you get to heaven, you are welcomed by the Jesus you're used to seeing in your imagination or the way he really looked. Or looks.

During our stay in Rome, I read an entry in our *Let's Go Europe* guidebook for one of the churches recommended for a visit: Il Gesù, which the book called a masterpiece of Baroque architecture and identified as the Mother Church for the Society of Jesus, aka the Jesuits. The full name of the church is the Church of the Most Holy Name of Jesus; in Italian it's Chiesa del Santissimo Nome di Gesù, almost always abbreviated as Il Gesù.

I read the entry in the guidebook and said to Jeanne, "*The Jesus*? What kind of name is that for a church?" We skipped it.

Once back in the States, I took a train to New York and stayed with Rob in the apartment of his uncle and aunt while we searched for a place to live. I had never set foot in a Manhattan apartment; in fact, only a few times in any apartment at all. None of my high school friends lived in an apartment, so when I watched sitcoms like *The Odd Couple* or *That Girl* or *The Courtship of Eddie's Father*, all 1970s staples where the characters lived in apartments—the first two in New York and the third in LA—I had a hard time imagining what apartment life would be like.

One Halloween during junior high school, along with some adventurous friends, we went trick-or-treating outside the boundaries of our neighborhood and ventured into some nearby apartment buildings. As we wandered up and down the halls I wondered: *Would it feel cramped to live in a few rooms? Not to have a lawn? How is your mail delivered? Would you know your neighbors? Where would you play in the summertime?* It seemed exotic.

Our temporary housing on Park Avenue was a high-end introduction to the world of New York apartments. I took a cab from Penn Station to the building and told the doorman, who wore a long, double-breasted greatcoat with gold buttons, the name of Rob's uncle.

"Sixth floor," he said, taking in my T-shirt and jeans and ratty nylon JanSport backpack.

"Which apartment?" I said.

He looked down at the floor to spare my blushes. "Sixth floor."

To my surprise, Rob's uncle and aunt owned a fabulous apartment occupying an entire floor, with original works of art, paintings and sculptures alike, from artists whose works I had seen only in museums. Rob and I spent a day or two on Park Avenue while we hunted for considerably more modest digs nearby.

I was grateful that I would be rooming with Rob. One of my housemates and a fellow Wharton student, he was (and is) easygoing, friendly, and funny. Rob had accepted a job at a midsize accounting firm, which would require him, like most recent hires, to spend much of his time studying for his CPA exams. He stood out in a crowd for his height—six feet seven to my five feet ten, if I stretched—but was distinguished more by his gentle demeanor.

But studying wouldn't be for a few months. For now, we had to find an apartment. Luckily, our friend Andy's stepmom was a real estate agent. Mrs. Schiff took us all over New York, which I had already started to refer to as the City.

Andy's stepmom was a bright, competent woman who wore her jet-black hair pulled tightly into a bun and, like most women in New York, sported an elegant black wardrobe. It was later explained to me that black was not only chic, but also hid the city's dirt and grime. In one day Rob and I checked out two apartments that she had selected. One was downtown on 14th Street, near Seventh Avenue, then a dodgy neighborhood on the edge of Greenwich Village. The apartment was improbably big, on the top floor of a walk-up with, we could barely believe it, a sauna. Despite the lavishness, it was cheap, because of the neighborhood.

The entrance of the building was recessed from the street, and I remarked that you might not be able to tell if someone were lying in wait for you late at night. "Well," she said, "when you walk home, you can always walk on the other side of the street and see if someone is there."

"The security," Rob recalled recently, "was the doorman across the street." This did not inspire confidence.

Farther uptown was a one-bedroom apartment on East 71st Street, between Second and Third Avenues, a safer neighborhood on the Upper East Side. With exposed brick (a big deal back then) but only one large bedroom, I wondered how we would fit. Andy's mom said that the living room was big enough to split into a living room and bedroom. Rob said he would be willing to pay a bit more and live in the large room if I'd take the living room. In a few days we had made our decision and told the landlord we would take the place. Then we moved back home for a few weeks, during which time I did some additional work with Peak Personnel, making money so that I could afford to move to New York to make money.

We moved in at the end of August, paying a security deposit of a month's rent, guaranteeing to our suspicious landlord that we wouldn't skip town without paying our rent.

Skipping town wouldn't have been difficult: Rob and I had few possessions. As agreed, we divided the living room in half, buying three cheap plywood bookcases that served as a divider and filled the room with a fresh woody smell. On one side was our couch, a chair, and a coffee table and credenza (the last two a gift from Rob's mom, a furniture saleswoman who purchased them from the company's outlet store), and on the other side were my mattress on a metal frame, an old desk, and a bureau.

During the many parties that we gave (which I remember happening only on hot summer nights when our GE air conditioner was broken), guests would spill out from the living room and end up in my bedroom, sometimes looking through my bureau and pulling out my underwear to hold up to the crowd. Once, one of my GE friends, after a few beers, climbed under the covers of my bed and shouted, "Look! I'm Jim Martin waking up late for work!" It grossed me out, so I washed the sheets the next day. Rob's mom also gave us a nice kitchen set, four cane-back chairs and a table, for our eat-in kitchen.

Like good 1980s yuppies, Rob and I put some framed fabric art on our walls and hung a few Patrick Nagel prints along with some Penn memorabilia. I decided that I would buy the prints and frame them and Rob could hang them. A few days after we moved in, I came home and found the art hung high on the wall.

"Rob," I said, "don't you know that you're supposed to hang photos at *eye level*?"

Rob, considerably taller, walked up to the photos, his face in front of a print a few inches above my head. "Eye level!"

The day we moved in, I walked out of my apartment and walked up and down East 71st Street, thinking, *I can't believe I'm living in New York!* Then, as now, this side street in Manhattan was mainly populated by high-priced apartments and town houses. Across the street was a town house whose owners had replaced the original square, paned windows with huge oval-shaped ones, which lent the place an insectlike appearance. We referred to it as the Bug House. The windows to our kitchen looked into a dark alley, which I found suitably urban.

As further testimony to my lack of religious awareness, I noticed that across the street was a place called Marymount Manhattan College. Flags flew from the facade of the building, which looked vaguely religious. Around the corner was an apartment building that also seemed to be part of Marymount, with a granite statue of Mary over the door. I had little clue what it was and even less interest. A few years after entering the Jesuits, I met a member of a religious order called the Religious of the Sacred Heart of Mary, also called the Marymount Sisters. At one point in the conversation, I mentioned I had lived on East 71st Street.

"Oh," she said delightedly, "right across the street from our college."

"Is that what that was?" I said.

When I mentioned the building with the statue of Mary, she told me it was a women's dorm. "You lived across from a Catholic college for two years and didn't know what it was?"

Rob recently reminded me that, for a time, he dated a woman in that building. "But I wasn't allowed past the lobby."

Rob and I quickly settled into a routine. When we were both home, I cooked (because I enjoyed it) and Rob washed the dishes (because we were dishwasher-less). To my surprise, Rob was such a desultory chef that when I was out and he was in, he would often resort to several cans of SpaghettiOs or, on one night, five hot dogs on five rolls, lined up on his plate.

Over the next two years, Rob and I grew close, as we worked our way up the corporate ladder(s), had fun, partied (often not together but with our work friends), and, overall, grew up. He told me recently that he remembered me as "loyal and kind," which I appreciated. And cheap. "Our friends in college used to say that if four of us went out to dinner and the bill was forty-four dollars, you would kick in ten," he told me recently. "My apologies if this is news to you."

It isn't. One source of either embarrassment or pride is that I never paid for pot during my high school, college, and postcollege years. I was being cheap, but not paying for drugs also allowed me to feel self-righteous. As if I could distance myself from any criminality by saying, "At least I never paid for it."

It was a perfect roommate situation. We gave each other dis-

How My Last Summer Job Turned Out

tance to spend time with other friends but spent plenty of time together too, going to the movies, shopping for groceries, and watching TV. We were partial to reruns of *The Honeymooners* and *The Odd Couple* and what are now called Britcoms, like *To the Manor Born* and *Good Neighbors*.

I also grew close to Rob's family, especially his parents, who would prove to be extremely supportive when I entered the Jesuits. Thanks to my Jewish friends, the most common reaction when I entered the Jesuits was "*Mazel tov!*" Rob told me recently that his parents, who have since died, reveled in the fact that they attended all three of what he called my "swearing-in ceremonies": First Vows as a Jesuit, my ordination as a deacon, and ordination as a priest.

Years later, when I was a Jesuit studying theology in Boston, Rob, who grew up nearby, invited me to his family's seder. At the time, I was in the middle of my Old Testament course and so at my lifetime peak of knowledge about the Hebrew Bible. At one point, Rob's mom started asking me questions about the Bible—not the traditional seder "Four Questions" that begin "What makes this night different from all other nights?" but general questions about the book of Exodus. I was able to field questions about Moses and Miriam, the Exodus and Passover with aplomb.

Rob's mom smiled at me approvingly and then turned to her Jewish son and said, "Rob, why don't you know as much about your own faith as your Catholic friend Jim?"

After dinner, the minute we stepped outside the front door, Rob laughed and said, "That's the last seder I ever invite *you* to!"

Try as I might, I don't remember any arguments with Rob. I'm sure we must have had some conflicts, but we were both too polite for arguing. One mild source of disagreement was my short-lived habit (which I had read about in a magazine and decided to try) of putting my underwear in the freezer on hot days. This was before the advent of air-conditioning on the subway and when men still wore suits and ties to work. Even my favorite lightweight khaki suit made me sweat as soon as I stepped onto the fetid subway platform. This practice lasted until I heard Rob bellow from the kitchen one morning, "Hey! Why is your underwear on the ice cube tray?"

The only time I saw Rob mildly cross was when he was studying for his CPA exam. I knew enough not to ask him how it went, and when he came home I asked, "How was it?"

"Over," he said. So I whipped up some chicken cutlets in cream of chicken soup to cheer him up in our little kitchen while we listened to Duran Duran on the radio, singing, "Hungry Like the Wolf." For me, the song seemed to define those years.

> Dark in the city, night is a wire
> Steam in the subway, earth is afire
> Do do do do do do do do do do do do do do

I didn't know what "night is a wire" meant, exactly. But I liked the refrain:

> In touch with the ground
> I'm on the hunt, I'm after you
> Smell like I sound, I'm lost in a crowd
> And I'm hungry like the *wooooolf.*

During those years, I felt if not like a wolf, then hungry. I was hungry to succeed at work, make money, win friends, be successful, whatever that meant. So did many of my friends. But it was nice to have someone normal—not a shark, not a wolf, not a jerk—to room with.

On my first day of work, a bright August day, I stopped at the corner newsstand. In my Jos. A. Bank suit ("I always picture you in a red-and-blue tie," Rob remembered; I was nothing if not a faithful Penn grad) I decided it would be good to start reading the local newspaper.

"The New York Times," I said brightly.

The newsstand owner laughed and said, "Kid, you're *in* New Yawk! It's just 'the Times'!"

So began my last summer job.

Entering the ornate art deco lobby of 570 Lexington Avenue at East 51st Street, then still called the GE Building, I felt like I had won the lottery. How could I have dithered over what job to take? I was working in *New York*! At *GE*! Of course I had worked hard in college (and also had some help from a neighbor's father who worked at GE and put in a good word), but I still felt lucky.

The director of the Financial Management Program, an affable man nicknamed "Sandy" Duncan, presumably because of his blond hair and not any resemblance to the then-popular actress, met me in the lobby and took me to his office on the twenty-first floor. Sandy worked in Financial Planning and Analysis with another guy nicknamed "Rusty" Nail, because of his red hair. Sandy, who was friendly and gracious and seemed much older but was probably only in his early thirties, told me how happy he was that I had joined them. "Me too!" I practically shouted.

As with most first days at any company, I spent the rest of the day focused on human resource issues: filling out this and that form. Finally, I signed a document saying that I would abide by the ethical rules of the company, got a photo taken for my ID (I was still sporting a college mustache, because I thought I looked too young, but my mother thought it made me look "too Italian"), and was shown around the offices. Sandy told me that my first "rotation" in the Financial Management Program would be in the Income Margin department on the seventh floor. Was that okay? Sure! *Did anyone notice my new Brooks Brothers tie?* I wondered.

At noon, on this sultry summer day, two other FMPs (as we were called) took me out to a cheap beer-and-burger restaurant of the kind that proliferated in Manhattan at the time, variously called Bun and Brew, Beer & Burger, Bun 'n' Beer, and so on. Though I was in tip-top drinking shape thanks to Penn, I found that after two pitchers of beer between the three of us, I was buzzed by the end of the hour-long meal. Lunch hour meant one hour, strictly enforced, so we hurried back.

Unfortunately, my first task that afternoon was reviewing some microfiche files, a long-ago way of storing information on film strips that were unspooled under a light source and projected onto a small desktop screen. In 1982, desktop computers were just being introduced. That meant we still used desktop calculators and recorded our accounting entries on long sheets with carbon copies. Microfiche readers were part of that ancient regime.

As I, still buzzed from lunch, rolled the microfiche spool and stared at the screen, with tiny numbers rushing by me like pills on an assembly line, I almost fell asleep. I went to the bathroom to splash cold water on my face and rinse out my mouth, terrified that someone would realize I was drunk and fire me. I didn't know that many of the employees (and executives) were just as buzzed as I was after lunch.

After returning from the bathroom, I sat down at my desk,

How My Last Summer Job Turned Out

looked out the window onto Lexington Avenue, and tried to sober up. My manager was a garrulous and efficient woman named Mary, whom I liked immediately. She was a Brooklynite who worked hard but didn't take anything too seriously.

GE was making a massive shift from its days as a safe, reliable, dependable, though somewhat stodgy, company presided over by the avuncular Reginald H. Jones into a more cutthroat and competitive firm managed by its newly appointed CEO, Jack Welch. As a result, many "old school" employees still worked there, making the office enjoyable.

Along with Mary, for example, I worked with Lois, a longtime GE employee. "I've got the meatball tattooed on my ass," she'd say, referring to the company's circular logo. She was fun, direct, and spoke with a flawless New York accent and was, not incidentally, a devoted admirer of Elvis Presley. She kept a framed photo of the King on her desk, and each year on the anniversary of his death she wore a black dress and black earrings. After lunch, she served us all a black cake (dark chocolate, in fact) while "Love Me Tender" played on a cassette player.

I was introduced to this tradition the next summer and was amazed not so much by the custom (working in my various summer jobs had given me a taste of plenty of personal quirkinesses) but that everyone, even at a Fortune 500 company, seemed unfazed. "I love Elvis Day," said Mary as she tucked into a slice of cake. On non-Elvis days, when one of the King's songs came on the radio, Lois would ask (expect, really) that everyone in the office would stop talking. This included, at least for Lois, phone conversations. If Lois was speaking on the phone, she would tell the caller that she had to go and hang up.

Lois worked with Sheila, who had a similar affection for Frank

Sinatra. (We were, however, permitted to talk during Frank's songs.) When Sheila was hired by GE in the 1960s, her co-workers suggested that she inform the management that she was unmarried. (Many managers at the time thought that single women made for more dedicated workers.) So Sheila officially remained single, and although she had worked for GE for decades, when her daughter visited the office, she was referred to as her niece, and the daughter's father as her brother. We all did the same to be polite. According to my sister, New York Life, the insurance company where she would eventually work, would fire women who got married, well into the 1960s.

As a trainee in the company's vaunted Financial Management Program, I would spend the next two years in a training program that moved me through "rotational job assignments" in finance and accounting, combined with finance and accounting courses, which they told us were every bit as good as an MBA. Rob and I would spend a good deal of our time in New York studying—him for the CPA exam and me for FMP courses. Still, while the CPA exam was only once a year, the FMP courses were constant. "You're the only one I know who studied business at Wharton," said Rob, "so he could get a job where he studied business."

Though I had spent the previous few years trying to avoid making stupid mistakes, I still made quite a few in my first days at GE.

In Income Margin, I worked with two other FMPs. One of them, Hisham, was a smart, friendly guy of Lebanese descent around my age whose last name was El-Azem. When he answered the phone, he would say "El-Azem," but I always I heard "LSM," which I assumed was yet another company acronym. Stepping into GE meant stepping into a sea of abbreviations. There was GETSCO (GE Technical Services), GEIC (GE Investment Corp), GECC (GE Credit Corp), and so on. About the only one we avoided was GENCO, the name of the fictional olive oil firm run by Don Corleone in *The Godfather*. There weren't many that started with an *L*, but what did I know?

So a few days into my job, I answered the phone and said confidently, "LSM!" After I hung up the phone, Hisham said, "Why did you answer the phone like that?" I flushed, as I often did when I knew that I had done something wrong. I thought back to the Bicentennial Wagon Train.

"That's the name of the department, isn't it?" I felt like a moron.

Hisham laughed. "No, that's *my* name!"

I would like to say that during the next two years, I carefully weighed my options for the future, reflecting on what life would bring and generally trying to meditate on who God was calling me to be. But that would not be the case.

Instead, the next two years were divided between working hard in my rotations, studying for our in-house exams, and drinking and spending time at a variety of clubs, most of which no longer exist.

So let us pause to mourn the passing of these early-1980s places for music, dancing, and drinking: 8BC (whose clever name meant you could never forget its location on East 8th Street between Avenues B and C), the Palladium, Area (in the no-man's-land neighborhood near the Holland Tunnel), CBGB, Limelight (a former church), the Garage, the vast Tunnel, Danceteria, the uber-preppy Surf Club (the rare dance club on the Upper East Side), and my favorite: the Pyramid Club, where I saw my first-ever drag show, watched a performance artist throw pieces of raw chicken into the dancing crowd, listened to "rants" (monologues with music), and danced to music I'd never heard before, shoulder to shoulder with the widest variety of people I'd ever danced with before or since: punk rockers with pierced lips, spiked hair, and sleeveless T-shirts; goths with jet-black T-shirts and torn jeans; gay men dressed like David Bowie; and yuppies with ties loosened and their Brooks Brothers jackets thrown on the floor. I went to the Pyramid Club as often as I could.

Down the street from the Pyramid Club was a Ukrainian diner/bar called Odessa, which had the most wonderful food: steaming pierogi, great scrambled eggs, and *kasha varnishkes*. When you entered, famished, late at night, especially in the winter, you wanted to stay forever in this warm place that smelled like coffee, bacon and eggs, and boiled cabbage.

The Pyramid Club and Odessa were in Alphabet City (so called because of its location at Avenues A, B, C, and D, east of First Avenue), which in the early 1980s was an arty, scuzzy, bohemian, rat-infested, and occasionally dangerous neighborhood. Often when I left the Pyramid Club in the wee hours, Avenue A was devoid of people, and lining its sidewalks were closed, abandoned, or shuttered buildings. I always kept "mug money" (twenty dollars stored inside my shoe) ready should I get mugged on my way back to the subway stop at Astor Place, a fifteen-minute walk through an unlit landscape of drug addicts, pushers, and other sketchy types. And cat-size rats.

One night, around 2 a.m., as I left the Pyramid Club, a police cruiser pulled up beside me on Avenue A. I was drunk so I thought that I was going to be arrested. I still felt a kind of instinctive guilt in these situations, even though I had done nothing wrong: "Forgive me, Officer, for I have sinned!"

Instead, a policeman rolled down the window and said, "Where are you going?"

"To the subway."

"Not at this time of night you're not. Get in."

Oh no! I was being arrested!

How My Last Summer Job Turned Out

Once I was inside the police cruiser, he and his partner told me that the neighborhood was too dangerous to walk around in. "Especially in a suit!" said the driver with a laugh. They drove me to Astor Place, and as I exited the car he said, "Be more careful, kid!" Every time I was called "kid" I felt like I was in a 1940s movie.

Most weekends I would hang out with a few of the twenty trainees in nearby bars, where there was free food during happy hours. In addition to clubbing there were always concerts downtown, though I never attended massive concerts in stadiums and arenas, thanks to their cost (my only one was Bruce Springsteen in Philadelphia, both enjoyable and impressive for its three-hour run time). I preferred smaller venues and somewhat lesser-known singers downtown: Suzanne Vega, Squeeze, Steve Forbert, the Washington Squares, or other folky artists at the Bottom Line, Webster Hall, the Lone Star Cafe, the Bitter End, the Village Vanguard, or Peppermint Lounge, all of which featured insanely expensive drinks. During the summers, there were free concerts in Central Park, baseball games at Yankee Stadium, and the occasional Broadway show. Most of these events were followed up by a visit to an East Side bar, many long gone: JG Melon, Dorrian's Red Hand, the Mad Hatter, the Beach Cafe, P. J. Clarke's, and the Old Stand, the last of which had the best happy hour hors d'oeuvres in Midtown.

During my time at Penn, I tried to avoid letting my parents see me (or hear me or know of me) getting drunk and certainly not high. But one night, coming back from an Upper East Side bar where I had drunk too much sambuca on a dare, I suddenly remembered that my father was going on a business trip the next day. My practice was to call to wish him a safe trip. Unthinkingly, I dialed the number from my bedroom, while I stared at three nickel-size stains of sambuca on my tie.

"Hi, Dad!" I said, and then started slurring my words.

Horrified, I thought, *I can easily speak clearly*, and tried. I could not.

"Are you *drunk*?" said my dad.

In the background my mom gasped. "Is Jimmy *drunk*?"

Then followed a lecture on why not to get drunk in front of my workmates. My dad, though a seasoned businessman, seemed unaware that this was not an offense at GE. "I hope you're not going to lose your job!" said my mom. Not at GE, of all places, I wanted to say.

New York for me at age twenty-one was close to perfect. I drew energy from the pace, the crowds, the noise, the music, and the feeling that I was living in the middle of everything that mattered. Discovering the newest restaurants, the hottest clubs, the most popular Broadway shows, and the latest movies. It was easy to get spoiled and self-satisfied. At one point, I ran across John Updike's observation that New Yorkers think that people living anywhere else in the country are, to some degree, "kidding." That sounded right. I started to call it "the City," as some of my Penn friends had.

I also started to imbibe some of the questionable ethics of the yuppie era. Once, my high school friend Greg was visiting from Massachusetts, where he was studying for his PhD. Greg was one of the kindest people I knew. On the way to a restaurant, we were walking down the street and approached a homeless man. I walked not only by him, but over him, stepping over his legs as he begged. "How can you do that?" said Greg.

"You get used to it," I said dismissively. I found myself doing things like that to impress others: something that seemed savvy when it was just mean.

My career at GE also coincided with the era of Reaganomics and

How My Last Summer Job Turned Out

the Age of the Yuppie. Enrollment at graduate and undergraduate business programs soared, and the yuppies disgorged by these schools were swallowed up by multinational corporations like GE, consulting firms, investment banks, and (even) commercial banks. Although my friends and I assiduously avoided the term "yuppie," which was seen as an insult, that's precisely what we were: young, urban professionals. "Corporate tool" was another epithet, with a double meaning: We were tools as in cogs in the corporate machine, but also tools as in jerks. (*Forbes*, the business magazine, capitalized on this epithet by puckishly calling itself the "Capitalist Tool.")

It's hard for me to remember exactly what I felt back then about the corporate world since my life is now so different. Recently, though, my longtime friend Peggy read an early version of this manuscript and offered a less biased view. (Along with a terrific memory, she's also blessed with letters I sent her from that time):

> You told me that protesters were once picketing out on the sidewalk in front of 570 Lex, just as you were entering the building. One protester snarled at you, "Do you know how many people GE can kill with one of their nuclear bombs?" to which you responded, "Do *you* know how much they pay their junior executives?" I thought at the time that your parents were happy that you worked for a Fortune 500 company, on the executive track, and you were happy if they were happy. I remember you cheerfully holding your paycheck for me to see, when you were a new GE employee. And since I came from a pro-business family, I wasn't raised with anti-capitalist views at home. So I was happy for you! But you weren't arrogant about having a lot of "stuff." You lived pretty simply, with Rob, and also when you moved out to Forest Hills. You

wanted to use your money for experiences (and fun parties), instead of expensive things.

In 1985, Rob and I, though still close, decided that we would not renew our two-year lease, despite two years of fun. Frankly, I couldn't remember what prompted this. I know that I moved to a place in Queens with some GE friends, but what instigated our rental breakup, I had forgotten. Rob explained in an email response to my query: "Because you were a frugal SOB and didn't want to pay the exorbitant NYC rents. Your decision to break up an extraordinary living situation forced my hand and led to my panic-stricken embarking on a housing search of my own. That culminated in my first real estate purchase on the island of Manhattan."

You may know where this story ends. After six years at GE, I would enter the Jesuit novitiate. At this point you may wonder: Were you thinking about the Jesuits or becoming a priest?

No.

If you had asked me if I wanted to be a priest in those days, I might have paused, for perhaps that desire was buried within me, but then I probably would have made a joke to cover it up. I went to Mass many Sundays at the Church of St. Vincent Ferrer, a church run by the Dominican Order, not far from my apartment. And as Peggy mentioned, even though I enjoyed my paycheck, and my new Brooks Brothers suits, I wasn't obsessed with owning and acquiring lots of "stuff." But between dating and drinking, I was hardly a monk, and my ignorance of Catholic life, and religious orders, was so vast that after I entered the novitiate, my novice director asked me where I went to Mass while I was living in New York. I said "St. Vincent Ferrer."

"Oh," he said, "the Dominican parish, right?"

"No," I said, "it was mostly Anglos, as I recall. Not too many Dominican people, as far as I remember."

He said, "No, I mean the Dominican *Order*."

"Uh, is it? What? They run the parish?"

"Didn't you notice their white habits?"

"I just saw them in their robes during Mass."

"Their vestments," he said. "Didn't you notice their habits when you saw them outside of Mass?"

Why, I asked, would I be speaking to a priest outside of Mass?

So I didn't know much about priests. For that matter, I didn't know much about Jesus, God, or the Bible. At one point, my friend Carol, my across-the-street neighbor in Plymouth Meeting, came to visit New York. (Carol was the one who had invited me to all those Presbyterian youth group ice-cream-eating, roller-skating socials.) We splurged on tickets for the Andrew Lloyd Webber and Tim Rice musical *Joseph and the Amazing Technicolor Dreamcoat*, which tells the story of Joseph in the book of Genesis, in which ten of his brothers sell him into slavery. At the intermission, I said to Carol, "What a great story! I wonder how it's going to end?"

"What do you mean?" said Carol. "It's the story of Joseph from the Old Testament."

"Yeah, I know," I said. "I wonder how it's going to end?"

So I didn't know much about the Bible, hardly anything about the priesthood, and even less about religious orders. When I prayed it was to ask God for things: help me pass my FMP exams or get a raise. That was the extent of my relationship with God. For now, I was happy to be in New York, more interested in having fun than discerning my future, and more interested in money than in God.

For now.

GE Capital, Stamford, Connecticut, 1985. Peak 1980s corporate fashion: pastel ties for the guys, shoulder pads for the women.

On the day of my First Vows as a Jesuit (in 1990, two years after this book ends), my friends from high school and college came to the Jesuit novitiate in Boston. Some of them laid bets on how long I would stay in the Jesuits. The longest estimate was six months.

CHAPTER 11

How the Ice Cream Inn Prepared Me for Life

AFTER I SPENT THREE YEARS AT 570 LEX, LIVING IN Manhattan for two years and commuting from Queens for the third, GE decided that it was time to close our office. The company was booming but Jack Welch was slashing anything, or anyone, he saw as deadwood. During our employee evaluations, your manager would rank you as a 1, 2, 3, or 4, with 1 being a "high pot" (high potential) and 4 being a "low pot." If you were a 4, you were rarely ever able to make it onto job slates for new openings and were thus encouraged to leave. On top of this, Jack (as we all called him, not out of any familiarity but because his stature was such that he needed only one name, like Elvis) decided that the lowest performing 10 percent of workers would be culled, like weaker animals in a herd. You either moved up in the company or left. "Up or out," as we said.

This was a dramatic change to the corporate culture of GE

under its previous CEO, Reginald H. Jones, whose very name bespoke a clubby, sedate, stable corporation where employees were content to spend their whole lives and were therefore willing to make great sacrifices—chief among them, moving their families all over the country, and sometimes around the world—for the reciprocal promise of GE's care for them. It was about fidelity: the employee to the company and the company to the employee. Like Lois, they would often say that they too had the GE logo tattooed on their butt.

Now Jack Welch was axing whole divisions. (His nickname, which he loathed, was Neutron Jack, after a bomb that would supposedly kill people but leave buildings standing.) GE's New York office handled the international finance and accounting work for the GE affiliates (aircraft engines, lighting, appliances, and so on), but Jack decided that could be done by the affiliates themselves. After graduating from the Financial Management Program, I spent a year on a special project, auditing the Plant and Equipment accounts for the building, to prepare for the building's eventual sale.

One day the manager of our division called us together into an auditorium and pointed to a column of numbers projected onto the back wall. "Here are how many people are working in this building now." He pointed to the number: four hundred, as I recall. "And here is how many will be left at the end of the year." The number was fifty. "Any questions?" The room fell silent, as many people who had worked their entire lives at GE contemplated their futures. It was especially difficult for people who had, under Reginald Jones, sacrificed so much. To be clear, many companies were going through the same "restructuring" in the early 1980s. At the same time, many took their cues from Jack Welch and GE. We FMP graduates were told that there was certainly a place for us in any of the GE affiliates. The older employees were not as lucky.

This transition involved, finally, a real reflection on what I was doing with my life. Finance and accounting paid well, but they were to me, in the end, rather dull. Business is a real vocation for a lot of people, but it increasingly seemed less so for me.

So I started job hunting in a desultory way, confident that GE would have an opening for me in Stamford, Connecticut, with GE Credit Corp (soon to be rebranded as GE Capital), the financial services arm of GE that began as a way to lend people money to purchase refrigerators and washing machines but then became in essence a full-fledged financial institution. GE Capital was the undisputed star of the GE empire, the fastest growing part of the company, and its contribution to the bottom line grew rapidly during the 1980s and 1990s. Decades later, however, GE would fail for many reasons, including selling off its stable divisions (small appliances, for example) and focusing overly on financial services. When the global financial crisis hit, GE, no longer as diversified, was therefore unable to weather the financial storms.

In the meantime, why not consider some other jobs? I stumbled upon an opening at the Museum of Modern Art, in its finance department. For a few days I enjoyed the idea of working at an office where I would be surrounded by Matisses and Cézannes. The job would involve a significant pay cut, but I figured it would be more enjoyable than GE. In the end, I was turned down for a novel reason. They explained that I was overqualified, and they were worried that I would leave for a higher-paying job.

GE Capital was a safer bet. There was even an opening in human resources, running the Financial Management Program for all of

Connecticut, which included the offices in Stamford (GE Capital) and Fairfield (corporate headquarters). There were roughly forty trainees to manage, with rotations all over the world: Stamford and Fairfield, but also Raleigh, London, and Frankfurt, those final three being plum assignments. Maybe, I thought, human resources would be more interesting than working directly in finance and accounting.

I enjoyed working in HR. The people were generally pleasant, though sadly, we did not celebrate Elvis Day. And I felt like I was making a difference by working with actual human beings, rather than toting up columns of numbers. The trainees were bright and motivated recent college grads, whom I enjoyed mentoring, even though I was just a few years older. It certainly beat bussing tables and standing in front of an assembly line. It even beat working in accounting and finance, which had begun to lose its appeal. Still, wasn't there more to life?

Another difference from my time in New York: I dealt with a few managers who were, frankly, mean. Remember the customer who burst into the back room to berate me for bussing the table during the Bicentennial Wagon Train? Or the golfer who made me stand in the rain while I held his golf clubs during a thunderstorm? From time to time, I saw replays of that kind of selfish disregard for others at GE, except now it happened in an air-conditioned office.

As an official HR person, I was privileged (or fated) to see what went on behind closed doors. At one point, a midlevel manager told me that he was planning to fire an employee without much cause. I reminded the manager that we had in fact just given this employee an incentive award for good performance. "I don't care," said the manager. "I wanna bounce him." I tried another tack: The employee had been there for many years and had a family. The manager was immovable. Finally, as a last resort, I pleaded, "Have some compassion." His two-word answer burned itself into my memory: "F—K compassion!"

My friend Peggy's less-biased memory of that time jibes with what I remember:

> You confided in me that sometimes news would come down from on high that you had to get rid of some worker, and you felt conflicted because you had an HR procedure that you had to warn them about first and give them a chance to improve their work output. Your HR training seemed to be thrown out the window. One day I met you at your parents' house to go out, and you and your mom told me about how bad things had gotten at work. People you fired were blaming and aiming at *you*, and you were stressed out about how to respond.

Add to that attitude the near-constant workload (most nights and many weekends), and despite the facts that I was paid well and had some wonderful friends with whom I often drove into New York to visit my favorite clubs, I started to feel that I was in the wrong place. All the stress brought on some stomach problems as well, which compounded my misery. At one point I got my first migraine and thought I was having a stroke. My doctor said, "You need to cut back."

Before we go further, I want to stress that not everyone at GE behaved badly. The vast majority of my fellow employees and bosses were kind, friendly, and ethical. Business, again, is a vocation for many people and an important way to contribute to the common good. GE made aircraft engines that got people to where they wanted to go, medical-imaging machines that saved lives, and power generators that provided energy and light for whole communities. And when I started there, they made light bulbs too. Some of my closest friends worked for GE for their entire adult lives. GE was not a hellscape of immoral people.

But there was enough mean, thoughtless, and immoral behavior to unsettle me. A few of the managers were truly jerks. Eventually, I started to wonder whether I wanted to advance in a company that rewarded ruthlessness, or at least tolerated it. And why was I working so hard for such a company?

At one point, I brought all the financial management trainees to GE's corporate headquarters in Fairfield, Connecticut, to hear a presentation from one of the company's top finance executives. After a rah-rah talk on the future of the company, he asked if there were any questions. One young trainee, a woman, noted that all the trainees were working considerable amounts of overtime without pay. "So I guess my question is—"

"I know what your question is," he said, cutting her off.

Everyone stared at him.

"Your question is: What does the company owe you in return?" He paused and gave an answer I will never forget.

"GE doesn't owe you a F—ING THING!"

The woman who asked the question was stunned into silence. A few of the trainees craned their necks toward me, seated in the back of the auditorium, to gauge my reaction. I was appalled but tried to look blasé.

I didn't mind working hard. I had worked hard since delivering papers, mowing lawns, and bussing tables, and my work ethic got me through my subsequent summer jobs and through high school and college. Working was part of life, and working hard was how you got ahead.

But I had never worked in a job that so thoroughly consumed me. During my time at 570 Lex in New York, we were tasked with completing the annual closing, when the company would tote up its yearly financial reports. This necessitated almost round-the-clock work for several weeks beginning at the end of December. Some of us checked into a divey hotel across the street because we were working so many late nights in a row. But that was once a year. At GE Capital, we seemed to work at that pace every day of the year—including weekends.

Between the stress of work and difficult managers, I realized that I was miserable. And because of the stomach problems, I stopped drinking. Beer, gin and tonics, and kamikazes were hardly healthy for my gut; and who likes to be hungover? Now in my mid-twenties, I found it took me longer to recover from late-night drinking than when I was in college. I stopped drinking almost completely, not out of moral compunction, but for purely physical reasons.

On one particularly stressful day I doodled on my desk blotter, "I hate my life." It seemed circular: I go to work so I can make money so I can support myself so I can go to work. A few days later, one of my friends was sitting at my desk playfully putting his feet on the desk, going through my drawers, mock-answering the phone, and pretending he was me. He glanced down at the blotting paper on my desk.

His face fell and he paused. "Do you really hate your life?"

One evening, after a long day at work, I went home, reheated some spaghetti and meatballs, and turned on the television. I flipped around aimlessly. I didn't watch much TV; usually I was either at work or out with friends. *Cheers* was on, but I had already seen the episode so I switched to PBS.

The sonorous voice of the veteran narrator Alexander Scourby filled the living room, and the first word out of his mouth was "Merton." Merton who?

The program was *Merton: A Film Biography*, a documentary about the Trappist monk Thomas Merton.

In sure, swift strokes the film recounted the story of Thomas Merton, a brilliant young man who "gave it all up" to enter a Trappist monastery in Kentucky. Something about the look on his face—calm, wise, peaceful—spoke to me. I wondered: *What did this guy know that I don't?* The monastery itself, a quiet place nestled amid rolling hills, was the picture of serenity. Suddenly I had a longing to visit there, to *live* there. It reminded me of my experience in the meadow way back in elementary school, a place I wanted to enter into, even possess.

I knew almost nothing about monastic life, other than having read *The Name of the Rose* a few years before, which alternately enchanted me and creeped me out. Umberto Eco's elegant 592-page novel about a murder in a medieval monastery was filled with monks both inspiring and insane.

But whatever it was that Merton had, I wanted. His life seemed beautiful, meaningful, even romantic in a way. Before I knew it, the movie was over. I went back to *Cheers* but couldn't get Thomas Merton out of my mind.

The next day I went to Barnes & Noble and searched for something about Merton. I had no idea if he was famous or not, and it took me a while to find the "Religion" section, but eventually I found his memoir *The Seven Storey Mountain*, published in 1948.

How the Ice Cream Inn Prepared Me for Life

That night, in bed, I started his book and within a few pages thought, *Why have I never read anything like this before? Why have I not learned about spirituality? Why have I not been interested in religion?*

It wasn't my parents' fault. They were good people. But, surprisingly for an Irish American father and an Italian American mother growing up in the 1930s and 1940s, neither was especially religious. My father attended a Catholic elementary school and Catholic high school run by the Christian Brothers, and his older sister, Marguerite, who helped raise him after their father's death, was devoutly religious. But he was not. My sister remembers my dad telling her that his own mother would clean linens for a Catholic sister she knew, so I suppose my grandmother was religious. For her part, my mother, perhaps because the Italian parish in her neighborhood (St. Lucy's in Manayunk) was so far away, wasn't especially devout either.

My longtime friend Peggy related this story about my mom, which I had never heard. The two were always close, and after my father died, Peggy would often take my mom out to dinner. She also had an astute observation about my dad:

> Your mom told me that your Sicilian grandfather had to get a "straw buyer" in order to purchase the house in Roxborough. She said that there was only one Catholic family on Rector Street, but they were Irish. A Sicilian family would not be welcome. Maybe your mom downplayed or rejected her religious background in order to fit in with her Protestant schoolmates in Roxborough. And your dad was probably like my dad. After a whole childhood of Catholic education, maybe a little rebellion was in order.

Around the time I discovered Thomas Merton, I was going to Mass most Sundays at St. Leo's, a pleasant parish with inspiring priests in Stamford. But I still saw God mainly as a remote judge. The idea that one could devote one's life to God seemed noble but distant, and for other people, people like Thomas Merton. For the saints. Not for me.

Merton's way of life, however, seemed infinitely more appealing than my own. So I started to think about doing something else, even though I couldn't imagine what that something else would be.

The problem was that I couldn't see a way out. My position at GE wasn't some summer job that I could toss aside for a different one next year. My question "How hard could it be?" returned. Only this time it wasn't about avoiding dogs on a paper route, dropping a banana split glass, or standing in the right spot on a golf green, but about something more fundamental to life: finding happiness. Happiness seemed hard. Living a meaningful life seemed out of reach, like a golf ball in a water hazard.

But I knew that Merton's life was more fulfilling than mine. So I started on a reading tour of his books, beginning with *The Seven Storey Mountain*, which recounted his journey from a jaded, dissatisfied, and unsettled young man to a contented Trappist monk. It is very much the book of a young person: clear and direct, with lots of black-and-white choices. In later life, Merton regretted some of the certainty of this book, which could be summarized as "world bad, monastery good." But it was just what I needed then: someone telling me that the world I was living in, the world of climbing and competition, wasn't perfect. I devoured the book in a few days. But not until I read Merton's *No Man Is an Island* did I come across the words that changed me.

How the Ice Cream Inn Prepared Me for Life

Let me put this into context. I'm a twenty-five-year-old corporate tool who has worked hard in a succession of summer jobs, studied hard in high school and college, and now has what he was aiming for all along: a promising financial career. My childhood dreams of being comfortably wealthy seemed within reach. (I could buy as many pup tents as I wanted.) I had plenty of wonderful friends too. But the focus of my life was work. And now work, around which my college education and the rest of life revolved, seemed to have failed me. Wharton set me on a conveyor belt that led to a high-paying job, but that job didn't seem to be what I wanted.

One night while reading *No Man Is an Island*, I came upon this passage: "Why do we have to spend our lives striving to be something that we would never want to be, if we only knew what we wanted? Why do we waste our time doing things which, if we only stopped to think about them, are just the opposite of what we were made for?"

Yes! I thought as I sat in bed. *That's me!*

But what *was* I made for? By now, I knew the answer was not working at GE.

Maybe, I thought, without knowing much about it, but based solely on Thomas Merton's life, I could become a priest.

More than forty years later, I can feel the strangeness of considering that path, as if I were joining the circus or trying out for the Phillies. Something so unexpected as to be almost laughable. True, I had worked in a variety of jobs in the past for which I was unprepared. But this was considering not just a different job, but a different life.

I knew no priests other than the ones I saw celebrating Mass on

Sundays. In the 1960s and 1970s, a priest from our parish church would visit our house once a year for the "block collection," when our family would sit uncomfortably in our living room and, at the end of a stilted discussion about how often we went to Mass and why my sister and I weren't going to Catholic school, my father would hand the priest an envelope with a cash donation and the whole family would kneel in front of the front door while the priest blessed us in the name of the Father, and of the Son, and of the Holy Spirit. But I don't think I ever spoke to a priest outside of that annual visit, the times (not many) I went to confession, and during Mass when I would say "Amen" after the priest said "the Body of Christ," when he held up the Eucharistic host.

I didn't know what priests *did*. I thought that they spent the whole week writing their homilies for Sunday Mass and on Saturdays heard confessions and maybe did a funeral or a wedding when needed. The idea never dawned on me that a parish priest manages the complex operation that is the parish (including its planning, finances, operations, and staff); visits parishioners in the hospital; and often helps to run a school, a soup kitchen, and all manner of adult education programs; along with myriad other duties. Today I know that parish priests are among the busiest people you'll ever meet.

I had almost no idea what religious orders were. Merton entered a Trappist monastery, and I knew that there were monks and maybe women monks too, or nuns (what did you even call them?), who, I supposed, sat in their rooms and prayed all day. I had heard of Franciscans, Dominicans, Jesuits, and by this point Trappists, but I didn't know what they *did*. I knew the Franciscans were poor and the Jesuits ran schools. That's about it. At one point I noticed in the parish bulletin at St. Leo's in Stamford that the names of some of the priests had initials after them: OFM, OP, SJ, which represented their religious orders (Order of Friars Minor, Order of Preachers, and Society of Jesus). I thought these were academic degrees. Maybe going to a Jesuit school meant you were a Jesuit?

Thus, I didn't know any priests, didn't know what they did, and didn't understand what a religious order was. Nevertheless, on the strength of one book, I talked to the local parish priest one day after Mass. "I think I might like to become a priest," I said, feeling silly for saying it.

The priest was enthusiastic, telling me, "In that case, you might want to contact the local vocations office here in the diocese." Then he thought for a moment. "And you might as well contact the Jesuits, up the street at Fairfield University." On such asides lives are changed.

A few days later, I met a priest at Fairfield, a Jesuit university thirty minutes from Stamford. He gave me some standard vocational literature about the Jesuits and took down my name and address after chatting with me for a few minutes. From the looks of the Jesuit brochures, young Jesuits divided their days evenly between praying and playing basketball (uh-oh).

In the cloistered safety of my Mazda GLC, I read about their vows of poverty, chastity, and obedience, which seemed weird. Life in a religious community seemed to promise no privacy and made me think of my parents' asking "Who's on the phone?" Their status as the largest men's missionary order was even worse: I didn't want to end up in some far-flung Nowheresville cut off from family and friends. I rethought my enthusiasm and tossed the brochure away as soon as I got home. But like clockwork over the next few months, vocational literature appeared in my mailbox. I was afraid that my roommates would see it and ask uncomfortable questions, so I tore each piece up at the mailbox and tossed it in the trash.

But the more I thought about it, the more I liked what I read. Even though I still knew little about the Jesuits, a life of service to God seemed more appealing than the life I was living as a young executive for GE. I started to read whatever I could about the Jesuits. And I started to think more and more about how I liked GE less and less.

A year or so after reading Thomas Merton, I swallowed my pride and asked to see the in-house staff psychologist at the Employee Assistance Program. Over the previous few years in Stamford, I had sent enough people to her, given all the stress at work.

She quickly sized me up as someone whose stress had led to physical problems, like migraines and stomach issues. She recommended that I see a psychologist named Anne who worked in an office with many macramé hangings and wicker chairs, in nearby Westport. Anne asked me to do biofeedback on a machine that monitored my heart rate and breathing and skin temperature, and the display screen nearly exploded and emitted a series of fast-paced, high-pitched beeps when she asked me about work. She recommended that I see another therapist, a kindly middle-aged man who worked from an office also in Westport.

I had never been to a therapist; the only model I had was the therapy scenario in the film *Ordinary People*, and so I figured that, like Conrad Jarrett, I would have a dramatic breakthrough when I realized something about my parents, which would end with my crying and ransacking the psychologist's poorly lit office out of anger or whatever pent-up emotion I was supposed to be feeling.

How the Ice Cream Inn Prepared Me for Life

The therapist simply asked me about my life today. Why did I feel such stress? (Work.) Why was I working at GE anyway? (What else would I do?) We dug deeper over the next few months, and eventually he asked me the question that changed my life. By that point, I had read enough about the Jesuits that it seemed a beautiful way to live, and I wanted to leave GE. But I was stuck.

"So, why are you working at GE if you don't like it?"

"I wouldn't know what else to do. I studied business. Wouldn't it be a waste of my education if I didn't work in business?"

"Not necessarily."

"Well, what would I do?"

Then he asked the question that I think every young person should be asked.

"What would you do if you could do anything you wanted to do?"

"Oh, that's easy," I said instantly. "I'd be a Jesuit."

"Then why don't you do that?"

Yeah, I thought with sudden clarity, *why don't I?*

I went back to my office and called the Jesuits and asked to begin the application process.

I'll spare you the details of what applications to the Society of Jesus entailed. In brief: completing a battery of interviews with a series of Jesuits; filling out a lengthy application form and writing a "spiritual autobiography"; visiting the Jesuit novitiate in Boston; and undergoing a medical examination and soliciting recommendations from family, friends, and co-workers. Rob jokingly sent me an altered copy of a generous recommendation that ended, "Signed, Rob, Jew." (The original included only his name.)

Finally, I took a battery of psychological exams. During the general intelligence test, I was asked all those questions from the psych experiments at Penn: "When was Goethe born?" "Where does rubber come from?" "How far is it from New York to Los Angeles?" I remembered the answers from my days at Penn. It wasn't exactly cheating, but I wouldn't have known them had I not looked them up in college. I felt guilty, but still, it couldn't hurt that the Jesuits thought they were admitting some kind of super genius.

One unnerving requirement was an eight-day silent retreat at the Campion Renewal Center in Weston, Massachusetts, a sprawling retreat house located on acres of beautiful fields and woodlands a few miles outside of Boston, not far from Lexington and Concord. I had heard of retreats but had no clue what one did at them. Sit in a chapel and pray with your eyes closed for hours on end? Wait for a vision? Voices? When I asked the Jesuits in Boston to fax me an agenda so that I could prepare for the week-plus away from work (a considerable amount of vacation time for a non-vacation event), the director of vocations, a cheerful, red-haired young priest named Jim whom I had met a few weeks before, said, "Oh, there's no agenda."

I thought: *No agenda? What's wrong with these people?*

My retreat director at Campion was a kind Jesuit priest named Ron who, as we sat in a small parlor on the first day, asked me to think about this question: "Who is God?"

Later, I sat on the broad, green lawn outside the retreat house on a sultry June day and tried to come up with the "right" answers: Creator of the Universe, Giver of Life, All-Powerful Being, etc. These I dutifully presented at our next meeting, as if I were answering a general intelligence test. Ron seemed satisfied with my answers but asked me to repeat the exercise, this time refining the question: "Who is Jesus?"

Ha! I thought. *A trick question.*

"Aren't they the same?" I said, wondering whether I was being tested. "Isn't Jesus *God*?"

"I see what you mean," said Ron. "But I'd like you to think about Jesus specifically."

When I told him I had a hard time concentrating on the first question, he said, "That's okay. Don't concentrate next time. Feel free to let your mind wander."

The next day I sat on the lawn, happy to work on my tan, and thought, *Who is Jesus?* The same type of list came into my mind: Son of God, Messiah, Judge.

Then an unusual word popped into my consciousness: "friend." It came to mind like a forgotten line of poetry or the lyric from a song you're trying to remember. Jesus as a friend? I had never thought about him like that before. But the more I thought about it, the more it made me happy to imagine him as a friend, someone to rely on in tough times. To talk with. To share your problems with. To spend time with. I lay back on a beach towel on the warm grass, looked up at the sky, and thought about that for a while and then returned to the task of drawing up my list of titles. Later on, in my little room, I wrote them down so I wouldn't forget.

The next day I returned to Ron and recited my list: Son of God, Messiah, Judge. Then I said, "You know, I had the funniest thought. The word 'friend' came into my mind." I told him how good it felt to think about that. And why it felt good to think about it. It calmed me.

He leaned back in his rocking chair and said, "I think you're beginning to pray."

It was a liberating moment. Ron wasn't telling me that what I was thinking was right or wrong, or Jesuit or not Jesuit. Rather, it was an invitation not simply to *think* things about God, but to *feel* them. To experience them. Later, he would invite me to see that these kinds of experiences might even be God's way of communicating with me. It seemed overwhelming, beautiful, and frightening that God might be doing that. Still, I was fascinated.

The next few days flew by, as I tried to listen, with Ron's help, to the faint sounds of God's voice in my life. He introduced me to the practice of Ignatian contemplation, that is, imagining yourself in a scene from the Gospels and seeing what comes up in prayer. A few years after I entered the Jesuits, I wrote about this practice in a book called *In Good Company*. Probably best to let my younger self describe what he felt:

> Most of the free time was given over to wandering the grounds and, especially, to prayer. Ron asked me to imagine various scenes from the New Testament. Then I would try to place myself somewhere in the scene and let my mind wander. Essentially, he had taken what I thought was a weakness—an overly active imagination and a wandering mind—and was helping me use it to experience God in a new way. I found that I could imagine scenes from the Gospels fairly easily: people's faces, their clothes, their voices, the smells of the place, the sounds, the landscape, the buildings. And when I had envisioned the whole scene and finally imagined myself therein, I was often surprised by my feelings and reactions. Sometimes I felt happy to be with Jesus, or, like his disciples, surprised and confused by his actions or words. Praying like this made me feel closer to God.

How the Ice Cream Inn Prepared Me for Life

After the retreat, Jim, the director of vocations, the person who, in a sense, recruits Jesuits, drove me to a Jesuit Ordination Mass, one of the church's grandest liturgies, at the College of the Holy Cross in Worcester, Massachusetts. During one part of the Mass the choir sang a beautiful setting of Psalm 27:

One thing I ask, this alone I seek,
To dwell in the house of the Lord, all my days.
For one day within Your temple, heals every day alone.
O Lord, bring me to Your dwelling.

Maybe that was what I was feeling decades ago in that meadow, when I wanted to understand the source of that happiness. Maybe all along it was a desire to be with God, to enter into God's "dwelling," though I couldn't have explained it like that back then.

The Mass left me in tears. By then, I wanted to join more than ever.

At the time, I felt myself being both pushed from GE, which seemed like a dead end, and pulled toward the Jesuits, which held out a strong, emotional, almost romantic appeal. I couldn't stop thinking about what it would be like to be a Jesuit. In the end, this was the "call": the happy inability to think of anything else. And this is how God calls to us. It's not (usually) about hearing voices or seeing visions. It's about a desire you discover within yourself. And this of course is God's desire for you. How else would God call you to something other than by awakening that desire within you?

Even after the retreat, however, the Jesuits appealed mainly because I admired what they *did*. You could be a Jesuit and a parish priest. You could be a Jesuit and a teacher. You could be a Jesuit and work in a retreat house. It seemed like a great *job*. Good things to *do*. Later I realized that it wasn't so much about what they did but about their way of looking at the world. It was less about their activities (which are important) and more about their spirituality, which can be summarized as finding God in all things. I entered because of what the Jesuits did, but I stayed because of who they are.

You might wonder: What enabled me to leave the corporate world, for which I had prepared for years, and join a religious order, for which I had prepared hardly at all? What changed?

The answer was that I was invited to consider that God was communicating with me.

When I was in that meadow near my elementary school as a boy, standing among the wildflowers and the grasshoppers, longing for more, there was, deep down, a sense of a call. I didn't understand it like that back then, but it was there. But there seemed to be a veil between God and me. God was still very much "out there." Celtic Christian traditions speak of "thin spaces," physical places where the distance between heaven and earth, between God and you, seems lessened. The meadow was one of those places for me, but God still felt distant.

At that moment, if you had asked me if God was calling to me, I probably would have thought it a silly question for two reasons. For one thing, God couldn't possibly care about me in that kind of personal way, and, for another, even if God did care in that way, and if he wanted to let me know he was there, he would have appeared in a vision or something. I would have laughed at the question and pedaled away on my Schwinn Speedster.

Later, as an adolescent and young adult, I believed that God was watching me for sure, judging me certainly, and interested in me maybe. But this was still a distant God. Not simply a concept or an idea—I believed in God as real—but a God who was so great that he (always he, or rather He) couldn't possibly take a personal interest in me other than in the vague (to me) way that he cared for all human beings. The idea that God would communicate with me seemed ridiculous. Also, borderline arrogant on my part.

Then, after Brad's death, God became an ogre, wantonly cruel. Why would I want to believe in, much less follow, a God who killed my friends? So in an instant, while I sat in that tasteful church during Brad's funeral, God seemed to move farther away. (My Jesuit brother Richard Leonard's insight comes to mind: If God feels far away, guess who moved?) A few months later, my friend Jacque's perspective—resting in gratitude for the blessings one had received even amid pain—helped me find a path out of that place of anger. Even so, God was still "out there." Far away. Other.

I knew that God became human in Jesus, so that we could come closer to God. But that was two thousand years ago. And I knew that I could encounter him, as we Catholics believe, in the Eucharist. And as I thought about it then: Jesus had lived, died, and risen again, but he wasn't physically *here*. He wasn't standing in front of me, as he had with his disciples. I knew he was *here* in the world in some vague way that I couldn't understand.

The notion that God would, through experiences in prayer and in daily life, want to communicate with me was absolutely life-changing. It was as if someone had tuned the radio to a station I hadn't known existed before.

I'm not saying that everything that came into my head during that retreat was a message from God. As a Jesuit friend likes to say, "Not every leaf that falls on the sidewalk in front of you is a message from the Almighty." But on that retreat Ron invited me to notice what was going on in my interior life, because this was indeed one way that God has of communicating with us. And why *wouldn't* God want to do that? It was just a matter of paying attention. Noticing.

Many of the books I've written focus on those themes: God's desire for us, God's way of communicating with us, and how to discern what's coming from God and what's coming just from our own thought processes, needs, and agendas.

During that initial retreat the veil that seemed to separate me from a deeper relationship with God was torn open. Or maybe, more gently, pulled aside. I was beginning to understand the longing that I felt in that meadow as a boy. And I could discern more about what that longing was coming from—or whom it was coming from.

I've never regretted the decision to leave GE and enter the Jesuits. The Jesuit life is not perfect (what life is?), but it's meant for me. Today it seems like it was preordained (no pun intended), but as you can tell from this book, it didn't seem like that at the time. While I have had occasional struggles and doubts, I know that entering the Jesuits was the best decision I've ever made.

Even if I probably didn't take enough time to make the decision. That may be my only regret about what we Jesuits call discernment. I probably spent more time deciding what car to buy. And after I entered the Jesuits, I met guys who had investigated all sorts of religious orders: Dominicans, Franciscans, Benedictines. I felt a bit outclassed. Then again, one guy who had explored five orders entered our novice class and left a few weeks later.

Nonetheless, I entered the novitiate on August 28, 1988, delighted. I had my fears about whether I would fit in, but again, I thought, *How hard could it be?*

Over the past four decades as a Jesuit I've learned a lot: about God, about Jesus, about the Bible, about the church, about other people, and about myself. I also learned more about work.

During the first year of my Jesuit novitiate in Boston, I worked at a hospital for seriously ill patients and then was sent on a four-month assignment to Kingston, Jamaica, to work with Mother Teresa's Sisters (the Missionaries of Charity), attending to the sick and dying, whom the sisters brought in from the streets to care for. The next year I worked in a homeless shelter in Boston and in a school for students from low-income families on the Lower East Side of New York City, a few blocks away from the Pyramid Club.

Over the next two years, after taking my First Vows as a Jesuit, and during my philosophy studies in Chicago, I worked with street-gang members in the inner city and at a homeless shelter helping men and women write résumés and get ready for job interviews. I was amazed that my Wharton background was coming in handy in, of all places, the Jesuits. ("God writes straight with crooked lines," my novice director said, quoting an old proverb.)

Then, as part of our "formation" (training), I worked for two years in Nairobi, Kenya, helping East African refugees start small businesses and earn a living for themselves. My Wharton background came in even handier there. After that, during my theology studies, back in Boston, I worked in a local prison as a chaplain. I was ordained eleven years after I entered the novitiate, in 1999, and was sent to work at *America* magazine.

Today I feel like I have several jobs: working at America Media (the parent company for *America*), writing books (the proceeds of which go to the magazine), and ministering with LGBTQ Catholics. As a priest, I'm involved with other jobs—ministries—as well: celebrating Masses, including funerals and weddings; baptizing babies; hearing confessions; offering spiritual direction and the like. And in my Jesuit community, I'm the house gardener. Not a job but still more work!

My friends will probably tell you that I work hard. Sometimes too hard. Workaholism is a trap for not a few Jesuits and priests. When you don't have a wife, husband, partner, children, or grandchildren to tell you to stop working so hard, it's easy to work to excess. Also, when you feel like you're working for God, you tend to work as hard as you can.

So whatever my many other faults, I'm not lazy. And my summer jobs, crazy and funny and varied as they were, had something to do with who I am. As we Jesuits would say, the lessons I learned helped to "form" me.

For one thing, I learned what it meant to work at a low-wage job, often side by side with people struggling to make better lives for themselves. I learned this not simply by standing next to people on the assembly line at Sharp, but also by working alongside the assistant managers or managers at the movie theater and the Ice Cream Inn, where Gladys wasn't rich; and at Western Savings Bank, where the tellers didn't have easy lives; and at the Cricket Club, where the older caddies, the Super Loopers, were still lugging around heavy bags well into middle age.

Those summers gave me a lifelong appreciation not only for hard work, but also for people who often didn't have as many options about where they worked. It was something I couldn't have learned in any book or economics class at Wharton. Even what I learned in my class on social stratification at Penn paled in comparison to standing next to someone on an assembly line and listening to their stories. "What would you do if you could do anything you wanted to do?" probably wasn't a question that they had the luxury of asking themselves. Or maybe they did ask themselves and the answer was a bitter "Not what I'm doing now." I didn't know everything about their lives, but I knew that I had a lot to be grateful for.

I also learned a lot about being mean. Or not being mean.

It's easy to be mean. Sometimes it feels like you're justified in doing so. I'm sure that the man who barged into the back room at the Ice Cream Inn, seething that his dinner had been ruined by a fifteen-year-old busboy, felt that he was in the right. But I'll never forget how he grinned when my manager half-heartedly indicated that I would be punished. From time to time, we may feel justified in being mean. We all get frustrated, on the job, in our families, or just walking around in the world; but being mean to someone—especially someone without any power—is never the answer.

When I was caddying at the Cricket Club, I discovered what it's like to be on the receiving end of snobbery, contempt, and pride—golfers not speaking to me, stiffing me on a tip, rolling their eyes when I said where I went to high school, laughing when I tried to keep up with their carts, or leaving me outside during an electrical storm. Some of those experiences were funny; others, not so much. Often during my summer jobs I said to myself, "I will never treat someone like I'm being treated." I will never make anyone's face blush in humiliation or cause them to burst into tears or feel small or ashamed of who they are. I am almost physically allergic to that today.

More important, I learned what it's like to be kind. From people like Mr. Clare at the Ice Cream Inn, who patiently showed me how to use a dishwasher and mop a floor; or Tommy at the Cricket Club, who carefully taught me the basics of golf; or Ethel at Western Savings Bank, who calmly stood up for me when a customer berated me. It's easy to be mean. It's better to be kind. Being kind isn't all of Christianity, but it's about 90 percent of it. And being kind to people who can't, in a sense, repay you is even more important. Jesus has a few parables about that, in fact.

Along the way, I learned basic job etiquette. For starters, be on time. At many of my summer jobs I "clocked in," sometimes with an actual time clock, like at Sharp or the movie theater. At every summer job I had after paperboy and lawn mower, you were expected to be on time. Many years later, at GE, my first manager said, "Five minutes early is on time."

"You don't think my time is valuable?" said one of my GE bosses to someone who came to a meeting five minutes late. (He never came late again.) Today, because so many people work online, with some employees working beyond their nine-to-five jobs, some argue that it's not fair to treat them like machines, punching in and out of a time clock. But my boss's question was a reasonable one. Today I'm something of a stickler for showing up on time.

Another lesson, less applicable to me now, since I love what I do, was learning how to enjoy the people if you don't enjoy the job. Perhaps the summer job I most despised was working at Sharp. It was both monotonous and tiring, as I stared at the clock on the wall, wondering when the day would come to an end. But I looked forward to my car rides with Kris, joking around with the other employees (and throwing a ruler into the machines occasionally), and sometimes getting high at lunch. You could hate

How the Ice Cream Inn Prepared Me for Life

the job but like the people, and here and there could be, thanks to them, a measure of comfort and camaraderie. Sometimes that's the only thing you have to hang on to in a bad job.

I learned to apologize after making a mistake. I should have apologized when I hit that woman on the head with a bussing tray at the Ice Cream Inn, lost a golf ball in the rough at the Cricket Club, miscounted a wad of bills at Western Savings Bank, or gave someone the wrong change at the ticket office at the Annenberg Center. It took time for me to learn the skill, or rather the virtue, of asking for forgiveness. Usually my first reaction when confronted with an error was to sputteringly defend myself. In time, I realized that as not only false (denying something that is true), but selfish. These days I'm quicker to apologize when I make a mistake.

At the same time, I learned not to apologize reflexively. When my neighbors berated me for asking them for money for a newspaper that they didn't subscribe to, I apologized. One night, after I returned from my paper route and told my dad about this, he said, "Why are you apologizing? You didn't do anything wrong." Here, apologizing was a kind of self-abasement designed to get people to like me, and encourage them to say, "You've done nothing wrong! You're a great kid!" But it was false. Now I try to apologize when it's called for, and for the right reason.

To that end, I learned not to be a doormat. It took time to realize the difference between apologizing and being humiliated. When I was standing under a thunderstorm at the Cricket Club, I (finally) knew enough to leave. No need to be a doormat, to let people mistreat you or, worse, to in any way abuse you. Everyone has dignity, including a caddy or a busboy.

I learned that it is okay not to know something. When I was confronted with something new, particularly a task I felt I might do poorly, I would resist doing it altogether. I had an almost visceral negative reaction to feeling ignorant. But on the job I was forced to learn to do all sorts of things that I had no experience with. I learned to say, "I don't know how to do this." Or, "Can you show me how?"

Maybe the most important thing I learned was to work hard. As my dad said often, "Why do you think they call it work? If it were fun, they'd call it play." Delivering a full sack of papers in the dark was hard work. Mowing lawns under the hot sun was hard work. Carrying a heavy bussing tray was hard work. So was lugging golf bags, balancing plates of food, popping corn for ten hours, standing in front of an assembly line, and even the more cerebral and less physically demanding tasks like working as a teller, as a (sort of) stockbroker, or in a box office. I learned to show up, work hard, and be conscientious. Thanks to the managers and assistant managers and fellow co-workers, and my parents too, I learned how to work.

Finally, here's something that would have surprised me as a teenager: I learned about gratitude. Some parts of these summer jobs were miserable. (I hope you found some parts funny too.) I didn't like getting chased by dogs, stung by bees, yelled at for bussing the wrong table; or cleaning up poop, trying to avoid being struck by lightning, staring at an assembly line for hours on end, and throwing up from touching dirty cash. If you had asked me, "Are you grateful for these jobs?" I would have lied and said yes. But if we were friends and I was being honest, I would probably have said, "No. I'm grateful for the money but not for the jobs. I'd rather sit on my back porch and read."

But today, when I think about sailing down our neighborhood street delivering papers on a cool fall evening; smelling the summery scent of a neighbor's newly mown lawn; seeing my friends enjoy their ice cream sundaes as they joked with me while I bussed tables; walking down a pristine green fairway on a warm summer's day with the sun at its zenith; laughing with the candy girls at the movie theater after eating pilfered M&M's; driving with Kris at breakneck speed to the factory with her radio blasting Supertramp; laughing with Ethel as she longed for Friday to come; and so many of the other experiences I've had during all those Junes, Julys, and Augusts—I experience real gratitude.

The jobs were hard and some funny things happened, but most of all I'm glad I met so many wonderful people who taught me about life, about work, and about working hard while I was young. I couldn't wait to leave most of those jobs, but I can look back on them now with fondness. I know why they call it work, but it could also be called grace.

On my first day in the Jesuit novitiate, we were told about *manualia*. It derives from the Latin word for "hands" and means housecleaning. Each weekend we cleaned the novitiate, with jobs divided among the novices by another novice who had the rather grand title of *manuductor*, from the Latin meaning the one who "leads by the hand," and who basically coordinated the house jobs. (A surprising amount of Latin was slung around the novitiate.)

One week the *manuductor* might assign you to clean the windows (which were abundant in the four-story former convent that served as the novitiate building). Another weekend you might polish the woodwork, including the banisters of the long wooden staircase. The next weekend your job might be washing the linens for the chapel. Bathroom duty was the worst but certainly not worse than my former bathroom duty at the Cinema on the Mall.

One Saturday I was assigned to clean the kitchen. The *manuductor*, a second-year novice, said he would teach me how. After breakfast, he led me into the kitchen and opened a closet door and pulled out the same kind of mop and bucket that I had used at my first real job, at the Ice Cream Inn.

It was a lot newer than the banged-up one Mr. Clare showed me when I was fifteen, but it was the same model: a long wooden mop with the cotton loop ends, which sat in a big yellow plastic bucket on wheels with the "side-attached" wringer. The older novice rolled it loudly out onto the linoleum kitchen floor, squirted in some cleaning fluid, and started filling it with water from a hose attached to a faucet inside the closet.

As the water loudly rushed into the bucket, I remembered mopping the floors of the Ice Cream Inn one evening after everyone else except Mr. Clare had left.

That didn't happen often. Usually all the employees stayed till closing, and even afterward some of the older boys would congregate outside by the dumpster and smoke cigarettes, swill some stale beer, smoke pot, or do whippets in the warm evening breezes.

But sometimes, usually on a weekday, it was just me and Mr. Clare closing up. He'd be quietly toting up the cash for the day, and I would fill the bucket with soapy water and mop up the spots of grease, the cigarette ashes, the melted ice cream, and the spilled wet nuts from the floors of the back room, the walk-in fridge, the kitchen area, and the dining room. Every few swipes I'd put the mop head back in the wringer, twist it hard, and lean on it with my whole body, like Mr. Clare had taught me. Then I'd start again.

One night my dad said that the car was acting up so he'd be

a little late. So I took my time, mopping slowly, slowly, slowly, careful to clean under the tables and get into all the corners. I was proud that I knew how to do it and could do it well. It reminded me of the need to stick with something even if it seemed hard to learn at first. And it felt satisfying to clean things, to get a paycheck, and to contribute a little to a place that gave people good food and a fun place to gather for a birthday, an anniversary, or a graduation and, in the process, experience a few moments of happiness, maybe even some lasting joy. Maybe they'd always remember that lunch or dinner at the Ice Cream Inn.

I remembered all that as I stood in the novitiate kitchen, just starting my new life.

"This kind of mop is a little complicated to use," said my Jesuit brother, as he turned off the spigot and maneuvered the bucket in front of me. "But you'll get the hang of it."

And, really, how hard could it be?

ACKNOWLEDGMENTS

THANKS TO MY MOM AND DAD FOR INSTILLING IN MY sister and me a strong work ethic. Further thanks for their driving me to job interviews and, especially before I could drive, to my summer jobs, and then, after I started those jobs, listening to me complain when I returned home. Thanks to my sister, Carolyn Martin Buscarino, for listening to me complain about how tired I was. Thanks to all the managers, assistant managers, and co-workers who put up with me as a teenager.

Several friends on a Facebook page for people from my hometown I thank for their memories of some of the long-forgotten places of employment, including the recipe for the Ice Cream Inn's Telstar ICI and the illicit movie theater titles on the Cinema on the Mall marquee (and commenting on the display of Nazi memorabilia from our history teacher). From that page, thanks to John Fetheringill, fellow paperboy on Kings Road, for reminding

Acknowledgments

me how we were paid (or, rather, not paid) for *The Advertiser* and *The Recorder*.

Also, thanks to Mark Apel, fellow Plymouth–Whitemarsh High School grad, for his memories of working at the Cinema on the Mall. Thanks to my cousin Ricky Spano for his memories of his brother, Tommy, and the Philadelphia Cricket Club and reminding me how early we had to get there. Thanks to Kris Juzaitis for her memories of the Sharp pill plant and reminding me that it was indeed a red Pinto that she drove. (I'm sorry that I smelled like cigarette smoke so early in the morning.) Thanks to my sister for her own memories of being a teller at the "drive-in" bank. Thanks to Bruce Zaharevitz and Andy Schiff for the details of our working together at the Annenberg box office. Thanks to Rob Schlakman for filling in some of the details of our apartment hunting and apartment dwelling in Manhattan. Thanks to John Olszewski, Gordon Freas, Bob Yarnall, and Greg White for reminding me of some of our more debauched escapades in those days (most of which were too risqué to make it into this book but the memories of which were enjoyable). Thanks to the University of Pennsylvania's Office of Student Employment for researching when I worked at the Financial Aid office. Thanks to my friends Carol Ash Pokorny, Peggy Pennacchi, John Olszewski, George Williams, Andy Schiff, Kris Juzaitis, Bruce Zaharevitz, Rob Schlakman, Chris Brown, Jim Ross, my cousins Rosie Spano Beddis and Tom Spano (Tommy's son), my sister, Carolyn, and my nephew Matthew Buscarino for reading this book in manuscript form and correcting any errors and adding a few stories that I had forgotten. Peggy's diary helped a great deal too.

As for the writing process, I thank two early readers, Jim Keane and Mary Karr; as well as my editor, Angela Guzman, and my friends at HarperOne, including Judith Curr, Laina Adler, Stephen Brayda, Jason Kayser, Courtney Nobile, Makenna Holford, Lisa Zuniga, Jessie Dolch, and Maya Alpert; my beloved literary agent Roger Freet, who died as this book was being completed and to whom I owe a great debt both personally and professionally; my new literary agent, Claudia Cross; my peerless copy editor Vinita Wright; my indefatigable fact-checker, Heidi Hill; and also Joseph McAuley, who painstakingly secured the permissions for all those 1970s and 1980s music lyrics.

Thanks to the people whose names I've forgotten, who were kind to me as a teenager, and who taught me how to mop floors, load dishwashers, pop corn, retrieve golf balls, tear pill packets, carry plates of food, count cash, write up a stock order, and all the rest. I met a lot of kind people during my summer jobs. I may not remember your names, but I'm grateful.

Finally, apologies to the woman I brained with my bussing tray, the neighbors who ended up with newspapers in their bushes, the customers whose lawns weren't edged well enough, the movie theater patrons whose candy boxes were emptied by me, the golfers to whom I gave the wrong clubs, the customers whose deposits I took too long to count, the investors who asked me questions I couldn't answer, the patrons whose tickets I misplaced, and, especially, the people whose meals I mistakenly bussed during the Bicentennial Wagon Train. Next time you see me, I'll treat you to a banana split with wet nuts.

CREDITS AND PERMISSIONS

THE AUTHOR GRATEFULLY ACKNOWLEDGES PERMISSION to publish lyrics from the following songs: "Alison," Words and Music by Elvis Costello (Copyright © 1977 by Universal Music Publishing MGB Ltd. Copyright Renewed All Rights in the United States Administered by Universal Music—MGB Songs International Copyright Secured All Rights Reserved Reprinted by Permission of Hal Leonard LLC); "The Logical Song," Words and Music by Richard Davies and Roger Hodgson (Copyright © 1979 ALMO MUSIC CORP. and DELICATE MUSIC. All Rights Administered by ALMO MUSIC CORP. All Rights Reserved Used by Permission Reprinted by Permission of Hal Leonard LLC); "Pump It Up," Words and Music by Elvis Costello (Copyright © 1978 by Universal Music Publishing MGB Ltd. All Rights in the United States and Canada Administered by Universal Music—MGB Songs International Copyright Secured All Rights Reserved Reprinted by Permission of Hal Leonard LLC); "Baker Street," Words and Music by Gerry Rafferty (Copyright © 1978 Stage Three Music (Catalogues) Limited All Rights Administered by BMG Rights Management (US) LLC All Rights Reserved Used by Permission Reprinted by Permission of Hal Leonard LLC); "We're All Alone," Words and Music by Boz Scaggs (Copyright

Credits and Permissions

© 1976 Boz Scaggs Music Copyright Renewed All Rights Administered by Spirit Four Music in the United States and Canada and Kobalt Music Group Ltd. for the rest of the world All Rights Reserved Used by Permission Reprinted by Permission of Hal Leonard LLC); "Afternoon Delight," Words and Music by Bill Danoff (Copyright © 1976 BMG Ruby Songs and Reservoir Media Management, Inc. Copyright Renewed All Rights for BMG Ruby Songs Administered by BMG Rights Management (US) LLC All Rights Reserved Used by Permission Reprinted by Permission of Hal Leonard LLC); "Hungry Like The Wolf," Words and Music by John Taylor, Andy Taylor, Nick Rhodes, Roger Taylor and Simon LeBon (Copyright © 1982 Gloucester Place Music Ltd. All Rights Administered by Sony Music Publishing (US) LLC, 424 Church Street, Suite 1200, Nashville, TN 37219 International Copyright Secured All Rights Reserved Reprinted by Permission of Hal Leonard LLC); "After the Gold Rush," Words and Music by Neil Young (Copyright 1970 Hipgnosis Side B and Broken Arrow Music Corporation Copyright Renewed All Rights Administered by Hipgnosis Songs Group All Rights Reserved Used by Permission Reprinted by Permission of Hal Leonard LLC).